Level 3

Microsoft®

Word

365
2019 Edition

Nita Rutkosky | **Audrey Roggenkamp**
Pierce College Puyallup
Puyallup, Washington

Ian Rutkosky
Pierce College Puyallup
Puyallup, Washington

PARADIGM
EDUCATION SOLUTIONS

St. Paul

Vice President, Content and Digital Solutions: Christine Hurney
Director of Content Development: Carley Fruzzetti
Developmental Editor: Jennifer Joline Anderson
Director of Production: Timothy W. Larson
Production Editor/Project Manager: Jen Weaverling
Senior Design and Production Specialist: Jack Ross
Cover and Interior Design: Valerie King
Copy Editor: Communicáto, Ltd.
Testers: Janet Blum, Traci Post
Indexer: Terry Casey
Vice President, Director of Digital Products: Chuck Bratton
Digital Projects Manager: Tom Modl
Digital Solutions Manager: Gerry Yumul
Senior Director of Digital Products and Onboarding: Christopher Johnson
Supervisor of Digital Products and Onboarding: Ryan Isdahl
Vice President, Marketing: Lara Weber McLellan
Marketing and Communications Manager: Selena Hicks

ISBN 978-0-76388-720-9 (print)
ISBN 978-0-76388-764-3 (digital)

© 2020 by Paradigm Publishing, LLC
875 Montreal Way
St. Paul, MN 55102
Email: CustomerService@ParadigmEducation.com
Website: ParadigmEducation.com

Brief Contents

Contents

Achieving Proficiency in Word

The Benchmark Series, *Microsoft® Word 365*, 2019 Edition, is designed for students who want to learn how to use Microsoft's powerful word processing program to create professional-looking documents for school, work, and personal communication needs. After successfully completing a course in Microsoft Word using this courseware, students can expect to be proficient in using Word to do the following:

- Create and edit memos, letters, flyers, announcements, and reports of varying complexity.
- Apply appropriate formatting elements and styles to a range of document types.
- Add graphics and other visual elements to enhance written communication.
- Plan, research, write, revise, design, and publish documents to meet specific information needs.
- Given a workplace scenario requiring a written solution, assess the communication purpose and then prepare materials that achieve the goal efficiently and effectively.

Well-designed pedagogy is important, but students learn technology skills through practice and problem solving. Technology provides opportunities for interactive learning as well as excellent ways to quickly and accurately assess student performance. To this end, this course is supported with Cirrus, Paradigm's cloud-based training and assessment learning management system. Details about Cirrus as well as its integrated student courseware and instructor resources can be found on page xii.

Proven Instructional Design

The Benchmark Series has long served as a standard of excellence in software instruction. Elements of the series function individually and collectively to create an inviting, comprehensive learning environment that leads to full proficiency in computer applications. The following visual tour highlights the structure and features that comprise the highly popular Benchmark model.

Microsoft

Word Level 3

Unit 1

Formatting with Special Features

Chapter 1 Designing with Styles

Chapter 2 Managing Merge Options

Chapter 3 Managing Macros

Chapter 4 Creating Forms

Unit Openers display the unit's four chapter titles. Each level of the course contains two units with four chapters each.

Chapter Openers Present Learning Objectives

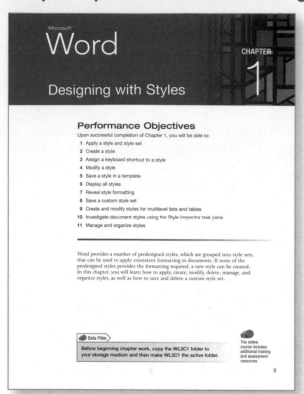

Chapter Openers present the performance objectives and an overview of the skills taught.

Data Files are provided for each chapter.

Activities Build Skill Mastery within Realistic Context

Multipart Activities provide a framework for instruction and practice on software features. An activity overview identifies tasks to accomplish and key features to use in completing the work.

Typically, a file remains open throughout all parts of the activity. Students save their work incrementally. At the end of the activity, students save, print, and then close the file.

Tutorials provide interactive, guided training and measured practice.

Quick Steps in the margins allow fast reference and review.

Hints offer useful tips on how to use software features efficiently and effectively.

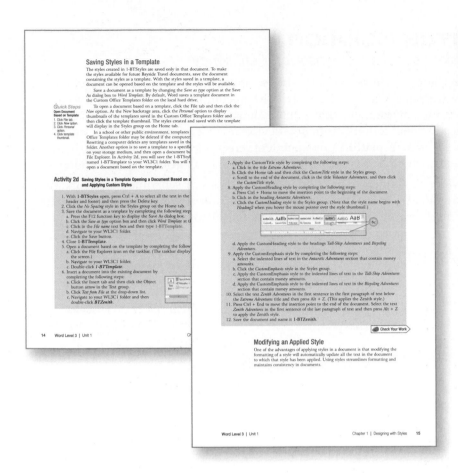

Step-by-Step Instructions guide students to the desired outcome for each activity part. Screen captures illustrate what the screen should look like at key points.

Between activity parts, the text presents instruction on the features and skills necessary to accomplish the next portion of the activity.

Magenta Text identifies material to type.

Check Your Work model answer images are available in the online course, and students can use those images to confirm they have completed the activity correctly.

Chapter Review Tools Reinforce Learning

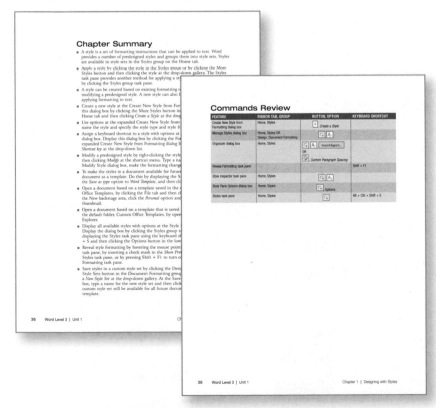

A **Chapter Summary** reviews the purpose and execution of key features.

A **Commands Review** summarizes visually the major software features and alternative methods of access.

The Cirrus Solution
Elevating student success and instructor efficiency

Powered by Paradigm, Cirrus is the next-generation learning solution for developing skills in Microsoft Office. Cirrus seamlessly delivers complete course content in a cloud-based learning environment that puts students on the fast track to success. Students can access their content from any device anywhere, through a live internet connection; plus, Cirrus is platform independent, ensuring that students get the same learning experience whether they are using PCs, Macs, or Chromebook computers.

Cirrus provides Benchmark Series content in a series of scheduled assignments that report to a grade book to track student progress and achievement. Assignments are grouped in modules, providing many options for customizing instruction.

Dynamic Training

The online Benchmark Series courses include interactive resources to support learning.

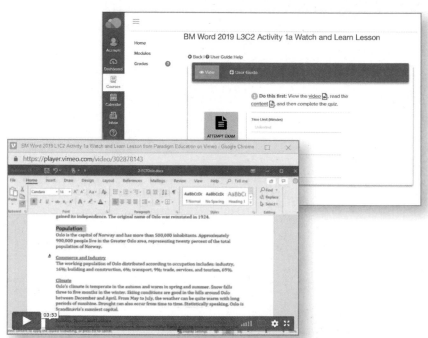

Watch and Learn Lessons include a video demonstrating how to perform the chapter activity, a reading to provide background and context, and a short quiz to check understanding of concepts and skills.

Guide and Practice Tutorials provide interactive, guided training and measured practice.

Hands On Activities enable students to complete chapter activities, compare their solutions against a Check Your Work model answer image, and submit their work for instructor review.

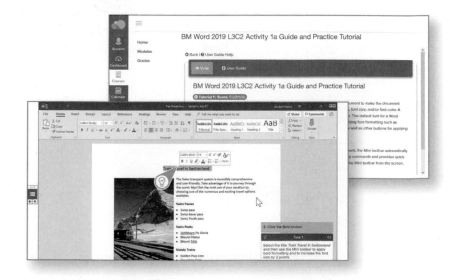

Chapter Review and Assessment

Review and assessment activities for each chapter are available for completion in Cirrus.

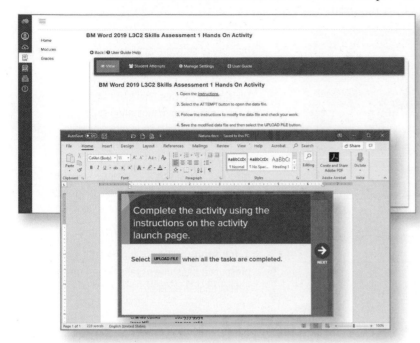

Knowledge Check matching exercises assess comprehension and recall of application features and functions as well as key terminology.

Skills Assessment Hands On Activity exercises evaluate the ability to apply chapter skills and concepts in solving realistic problems. Each is completed live in Microsoft Word and is uploaded through Cirrus for instructor evaluation.

Visual Benchmark assessments test problem-solving skills and mastery of application features.

A **Case Study** requires analyzing a workplace scenario and then planning and executing a multipart project. Students search the web and/or use the program's Help feature to locate additional information required to complete the Case Study.

Exercises and **Projects** provide opportunities to develop and demonstrate skills learned in each chapter. Each is completed live in Microsoft Word and is automatically scored by Cirrus. Detailed feedback and how-to videos help students evaluate and improve their performance.

Skills Check Exams evaluate students' ability to complete specific tasks. Skills Check Exams are completed live in Microsoft Word and are scored automatically. Detailed feedback and instructor-controlled how-to videos help student evaluate and improve their performance.

Multiple-choice **Concepts Exams** assess understanding of key commands and concepts presented in each chapter.

Unit Review and Assessment

Review and assessment activities for each unit of each Benchmark course are also available for completion in Cirrus.

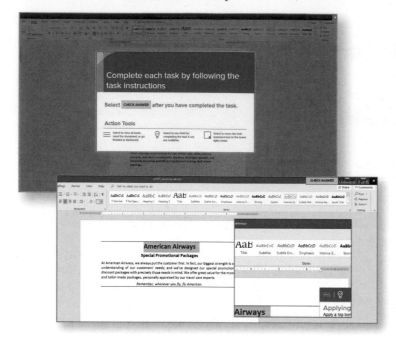

Assessing Proficiency exercises check mastery of software application functions and features.

Writing Activities challenge students to use written communication skills while demonstrating their understanding of important software features and functions.

Internet Research assignments reinforce the importance of research and information processing skills along with proficiency in the Office environment.

A **Job Study** activity at the end of Unit 2 presents a capstone assessment requiring critical thinking and problem solving.

Unit-Level Projects allow students to practice skills learned in the unit. Each is completed live in Microsoft Word and automatically scored by Cirrus. Detailed feedback and how-to videos help students evaluate and improve their performance.

Student eBook

The Student eBook, accessed through the Cirrus online course, can be downloaded to any device (desktop, laptop, tablet, or smartphone) to make Benchmark Series content available anywhere students wish to study.

Instructor eResources

Cirrus tracks students' step-by-step interactions as they move through each activity, giving instructors visibility into their progress and missteps. With Exam Watch, instructors can observe students in a virtual, live, skills-based exam and join remotely as needed—a helpful option for struggling students who need one-to-one coaching, or for distance learners. In addition to these Cirrus-specific tools, the Instructor eResources for the Benchmark Series include the following support:

- Planning resources, such as lesson plans, teaching hints, and sample course syllabi
- Delivery resources, such as discussion questions and online images and templates
- Assessment resources, including live and annotated PDF model answers for chapter work and review and assessment activities, rubrics for evaluating student work, and chapter-based exam banks in RTF format

About the Authors

Nita Rutkosky began her career teaching business education at Pierce College in Puyallup, Washington, in 1978 and holds a master's degree in occupational education. In her years as an instructor, she taught many courses in software applications to students in postsecondary information technology certificate and degree programs. Since 1987, Nita has been a leading author of courseware for computer applications training and instruction. Her current titles include Paradigm's popular Benchmark Series, Marquee Series, and Signature Series. She is a contributor to the Cirrus online content for Office application courses and has also written textbooks for keyboarding, desktop publishing, computing in the medical office, and essential skills for digital literacy.

Audrey Roggenkamp holds a master's degree in adult education and curriculum and has been an adjunct instructor in the Business Information Technology department at Pierce College in Puyallup, Washington, since 2005. Audrey has also been a content provider for Paradigm Education Solutions since 2005. In addition to contributing to the Cirrus online content for Office application courses, Audrey co-authors Paradigm's Benchmark Series, Marquee Series, and Signature Series. Her other available titles include *Keyboarding & Applications I* and *II* and *Using Computers in the Medical Office: Word, PowerPoint®, and Excel®*.

Ian Rutkosky has a master's degree in business administration and has been an adjunct instructor in the Business Information Technology department at Pierce College in Puyallup, Washington, since 2010. In addition to joining the author team for the Benchmark Series and Marquee Series, he has co-authored titles on medical office computing and digital literacy and has served as a co-author and consultant for Paradigm's Cirrus training and assessment software.

Microsoft®

Word Level 3

Unit 1

Formatting with Special Features

Microsoft®

Word

Designing with Styles

Performance Objectives

Upon successful completion of Chapter 1, you will be able to:

1 Apply a style and style set
2 Create a style
3 Assign a keyboard shortcut to a style
4 Modify a style
5 Save a style in a template
6 Display all styles
7 Reveal style formatting
8 Save a custom style set
9 Create and modify styles for multilevel lists and tables
10 Investigate document styles using the Style Inspector task pane
11 Manage and organize styles

Word provides a number of predesigned styles, which are grouped into style sets, that can be used to apply consistent formatting in documents. If none of the predesigned styles provides the formatting required, a new style can be created. In this chapter, you will learn how to apply, create, modify, delete, manage, and organize styles, as well as how to save and delete a custom style set.

 Data Files

Before beginning chapter work, copy the WL3C1 folder to your storage medium and then make WL3C1 the active folder.

The online course includes additional training and assessment resources.

Activity 1 **Format a Study Adventure Document with Styles** **1 Part**

You will open a document containing information on an African Study Adventure program, change the style set, and apply styles.

Tutorial

Review: Applying Styles and Style Sets

Formatting with Styles

A style is a set of formatting instructions that can be applied to text. Word provides a number of predesigned styles and groups those that apply similar formatting into style sets. Whereas a theme changes the overall colors, fonts, and effects used in a document, a style set changes the font and paragraph formatting for the document. Using the styles within a style set, formatting can be applied to a document to give it a uniform and professional appearance. Change the style set by clicking the Design tab and then clicking a style set in the style sets gallery.

Displaying Styles in a Style Set

The styles in a style set are available in the Styles group on the Home tab. Generally, the visible styles include Normal, No Spacing, Heading 1, Heading 2, Title, Subtitle, and Subtitle Emphasis. (Depending on the monitor and screen resolution, more or fewer styles may display in the Styles group.) The styles change to reflect the style set that has been applied to the active document. Click the More Styles button in the Styles group and a drop-down gallery displays containing all the styles available in the default style set. Hover the mouse pointer over a style in the drop-down gallery to see how the style will format the text in the document.

Another method for displaying additional styles is to click either the up arrow or the down arrow at the right of the styles. Clicking the down arrow scrolls down the styles, displaying subsequent rows of styles. Clicking the up arrow scrolls up, displaying previous rows of styles.

Applying a Style

Quick Steps

Apply Style
Click style in Styles group on Home tab.
OR
1. Click More Styles button in Styles group on Home tab.
2. Click style.
OR
1. Display Styles task pane.
2. Click style in task pane.

Hint You can also display the Styles task pane by pressing Alt + Ctrl + Shift + S.

Several methods are available for applying styles to the text in a document. Apply a style by clicking the style in the Styles group on the Home tab or by clicking the More Styles button and then clicking the style at the drop-down gallery. The Styles task pane provides another method for applying a style. Display the Styles task pane, shown in Figure 1.1, by clicking the Styles group task pane launcher.

Each style in the currently selected style set displays in the task pane followed by the paragraph symbol (¶), indicating that the style applies paragraph formatting, or the character symbol (**a**), indicating that the style applies character formatting. If both characters display to the right of a style, the style applies both paragraph and character formatting. In addition to displaying styles that apply formatting, the Styles task pane also displays a *Clear All* option that removes all formatting from the selected text.

Hover the mouse pointer over a style in the Styles task pane and a ScreenTip displays with information about the formatting applied by the style. Apply a style in the Styles task pane by clicking the style. Close the Styles task pane by clicking the Close button in the upper right corner of the task pane.

Figure 1.1 Styles Task Pane

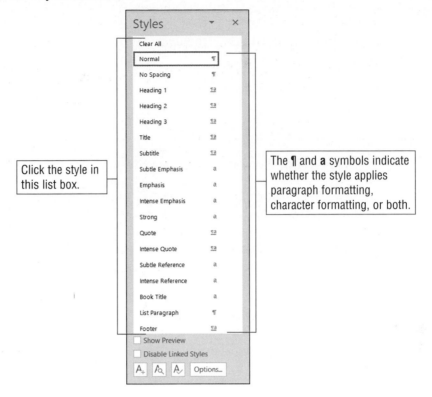

Click the style in this list box.

The ¶ and **a** symbols indicate whether the style applies paragraph formatting, character formatting, or both.

Activity 1 Applying a Style Set and Styles

Part 1 of 1

1. Open **BTAdventures** and then save it with the name **1-BTAdventures**.
2. Apply a different style set by clicking the Design tab and then clicking the *Black & White (Word)* style set in the Styles group (eighth option in the style sets gallery).
3. Move the insertion point to the end of the document and then select the last paragraph of text.
4. Apply styles using the Styles task pane by completing the following steps:
   a. Click the Home tab and then click the Styles group task pane launcher. (This displays the Styles task pane.)
   b. If necessary, scroll down the Styles task pane list box and then click the *Subtle Reference* style. (Notice that the style is followed by the character symbol **a**, indicating that the style applies character formatting.)
   c. Select the bulleted text below the heading *Disneyland Adventure* and then click the *Subtle Emphasis* style in the Styles task pane.
   d. Apply the Subtle Emphasis style to the bulleted text below the heading *Florida Adventure* and the heading *Cancun Adventure*.
   e. Select the quote by Mark Twain and his name at the beginning of the document and then click the *Quote* style in the Styles task pane.
   f. After noticing the formatting of the quote, remove the formatting by making sure the text is selected and then clicking *Clear All* at the top of the Styles task pane.

4b

g. With the Mark Twain quote still selected, click the *Intense Quote* style in the Styles task pane.

h. Click in the document to deselect the text.

i. Close the Styles task pane.

5. Save, print, and then close **1-BTAdventures**.

Activity 2 **Create and Modify Styles for Bayside Travel Documents**   **9 Parts**

You will create and apply custom styles to Bayside Travel documents. You will assign a keyboard shortcut to a style, save styles in a template, display all styles, and reveal formatting. You will also modify the styles, save the styles in a style set, and then delete the style set.

Applying and
Modifying a Style

Creating a Style

If the predesigned styles provided by Word do not contain the desired formatting, a new style can be created. Create a style based on existing formatting, create a new style and apply all the formatting, or modify an existing style.

Creating a New
Style

Creating a Style Based on an Existing Style

To create a style based on an existing style, apply the style to text, make the formatting changes, and then select the text. Click the More Styles button in the styles gallery in the Styles group and then click *Create a Style* at the drop-down gallery. At the Create New Style from Formatting dialog box, type a name for the new style in the *Name* text box and then click OK.

Creating a Style Based on Existing Formatting

Quick Steps

Create Style Based on Existing Style

1. Apply style to text.
2. Make formatting changes.
3. Select text.
4. Click More Styles button in Styles group.
5. Click *Create a Style*.
6. Type name for new style.
7. Click OK.

Create Style Based on Existing Formatting

1. Apply formatting to text.
2. Select text.
3. Click More Styles button in Styles group.
4. Click *Create a Style*.
5. Type name for new style.
6. Click OK.

To create a style based on existing formatting, apply the specific formatting to text in a document and then select the text. Click the More Styles button in the Styles group on the Home tab and then click *Create a Style* at the drop-down gallery. At the Create New Style from Formatting dialog box, shown in Figure 1.2, type a name for the new style in the *Name* text box and then click OK. The style is inserted in the styles gallery and is available for use in the current document.

Figure 1.2 Create New Style from Formatting Dialog Box

Type a name for the new style in this text box.

This preview area displays the formatting applied by the style.

1. Open **BTStyles** and then save it with the name **1-BTStyles**.
2. Create a style based on the formatting of the text *CustomTitle* by completing the following steps:
   a. Click the Show/Hide ¶ button in the Paragraph group on the Home tab to turn on the display of nonprinting characters.
   b. Select the text *Custom Title*. (Make sure you select the paragraph symbol [¶] after *Title*.)
   c. Click the More Styles button in the Styles group on the Home tab.
   d. Click *Create a Style* at the drop-down gallery.
   e. At the Create New Style from Formatting dialog box, type CustomTitle in the *Name* text box.
   f. Click OK.
   g. Click the Show/Hide ¶ button to turn off the display of nonprinting characters.
3. Save **1-BTStyles**.

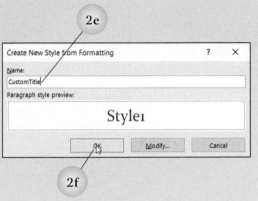

Creating a New Style

A new style can be created without first applying formatting to text. To do this, click the More Styles button in the Styles group on the Home tab and then click *Create a Style* at the drop-down gallery. At the Create New Style from Formatting dialog box, click the Modify button. This displays an expanded Create New Style from Formatting dialog box, as shown in Figure 1.3. At this dialog box, type a name for the new style in the *Name* text box and then use the *Style type* option box to specify the type of style being created. Click the *Style type* option box arrow and a drop-down list displays with options for creating a paragraph style, character style, linked style (both paragraph and character styles), table style, or list style. Choose the option that identifies the type of style being created.

The *Style based on* option has a default setting of ¶ *Normal*. A new style can be based on an existing style. To do this, click the *Style based on* option box arrow and then click the style at the drop-down list. For example, a new style can be based on a predesigned style, such as the Heading 1 style. Click *Heading 1* style at the drop-down list and the formatting settings of the Heading 1 style display in the Create New Style from Formatting dialog box. Apply additional formatting at the dialog box to modify the formatting of the Heading 1 style. If a predesigned style contains some of the formatting for the new style, choosing the predesigned style at the *Style based on* option box drop-down list saves formatting time.

Use the *Style for following paragraph* option to specify what style to use for the next paragraph in the document when the Enter key is pressed. For example, a style can be created that formats a caption heading and is then followed by a style that applies paragraph formatting to the text after the caption heading (such as italic formatting or a specific font and font size). In this situation, the style would be created that applies the specific paragraph formatting to the text that follows a caption heading. The caption heading style would be created and then the *Style for following paragraph* option would specify that the paragraph style is applied when the Enter key is pressed after applying the caption heading style.

Figure 1.3 Expanded Create New Style from Formatting Dialog Box

Type a name for the style in this text box.

Choose a style type in this option box, such as paragraph and/or character, table, or list.

Use option boxes and buttons in this section to apply formatting style.

Choose a style in this option box on which to base the new style.

Click this button to display a list of formatting options.

The Create New Style from Formatting dialog box contains a number of options for specifying formatting for the new style. Use options in the *Formatting* section to apply character and paragraph formatting, such as changing the font, font size, font color, and font effects and changing the paragraph alignment, spacing, and indenting. Click the Format button in the lower left corner of the dialog box and a drop-down list displays with a number of formatting options. Use options at this drop-down list to specify formatting for the style with options in dialog boxes such as the Font, Paragraph, Tabs, Borders, Language, and Frame dialog boxes.

Unless the Create New Style from Formatting dialog box has been customized, the *Add to the Styles gallery* check box in the lower left corner of the dialog box contains a check mark. With this option active, the new style will display in the Styles group on the Home tab. Additionally, the *Only in this document* option is active. With this option active, the new style is saved only with the current document.

To make the style available for new documents based on the Normal template, click the *New documents based on this template* option. If a style is created in a template other than the Normal template, the style is available in the template or any other document based on the template with either option active. For example, in Activity 2, styles are created in the 1-BTStyles document and then the document is saved as a template named 1-BTTemplate. The styles created in the activity will be available in any document based on the 1-BTTemplate.

The *Automatically update* check box is empty by default. Insert a check mark in this check box and a style applied to text will be updated when changes are made to the style. Keep this option inactive if text should retain the original style formatting.

Assigning a Keyboard Shortcut to a Style

Consider assigning a keyboard shortcut to a style that is applied on a regular basis. A keyboard shortcut can be assigned to a style using any of the following combinations:

Alt + letter

Alt + Ctrl + letter

Alt + Shift + letter

Ctrl + Shift + letter

Alt + Ctrl + Shift + letter

Word already uses many combinations for Word functions. For example, pressing Ctrl + Shift + F displays the Font dialog box.

Assign a keyboard shortcut to a style by clicking the Format button at the bottom of the expanded Create New Style from Formatting dialog box as shown in Figure 1.3 (on page 8) and then clicking *Shortcut key* at the drop-down list. This displays the Customize Keyboard dialog box, shown in Figure 1.4. With the insertion point positioned in the *Press new shortcut key* text box, press the specific keys. Word inserts the message *Currently assigned to* below the *Current keys* list box. If the keyboard shortcut is already assigned to a command, the command is indicated after the *Currently assigned to* message. If the shortcut has not been assigned to any command, *[unassigned]* displays after the *Currently assigned to* message. When assigning a keyboard shortcut, use an unassigned combination of keystrokes.

Figure 1.4 Customize Keyboard Dialog Box

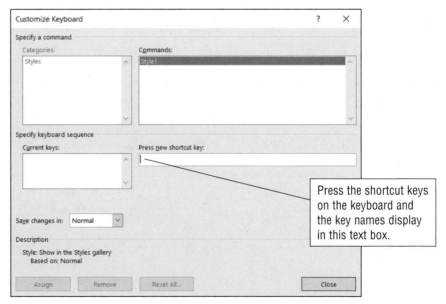

Press the shortcut keys on the keyboard and the key names display in this text box.

1. With **1-BTStyles** open, press Ctrl + End to move the insertion point to the end of the document.
2. Click the More Styles button in the Styles group.
3. Click *Create a Style* at the drop-down gallery.
4. At the Create New Style from Formatting dialog box, type CustomEmphasis in the *Name* text box.
5. Click the Modify button.

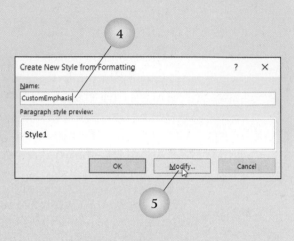

6. At the expanded Create New Style from Formatting dialog box, make the following changes:
   a. Click the *Font Size* option box arrow and then click *12* at the drop-down list.
   b. Click the *Font Color* option box arrow and then click the *Dark Blue* color (ninth option in the *Standard Colors* section).
   c. Click the Format button at the bottom of the Create New Style from Formatting dialog box and then click *Font* at the drop-down list.

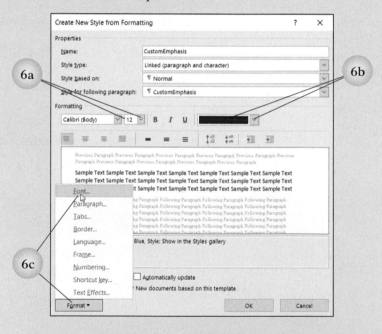

   d. At the Font dialog box, click the *Small caps* check box to insert a check mark and then click OK to close the dialog box.
   e. Click the Format button and then click *Paragraph* at the drop-down list.
   f. At the Paragraph dialog box with the Indents and Spacing tab selected, click the *Left* measurement box up arrow in the *Indentation* section until *0.3"* displays.
   g. Select the current measurement in the *After* measurement box in the *Spacing* section and then type 3.
   h. Click OK to close the Paragraph dialog box.
   i. Click OK to close the Create New Style from Formatting dialog box.

7. Create a character style and assign a keyboard shortcut to it by completing the following steps:

   a. Click the *No Spacing* style in the Styles group on the Home tab.

   b. Click the More Styles button in the Styles group and then click *Create a Style* at the drop-down gallery.

   c. At the Create New Style from Formatting dialog box, type Zenith in the *Name* text box.

   d. Click the Modify button.

   e. At the Create New Style from Formatting dialog box, click the *Style type* option box arrow and then click *Character* at the drop-down list.

   f. Click the *Font* option box arrow, scroll down the drop-down list, and then click *Imprint MT Shadow*.

   g. Click the Format button at the bottom of the dialog box and then click *Font* at the drop-down list.

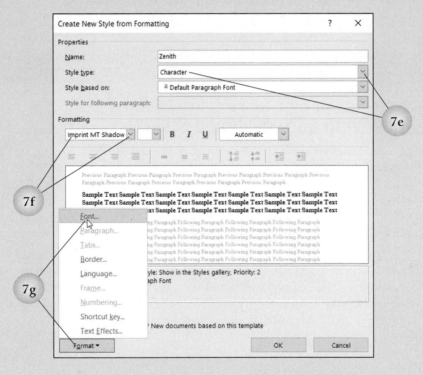

   h. At the Font dialog box, click the *Small caps* check box (displays with a solid square inside) to insert a check mark.

   i. Click OK to close the dialog box.

   j. Click the Format button and then click *Shortcut key* at the drop-down list.

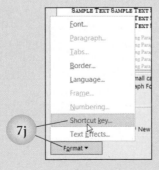

k. At the Customize Keyboard dialog box with the insertion point positioned in the *Press new shortcut key* text box, press the keys Alt + Z.

l. Check to make sure *[unassigned]* displays after *Currently assigned to*.

m. Click the Assign button.

n. Click the Close button to close the Customize Keyboard dialog box.

o. Click OK to close the Create New Style from Formatting dialog box.

8. Save **1-BTStyles**.

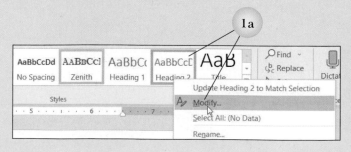

 Tutorial

Modifying a Predesigned Style

Ǫuick Steps

Modify Predesigned Style
1. Right-click style in Styles group or Styles drop-down gallery.
2. Click *Modify*.
3. Type new name for style.
4. Make changes.
5. Click OK.

Modifying a Predesigned Style

If a predesigned style contains most of the desired formatting, modify the style to create a new style. To do this, right-click the style in the Styles group and then click *Modify* at the shortcut menu. This displays the Modify Style dialog box, which contains the same options as the Create New Style from Formatting dialog box. Type a new name in the *Name* text box, make the desired changes, and then click OK.

Another method for modifying a predesigned style is to update the style to match selected text. To do this, apply a predesigned style to text, such as the Heading 1 style. Apply additional formatting to the text and then select the text. Right-click the *Heading 1* style in the Styles group and then click the *Update Heading 1 to Match Selection* option at the shortcut menu.

Activity 2c Modifying a Predesigned Style   Part 3 of 9

1. With **1-BTStyles** open, modify the Heading 2 style by completing the following steps:
   a. Right-click the *Heading 2* style in the Styles group on the Home tab and then click *Modify* at the shortcut menu.

b. At the Modify Style dialog box, type CustomHeading in the *Name* text box.

c. Click the *Font* option box arrow and then click *Constantia* at the drop-down list.

d. Click the Italic button to apply italic formatting.

e. Click the *Font Color* option box arrow and then click the *Dark Blue* color (ninth option in the *Standard Colors* section).

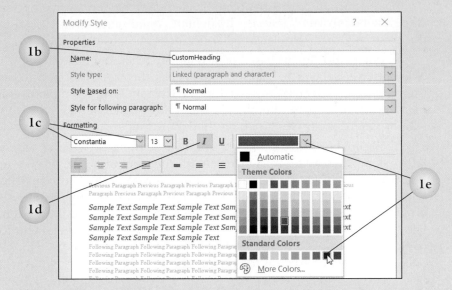

f. Click the Format button at the bottom of the dialog box and then click *Paragraph* at the drop-down list.

g. At the Paragraph dialog box with the Indents and Spacing tab selected, select the current measurement in the *After* measurement box in the *Spacing* section and then type 6.

h. Click OK to close the Paragraph dialog box.

i. Click the Format button at the bottom of the dialog box and then click *Border* at the drop-down list.

j. At the Borders and Shading dialog box, click the Shading tab.

k. Click the *Fill* option box arrow and then click the *Blue, Accent 1, Lighter 80%* color (fifth column, second row in the *Theme Colors* section).

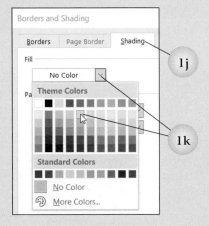

l. Click OK to close the Borders and Shading dialog box.

m. Click OK to close the Modify Style dialog box.

2. Save **1-BTStyles**.

Saving Styles in a Template

The styles created in 1-BTStyles are saved only in that document. To make the styles available for future Bayside Travel documents, save the document containing the styles as a template. With the styles saved in a template, a document can be opened based on the template and the styles will be available.

Save a document as a template by changing the *Save as type* option at the Save As dialog box to *Word Template*. By default, Word saves a template document in the Custom Office Templates folder on the local hard drive.

Quick Steps

Open Document Based on Template
1. Click File tab.
2. Click *New* option.
3. Click *Personal* option.
4. Click template thumbnail.

To open a document based on a template, click the File tab and then click the *New* option. At the New backstage area, click the *Personal* option to display thumbnails of the templates saved in the Custom Office Templates folder and then click the template thumbnail. The styles created and saved with the template will display in the Styles group on the Home tab.

In a school or other public environment, templates saved in the Custom Office Templates folder may be deleted if the computer is reset on a regular basis. Resetting a computer deletes any templates saved in the Custom Office Templates folder. Another option is to save a template to a specific folder, such as a folder on your storage medium, and then open a document based on the template using File Explorer. In Activity 2d, you will save the 1-BTStyles document as a template named 1-BTTemplate to your WL3C1 folder. You will then use File Explorer to open a document based on the template.

Activity 2d Saving Styles in a Template Opening a Document Based on a Template, and Applying Custom Styles

Part 4 of 9

1. With **1-BTStyles** open, press Ctrl + A to select all the text in the document (except the header and footer) and then press the Delete key.
2. Click the *No Spacing* style in the Styles group on the Home tab.
3. Save the document as a template by completing the following steps:
   a. Press the F12 function key to display the Save As dialog box.
   b. Click the *Save as type* option box and then click *Word Template* at the drop-down list.
   c. Click in the *File name* text box and then type 1-BTTemplate.
   d. Navigate to your WL3C1 folder.
   e. Click the Save button.
4. Close **1-BTTemplate**.
5. Open a document based on the template by completing the following steps:
   a. Click the File Explorer icon on the taskbar. (The taskbar displays along the bottom of the screen.)
   b. Navigate to your WL3C1 folder.
   c. Double-click *1-BTTemplate*.
6. Insert a document into the existing document by completing the following steps:
   a. Click the Insert tab and then click the Object button arrow in the Text group.
   b. Click *Text from File* at the drop-down list.
   c. Navigate to your WL3C1 folder and then double-click **BTZenith**.

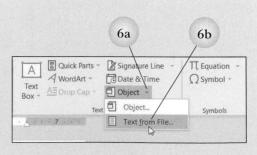

7. Apply the CustomTitle style by completing the following steps:
   a. Click in the title *Extreme Adventures*.
   b. Click the Home tab and then click the *CustomTitle* style in the Styles group.
   c. Scroll to the end of the document, click in the title *Volunteer Adventures*, and then click the *CustomTitle* style.
8. Apply the CustomHeading style by completing the following steps:
   a. Press Ctrl + Home to move the insertion point to the beginning of the document.
   b. Click in the heading *Antarctic Adventures*.
   c. Click the *CustomHeading* style in the Styles group. (Note that the style name begins with *Heading2* when you hover the mouse pointer over the style thumbnail.)

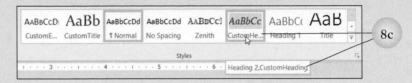

   d. Apply the CustomHeading style to the headings *Tall-Ship Adventures* and *Bicycling Adventures*.
9. Apply the CustomEmphasis style by completing the following steps:
   a. Select the indented lines of text in the *Antarctic Adventures* section that contain money amounts.
   b. Click the *CustomEmphasis* style in the Styles group.
   c. Apply the CustomEmphasis style to the indented lines of text in the *Tall-Ship Adventures* section that contain money amounts.
   d. Apply the CustomEmphasis style to the indented lines of text in the *Bicycling Adventures* section that contain money amounts.
10. Select the text *Zenith Adventures* in the first sentence in the first paragraph of text below the *Extreme Adventures* title and then press Alt + Z. (This applies the Zenith style.)
11. Press Ctrl + End to move the insertion point to the end of the document. Select the text *Zenith Adventures* in the first sentence of the last paragraph of text and then press Alt + Z to apply the Zenith style.
12. Save the document and name it **1-BTZenith**.

Check Your Work

Modifying an Applied Style

One of the advantages of applying styles in a document is that modifying the formatting of a style will automatically update all the text in the document to which that style has been applied. Using styles streamlines formatting and maintains consistency in documents.

1. With **1-BTZenith** open, edit the CustomTitle style to change the font size and alignment by completing the following steps:
   a. Right-click the *CustomTitle* style in the *Styles* gallery in the Styles group on the Home tab.
   b. Click *Modify* at the shortcut menu.
   c. At the Modify Style dialog box, change the font size to 22 points.
   d. Click the Align Left button in the *Formatting* section.
   e. Click OK to close the Modify Style dialog box.
2. Scroll through the document and notice that the modified custom title style is applied to both titles in the document.
3. Save **1-BTZenith**.

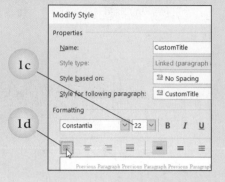

> Check Your Work

Displaying All Styles

Each style set contains a title style and body text style, a number of heading level styles, and other styles that are designed to work together in a single document. Only the styles for the currently selected style set display in the *Styles* drop-down gallery or Styles task pane. Display all available styles with options at the Style Pane Options dialog box, shown in Figure 1.5. Display this dialog box by clicking the Styles group task pane launcher or pressing the keyboard shortcut Alt + Ctrl + Shift + S to display the Styles task pane and then clicking the Options button in the lower right corner of the task pane.

To display all available styles, click the *Select styles to show* option box arrow and then click *All styles* at the drop-down list. Specify how the styles are sorted in the Styles task pane with the *Select how list is sorted* option.

Figure 1.5 Style Pane Options Dialog Box

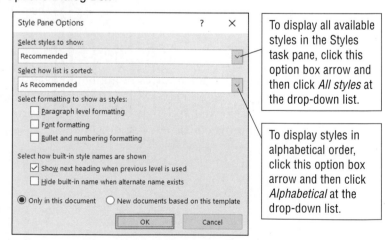

To display all available styles in the Styles task pane, click this option box arrow and then click *All styles* at the drop-down list.

To display styles in alphabetical order, click this option box arrow and then click *Alphabetical* at the drop-down list.

1. With **1-BTZenith** open, display all available styles in the Styles task pane by completing the following steps:
   a. Click the Styles group task pane launcher.
   b. Click the Options button in the lower right corner of the Styles task pane.
   c. At the Style Pane Options dialog box, click the *Select styles to show* option box arrow and then click *All styles* at the drop-down list.
   d. Click the *Select how list is sorted* option box arrow and then click *Alphabetical* at the drop-down list.
   e. Click OK to close the dialog box.

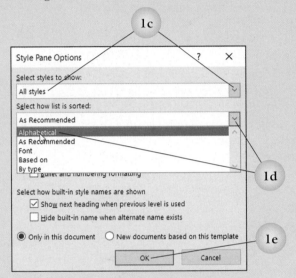

2. Apply styles by completing the following steps:
   a. Select the lines of text in the *Antarctic Adventures* section that contain money amounts.
   b. Click the *Body Text Indent* style.
   c. Click the *Book Title* style.
   d. Apply the Body Text Indent and Book Title styles to the two other sections of text that contain money amounts.
3. Save and then print **1-BTZenith**.

Revealing Style Formatting

Hover the mouse pointer over a style in the Styles task pane and a ScreenTip displays with information about the formatting applied by the style. Refer to the styles gallery in the Styles group to see a visual representation of the formatting applied by each style. Other methods for displaying a visual representation of styles include inserting a check mark in the *Show Preview* check box in the Styles task pane and displaying the Reveal Formatting task pane by pressing Shift + F1.

1. With **1-BTZenith** open, view the styles in the Styles task pane by completing the following steps:
   a. With the Styles task pane open, click the *Show Preview* check box to insert a check mark.
   b. Scroll through the list box to see how styles display with the preview feature turned on.
   c. Click the *Show Preview* check box to remove the check mark.
   d. Close the Styles task pane.
2. Display style formatting in the Reveal Formatting task pane by completing the following steps:
   a. Press Shift + F1 to turn on the display of the Reveal Formatting task pane.
   b. Click the *Distinguish style source* check box to insert a check mark.
   c. Click in the title *Extreme Adventures* and notice the formatting applied by the style displayed in the Reveal Formatting task pane.
   d. Click in the heading *Antarctic Adventures* and notice the formatting applied by the style displayed in the Reveal Formatting task pane.
   e. Click other text in the document and view the formatting.
   f. Click the *Distinguish style source* check box to remove the check mark.
   g. Press Shift + F1 to turn off the display of the Reveal Formatting task pane.
3. Save **1-BTZenith**.

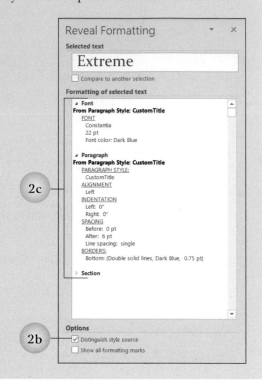

 Tutorial

Saving, Applying, and Deleting a Custom Style Set

Saving a Custom Style Set

Word provides a number of predesigned styles and groups styles that apply similar formatting into style sets. These style sets are available in the style sets gallery in the Document Formatting group on the Design tab. In addition to the style sets provided by Word, styles can be created and then saved into a custom style set. For example, the styles saved in the template 1-BTTemplate can be saved as a custom style set. The advantage to creating a custom style set is that the set is saved in the Normal template and is available for all documents, not just documents based on a specific template.

Quick Steps

Save Custom Style Set
1. Click Design tab.
2. Click More Style Sets button in Document Formatting group.
3. Click *Save as a New Style Set*.
4. Type custom style set file name.
5. Click Save button.

To save styles in a custom style set, click the Design tab, click the More Style Sets button at the right side of the style sets gallery in the Document Formatting group, and then click *Save as a New Style Set* at the drop-down gallery. This displays the Save as a New Style Set dialog box and makes the QuickStyles subfolder on the local hard drive the active folder. The *Save as type* option at the dialog box is set at *Word Templates*. The custom style set is saved as a template that is available with the Normal template, which is the default template on which most documents are based. Type a name for the style set in the *File name* text box and then press the Enter key or click the Save button. The custom style set will be available in the style sets gallery in the Document Formatting group on the Design tab for all documents.

Changing Default Settings

If a predesigned or custom style set is applied to most documents, it can be specified as the default style set for all future documents. Change the default style set with the Set as Default button in the Document Formatting group on the Design tab. In addition to changing the default style set, default settings can be changed by making changes to the theme, theme colors, theme fonts, theme effects, and paragraph spacing in a document. Click the Set as Default button and a confirmation message displays asking if the current style set and theme should be the default. At this message, click Yes.

When the current style set, themes, theme colors, theme fonts, theme effects, and paragraph spacing are specified as the default, the changes are made to the Normal template. To return to the original default settings, open a document that was created before the default settings were changed, click the Set as Default button in the Document Formatting group on the Design tab, and then click Yes at the confirmation message.

Activity 2h **Saving Styles in a Custom Style Set**   Part 8 of 9

1. With **1-BTZenith** open, save the styles in a custom style set by completing the following steps:
   a. Click the Design tab.
   b. Click the More Style Sets button at the right side of the style sets gallery in the Document Formatting group.
   c. Click the *Save as a New Style Set* option at the drop-down gallery.
   d. At the Save as a New Style Set dialog box, type XXX-BTStyles (typing your initials in place of the *XXX*) and then press the Enter key.

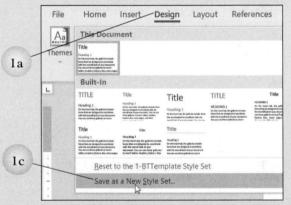

2. Save, print, and then close **1-BTZenith**.
3. Open **BTVacations** and then save it with the name **1-BTVacations**.
4. Apply the XXX-BTStyles custom style set (where your initials display in place of the *XXX*) by completing the following steps:
   a. Click the Design tab.
   b. Click the More Style Sets button in the Document Formatting group.
   c. Click the *XXX-BTStyles* custom style set (where your initials display in place of the *XXX*) in the *Custom* section of the drop-down gallery.
5. Click the Home tab and then apply the following styles to the specified text:
   a. Apply the CustomTitle style to the title *Vacation Adventures*.

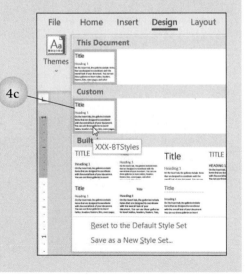

b. Apply the CustomHeading style to the headings *Disneyland Adventure*, *Florida Adventure*, and *Cancun Adventure*.

c. Apply the CustomEmphasis style to the bulleted text below the *Disneyland Adventure* heading, *Florida Adventure* heading, and *Cancun Adventure* heading.

6. Save and then print **1-BTVacations**.

Deleting a Custom Style Set

Quick Steps
Delete Custom Style Set
1. Click Design tab.
2. Click More Style Sets button in Document Formatting group.
3. Right-click custom style set in *Custom* section.
4. Click *Delete*.
5. Click Yes.

If a custom style set is no longer needed, delete it at the style sets drop-down gallery. To do this, click the Design tab and then click the More Style Sets button in the Document Formatting group. At the drop-down gallery, right-click the custom style set in the *Custom* section and then click *Delete* at the shortcut menu. At the confirmation message, click Yes.

Activity 2i Deleting a Custom Style Set   Part 9 of 9

1. With **1-BTVacations** open, delete the XXX-BTStyles custom style set (where your initials display in place of the *XXX*) by completing the following steps:

a. Click the Design tab.

b. Click the More Style Sets button in the Document Formatting group.

c. Right-click the *XXX-BTStyles* custom style set (where your initials display in place of the *XXX*) in the *Custom* section of the drop-down gallery.

d. Click *Delete* at the shortcut menu.

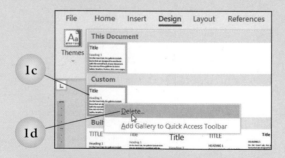

e. At the message that displays, click Yes.

2. Save and then close **1-BTVacations**.

Creating Styles for Lists and Tables

In addition to custom character and paragraph styles and style sets, custom styles can be created for multilevel lists and tables. These styles cannot be saved to the Styles group or style sets gallery, but they can be saved in the current document or in a template.

Tutorial

Creating a
Multilevel List Style

Creating a Multilevel List Style

Word provides a number of predesigned list styles that can be applied to text in a document. These styles are generally paragraph styles that apply formatting to text such as paragraph indenting and spacing and that apply formatting only to one level of the list. To create a multilevel list style that applies formatting to more than one level, create the style at the Define New List Style dialog box, shown in Figure 1.6. Display this dialog box by clicking the Multilevel List button in the Paragraph group on the Home tab and then clicking *Define New List Style* at the drop-down list. A multilevel list style can also be created at the Create New Style from Formatting dialog box by changing the *Style type* option to *List*.

Multilevel List

Figure 1.6 Define New List Style Dialog Box

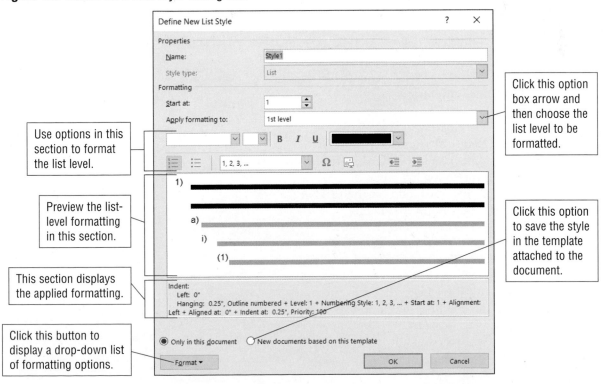

The Define New List Style dialog box (and the Create New Style from Formatting dialog box with *List* selected as the *Style type* option) contains the same options as the Create New Style from Formatting dialog box with *Paragraph*, *Character*, or *Linked (paragraph and character)* selected along with some additional options, such as the *Start at* and *Apply formatting to* options. By default, the *Apply formatting to* option is set at *1st level*. With this option selected, apply the formatting for the letter, number, or symbol that begins the first level of the list. (The formatting applied affects only the letter, number, or symbol—not the following text.)

After specifying formatting for the first level, click the *Apply formatting to* option box arrow, click *2nd level* at the drop-down list, and then apply the formatting for the second level. Continue in this manner until formatting has been applied to the desired number of levels.

Updating a Template with an Updated Style

Create a style in a document based on a template and the style can be saved in the template, making it available for any future documents created with that template. A document based on a template is attached to the template. To save a style in a template, open a document based on the template, create the style, and then click the *New documents based on this template* option at the Create New Style dialog box. When the document is saved, a message displays asking if the attached document template should be updated. At this message, click Yes.

Activity 3a **Saving a Document as a Template and Creating and Applying a Multilevel List Style**

Part 1 of 6

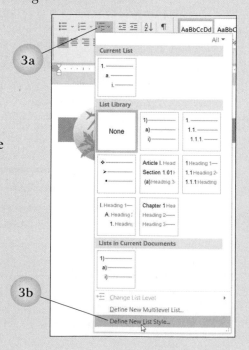

1. Open **BTListTableTemplate** and then save it as a template by completing the following steps:
   a. Press the F12 function key to display the Save As dialog box.
   b. At the Save As dialog box, click the *Save as type* option box and then click *Word Template* at the drop-down list.
   c. Click in the *File name* text box and then type 1-BTListTableTemplate.
   d. Navigate to your WL3C1 folder.
   e. Click the Save button.
   f. Close **1-BTListTableTemplate**.
2. Open a document based on **1-BTListTableTemplate** by completing the following steps:
   a. Click the File Explorer icon on the taskbar.
   b. Navigate to your WL3C1 folder.
   c. Double-click *1-BTListTableTemplate*.
3. At the document based on the template, create a multilevel list style by completing the following steps:
   a. Click the Multilevel List button in the Paragraph group on the Home tab.
   b. Click the *Define New List Style* option at the bottom of the drop-down list.

c. At the Define New List Style dialog box, type BTMultilevelList in the *Name* text box.

d. Click the Bold button.

e. Click the option box arrow right of the option box containing *1, 2, 3, ...* and then click *A, B, C, ...* at the drop-down list.

f. Click the *Font Color* option box arrow and then click the *Dark Blue* color (ninth option in the *Standard Colors* section).

g. Click the *Apply formatting to* option box arrow and then click *2nd level* at the drop-down list.

h. Click the Symbol button below the *Font Color* option.

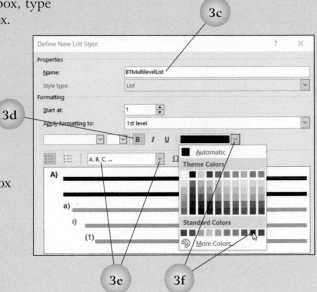

i. At the Symbol dialog box, change the font to Wingdings, double-click the current number in the *Character code* text box, type 173 to select the ✹ symbol, and then click OK.

j. At the Define New List Style dialog box, click the Bold button and then change the font color to Dark Blue.

k. Click the *Apply formatting to* option box arrow and then click *3rd level* at the drop-down list.

l. Click the Symbol button.

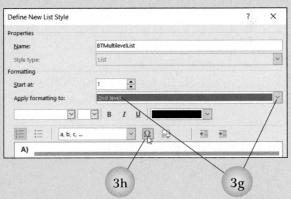

m. At the Symbol dialog box, make sure that Wingdings is selected as the font, double-click the current number in the *Character code* text box, type 252 to select the ✓ symbol, and then click OK.

n. At the Define New List Style dialog box, click the Bold button and then make sure the font color is Dark Blue.

o. Click *New documents based on this template* near the bottom of the dialog box.

p. Click OK to close the Define New List Style dialog box.

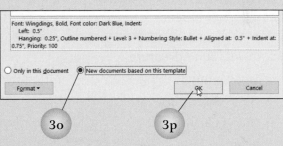

4. Close the document without saving it. At the message asking if you want to save changes to 1-BTListTableTemplate, click the Save button.

5. Open a document based on the template by completing the following steps:
   a. Click the File Explorer icon on the taskbar.
   b. Navigate to your WL3C1 folder.
   c. Double-click *1-BTListTableTemplate*.

6. Insert a document into the current document by completing the following steps:
   a. Click the Insert tab.
   b. Click the Object button arrow and then click *Text from File* at the drop-down list.
   c. Navigate to your WL3C1 folder and then double-click *BTTourList*.

7. Apply the multilevel style you created by completing the following steps:
   a. Select the text that was just inserted.
   b. Click the Home tab and then click the Multilevel List button in the Paragraph group.
   c. If necessary, scroll down the drop-down list and then click the multilevel list style you created (in the *List Styles* section). (Hover the mouse pointer over the multilevel list and a ScreenTip will display with the style name.)

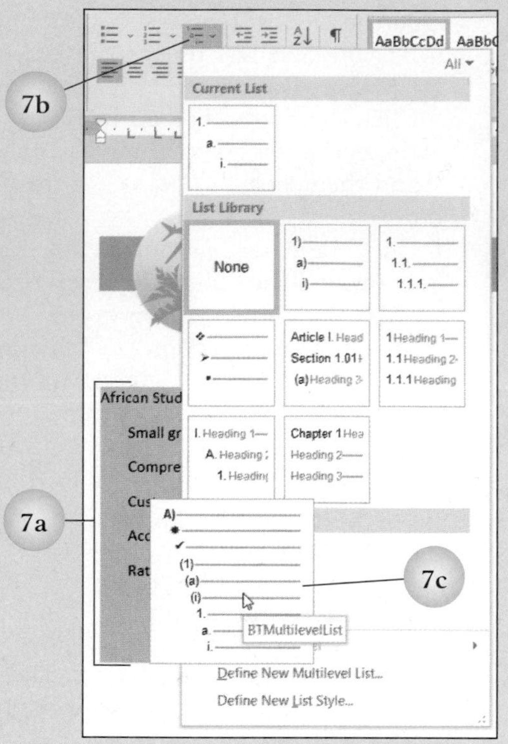

8. Add the text shown in Figure 1.7 to the document by completing the following steps:
   a. Move the insertion point so it is immediately right of the text *Double-occupancy rate: $2,755* and then press the Enter key. (This moves the insertion point down to the next line and inserts a check mark bullet.)
   b. Click the Decrease Indent button in the Paragraph group on the Home tab two times to move the insertion point to the left margin. (This inserts *B)* in the document.)
   c. Type the text shown in Figure 1.7. (When typing the text, click the Increase Indent button to move the insertion point to the next level.)

9. Click the Design tab, click the Paragraph Spacing button in the Document Formatting group, and then click *Double* at the drop-down gallery.

10. Save the document in your WL3C1 folder and name it **1-BTTours**.

11. Print and then close **1-BTTours**.

Check Your Work

Figure 1.7 Activity 3a

Southwest Sun Adventure
   Small groups
   Guided day trips
   Grand Canyon vistas
   Bilingual tour guides
   Rates
      Single-occupancy rate: $1,450
      Double-occupancy rate: $1,249

Creating a Table Style

The Table Tools Design tab contains a number of predesigned styles that can be applied to a table. If none of these styles applies the desired formatting to a table, create a custom table style.

Create a table style at the Create New Style from Formatting dialog box with *Table* selected in the *Style type* option box, as shown in Figure 1.8. Display this dialog box by clicking the More Styles button in the Styles group on the Home tab and then clicking *Create a Style*. At the Create New Style from Formatting dialog box, click the Modify button. Click the *Style type* option box arrow and then click *Table* at the drop-down list. This dialog box can also be displayed by inserting a table in the document, clicking the More Table Styles button in the Table Styles group on the Table Tools Design tab, and then clicking *New Table Style* at the drop-down list.

The Create New Style from Formatting dialog box with *Table* selected as the style type contains options for formatting the entire table or specific portions of the table. By default, *Whole table* is selected in the *Apply formatting to* option. With this option selected, any formatting options that are chosen will affect the entire table. To format a specific part of the table, click the *Apply formatting to* option box arrow and then click the desired option at the drop-down list. Use options at this drop-down list to specify formatting for sections in the table, such as the header row, total row, first column, last column, odd banded rows, even banded rows, and so on.

Figure 1.8 Create New Style from Formatting Dialog Box with the *Table* Style Type Selected

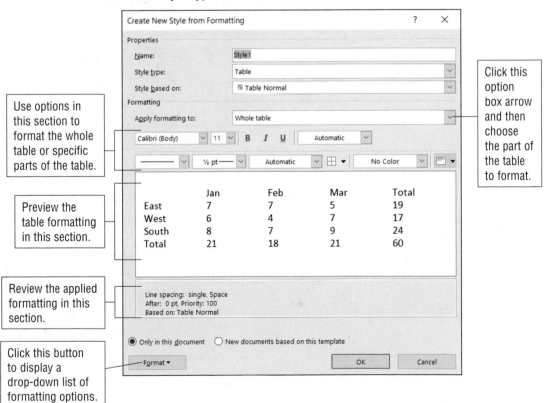

1. Display the Open dialog box and then open **1-BTListTableTemplate** located in your WL3C1 folder. (If the template is not visible, click the option box to the right of the *File name* text box at the Open dialog box and then click *All Files* at the drop-down list.)
2. Create a table style by completing the following steps:
   a. Click the More Styles button in the Styles group on the Home tab and then click *Create a Style* at the drop-down list.
   b. At the Create New Style from Formatting dialog box, type BTTable in the *Name* text box.
   c. Click the Modify button.
   d. At the Create New Style from Formatting dialog box, click the *Style type* option box arrow and then click *Table* at the drop-down list.

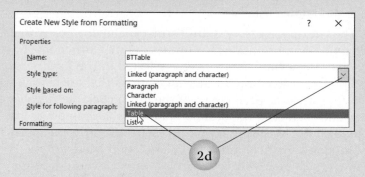

   e. Make sure *Whole table* is selected in the *Apply formatting to* option box.
   f. Click the *Font* option box arrow and then click *Constantia* at the drop-down list.
   g. Click the *Font Size* option box arrow and then click *12* at the drop-down list.
   h. Click the *Font Color* option box arrow and then click the *Dark Blue* color (ninth color option in the *Standard Colors* section).
   i. Click the Border button arrow and then click *All Borders* at the drop-down list. (See the image below to locate the button.)

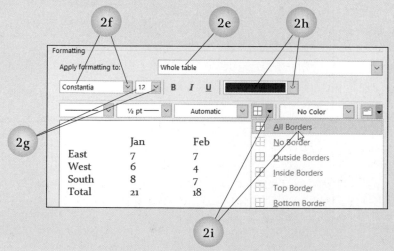

j. Click the *Apply formatting to* option box arrow and then click *Header row* at the drop-down list.

k. Click the *Font Size* option box arrow and then click *14* at the drop-down list.

l. Click the Bold button.

m. Click the *Fill Color* option box arrow and then click *Orange, Accent 2, Lighter 40%* (sixth column, fourth row in the *Theme Colors* section).

n. Click the Alignment button arrow immediately right of the *Fill Color* option and then click *Align Center* at the drop-down list.

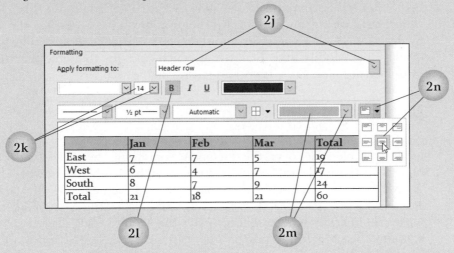

o. Click the *Apply formatting to* option box arrow and then click *Even banded rows* at the drop-down list.

p. Click the *Fill Color* option box arrow and then click *Orange, Accent 2, Lighter 80%* (sixth column, second row in the *Theme Colors* section).

q. Click OK to close the Create New Style from Formatting dialog box.

3. Save and then close **1-BTListTableTemplate**.

4. Open a document based on the template by completing the following steps:

a. Click the File Explorer icon on the taskbar.

b. Navigate to your WL3C1 folder.

c. Double-click **1-BTListTableTemplate**.

5. Insert a document into the current document by completing the following steps:

a. Press the Enter key two times and then click the Insert tab.

b. Click the Object button arrow in the Text group and then click *Text from File* at the drop-down list.

c. Navigate to your WL3C1 folder and then double-click **BTAdvTables**.

6. Apply the table style you created by completing the following steps:

a. Click in any cell in the top table.

b. Click the Table Tools Design tab.

c. In the Table Styles group, click the table style you created. (Your table style should be the first thumbnail in the group. If it is not, click the More Table Styles button in the Table Styles group and then click your table style at the drop-down gallery. To find your table style, hover the mouse pointer over a table and wait for the ScreenTip to display the style name.)

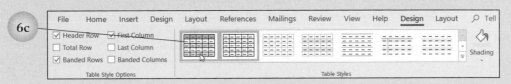

7. Apply your table style to the two other tables in the document.
8. Save the document and name it **1-BTTables**.
9. Print **1-BTTables**.

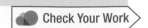

Modifying a Multilevel List Style

Like other styles, a multilevel list style can be modified. To do this, click the Multilevel List button, scroll down the drop-down list to display the style to be modified, right-click the style, and then click *Modify* at the shortcut menu. This displays the Modify Style dialog box, which contains the same formatting options as the Create New Style from Formatting dialog box.

Modifying a Table Style

A custom table style or one of the predesigned table styles can be modified. To modify a table style, open the document containing the table style. Click in a table with that style applied or insert a new table in the document. Click the Table Tools Design tab, right-click the table style, and then click *Modify Table Style* at the shortcut menu. (If the table style is not visible, click the More Table Styles button in the Table Styles group.) This displays the Modify Style dialog box, which contains the same formatting options as the Create New Style from Formatting dialog box.

Activity 3c **Modifying a Table Style**   *Part 3 of 6*

1. With **1-BTTables** open, save it with the name **1-BTTablesModified**.
2. Modify the table style you created by completing the following steps:
   a. Click in any cell in the top table.
   b. Click the Table Tools Design tab.
   c. Right-click your table style and then click *Modify Table Style* at the shortcut menu. (Your table style should be the first thumbnail in the Table Styles group. If your table style is not visible, click the More Table Styles button in the Table Styles group and then locate your table style.)

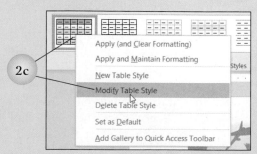

   d. At the Modify Style dialog box, click the Format button in the lower left corner of the dialog box and then click *Table Properties* at the drop-down list.

e. At the Table Properties dialog box with the Table tab selected, click the *Center* option in the *Alignment* section.

f. Click OK to close the Table Properties dialog box.

g. Click the *Apply formatting to* option box arrow and then click *Odd banded rows* at the drop-down list.

h. Click the *Fill Color* option box arrow and then click *Blue, Accent 1, Lighter 80%* (fifth column, second row in the *Theme Colors* section).

i. Click the *New documents based on this template* option (at the bottom of the dialog box).

j. Click OK to close the Modify Style dialog box. (Notice that the formatting changes for all three tables in the document because the table style is applied to each table.)

2e

3. Select the second row in the top table of the document, press Ctrl + B to apply bold formatting, and then press Ctrl + E to center the text in the cells.

4. Apply bold formatting to and center-align the second row in the middle table and the second row in the bottom table.

5. Save and then print **1-BTTablesModified**. (If a message displays asking if you want to save the changes to the template, click Yes.)

6. Close **1-BTTablesModified**.

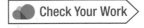
Check Your Work

Using the Style Inspector Task Pane

When working with styles and creating and applying styles to documents, a situation may arise in which multiple styles have been applied to the text. If multiple styles are applied and the formatting is not what is intended, investigate the document styles using the Style Inspector task pane.

Quick Steps

Display Style Inspector Task Pane

1. Click Styles group task pane launcher.
2. Click Style Inspector button.

Display the Style Inspector task pane by clicking the Styles group task pane launcher to display the Styles task pane and then clicking the Style Inspector button at the bottom of the task pane. The Style Inspector task pane displays paragraph- and text-level formatting for the paragraph where the insertion point is positioned. Figure 1.9 displays the Style Inspector task pane with the insertion point positioned in the title in 1-BTZenith.

The *Paragraph formatting* option box and the *Text level formatting* option box display style formatting applied to the selected text or character where the insertion point is positioned. A box displays below each option that contains the word *Plus:* followed by any additional formatting that is not specific to the style formatting.

Hover the mouse pointer over the *Paragraph formatting* option box or *Text level formatting* option box and a down arrow displays. Click the arrow and a drop-down list displays with options for clearing the formatting applied to the text, applying a new style, and displaying the Reveal Formatting task pane. Click the New Style button right of the Reveal Formatting button and the Create New Style from Formatting dialog box displays.

Use the buttons right of the *Paragraph formatting* option box to return the paragraph style back to the Normal style and clear any paragraph formatting applied to the text. Use the buttons right of the *Text level formatting* option box to clear character formatting applied to text.

Figure 1.9 Style Inspector Task Pane

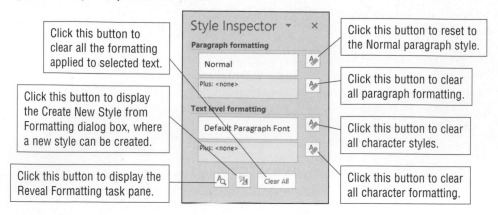

Click this button to clear all the formatting applied to selected text.

Click this button to display the Create New Style from Formatting dialog box, where a new style can be created.

Click this button to display the Reveal Formatting task pane.

Click this button to reset to the Normal paragraph style.

Click this button to clear all paragraph formatting.

Click this button to clear all character styles.

Click this button to clear all character formatting.

Activity 3d Using the Style Inspector Task Pane

1. Open **1-BTZenith** and then save it with the name **1-BTZenithAdvs**.
2. Make sure the insertion point is positioned at the beginning of the title *Extreme Adventures*.
3. Click the Styles group task pane launcher. (This displays the Styles task pane.)
4. Display the Style Inspector task pane by clicking the Style Inspector button at the bottom of the Styles task pane.
5. At the Style Inspector task pane, hover the mouse pointer over the *Paragraph formatting* option box and then look at the information about the custom title style in the ScreenTip.
6. Click in the heading *Antarctic Adventures*.
7. Hover the mouse pointer over the *Paragraph formatting* option and then look at the information that displays about the custom heading.
8. Remove paragraph and character styles and apply a style to the text in the document by completing the following steps:
   a. Select the indented lines of text in the *Antarctic Adventures* section that contain money amounts.
   b. Remove the paragraph style from the text by clicking the Reset to Normal Paragraph Style button right of the *Paragraph formatting* option box.
   c. Remove the character style from the text by clicking the Clear Character Style button right of the *Text level formatting* option box.
   d. Click the *Block Text* style in the Styles task pane.
9. Select the indented lines of text in the *Tall-Ship Adventures* section that contain money amounts and then complete Steps 8b through 8d to remove styles and apply a style.

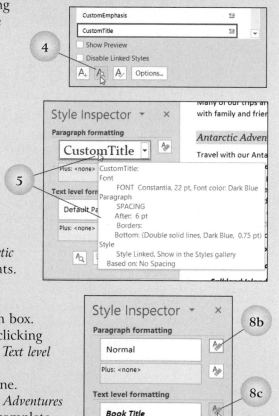

10. Select the lines of text in the *Bicycling Adventures* section that contain money amounts and then complete Steps 8b through 8d to remove styles and apply a style.
11. Close the Style Inspector task pane. (Leave the Styles task pane open.)
12. Save **1-BTZenithAdvs**.

 Check Your Work

 Tutorial
Managing Styles

 Paragraph Spacing

Q̃uick Steps

Display Manage Styles Dialog Box
1. Click Styles group task pane launcher.
2. Click Manage Styles button.

Managing Styles

The Manage Styles dialog box provides one location for managing all styles. Display this dialog box, shown in Figure 1.10, by clicking the Manage Styles button at the bottom of the Styles task pane or by clicking the Paragraph Spacing button in the Document Formatting group on the Design tab and then clicking *Custom Paragraph Spacing* at the drop-down gallery.

The options available in the Manage Styles dialog box vary depending on which tab is selected. Select the Edit tab and options are available to sort styles, select a style to edit and modify, and create a new style.

Click the Recommend tab and options display for specifying which styles to display in the Styles pane and in what order. With the Recommend tab selected, styles display in the list box preceded by priority numbers. Styles display in ascending order, with the styles preceded by the lowest numbers displaying first. The priority of a style can be changed by clicking the style in the list box and then clicking the Move Up button, Move Down button, or Move Last button, or a value number can be assigned with the Assign Value button.

With the Restrict tab selected, access to styles can be permitted or restricted. This allows control over which styles other individuals can apply or modify in a document.

Figure 1.10 Manage Styles Dialog Box

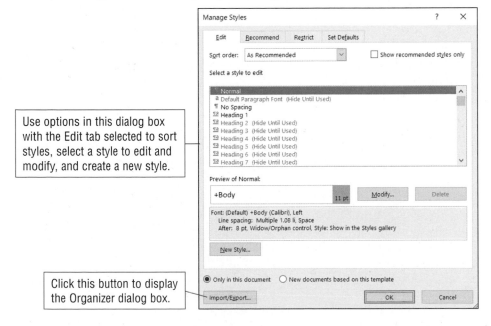

Use options in this dialog box with the Edit tab selected to sort styles, select a style to edit and modify, and create a new style.

Click this button to display the Organizer dialog box.

Click the Set Defaults tab to display character and formatting options and specify whether changes made in the dialog box will affect the current document or all documents based on the current document. If the default document is being used, changes will affect the Normal template.

Activity 3e Managing Styles

1. With **1-BTZenithAdvs** open, make sure the Styles task pane displays. (If not, click the Styles group task pane launcher.)
2. Click in the first paragraph of text. (Do not click a title or heading.)
3. Click the Manage Styles button (located to the left of the Options button at the bottom of the Styles task pane).
4. At the Manage Styles dialog box, make sure the Edit tab is active. (If not, click the Edit tab.)
5. Click the *Show recommended styles only* check box to insert a check mark. (This causes only the styles recommended by Word [along with your custom styles] to display in the *Select a style to edit* list box.)
6. Make sure *As Recommended* is selected in the *Sort order* option box. (If not, click the *Sort order* option box arrow and then click *As Recommended* at the drop-down list.)
7. Create a new style by completing the following steps:
   a. Click the New Style button near the lower left corner of the dialog box.

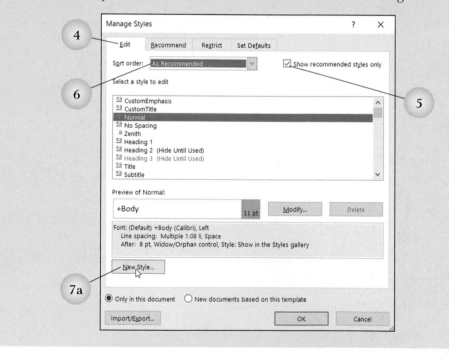

b. At the Create New Style from Formatting dialog box, type CoNameEmphasis in the *Name* text box.

c. Click the *Style type* option box arrow and then click *Character* at the drop-down list.

d. Click the Bold button in the *Formatting* section of the dialog box.

e. Click the Italic button.

f. Click the *Font Color* option box arrow and then click the *Dark Blue* color (ninth option in the *Standard Colors* section).

g. Click the *Add to the Styles gallery* check box in the lower left corner of the dialog box to insert a check mark. (Skip this step if the check box already contains a check mark.)

h. Click OK to close the Create New Style from Formatting dialog box.

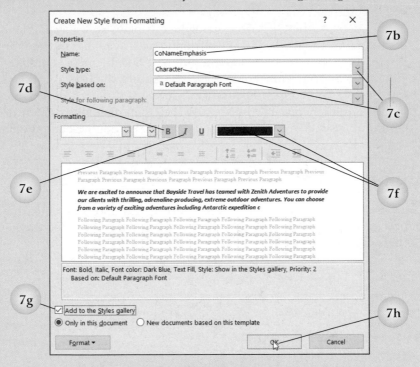

8. Specify that you want the CoNameEmphasis style to be prioritized as number 1 by completing the following steps:

a. At the Manage Styles dialog box, click the Recommend tab.

b. Make sure the CoNameEmphasis style is selected in the list box.

c. Click the Move Up button. (Notice that the CoNameEmphasis style moves to near the top of the list.)

d. Click OK to close the Manage Styles dialog box.

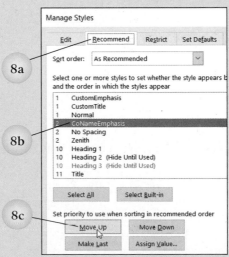

9. Select the company name *Bayside Travel* in the first paragraph of the document and then apply the CoNameEmphasis style.

10. Select the company name *Bayside Travel* in the last paragraph of the document and then apply the CoNameEmphasis style.

11. Close the Styles task pane.

12. Save, print, and then close **1-BTZenithAdvs**.

Check Your Work

Copying Styles Between Documents and Templates

Quick Steps

Display Organizer Dialog Box
1. Click Styles group task pane launcher.
2. Click Manage Styles button.
3. Click Import/Export button.

A style (or styles) created for a specific document or template can be copied to the default template, the Normal template, or another template. Copy the style using the Organizer dialog box with the Styles tab selected, as shown in Figure 1.11. Display this dialog box by clicking the Import/Export button at the Manage Styles dialog box.

At the Organizer dialog box with the Styles tab selected, copy a style from a document or template to another document or template and then delete and rename the styles. To copy a style, click the style in the list box at the left and then click the Copy button between the two list boxes. Complete similar steps to delete a style.

By default, the Organizer dialog box displays styles available in the open document in the list box at the left and styles available in the Normal template in the list box at the right. Choose a different document or template by clicking the Close File button. This removes the styles from the list box and changes the Close File button to the Open File button. Choose a different document or template by clicking the Open File button. At the Open dialog box, navigate to the folder containing the document or template and then double-click the document or template.

Renaming Styles

To rename a style, click the style in the list box and then click the Rename button between the two list boxes. At the Rename dialog box, type the new name and then press the Enter key.

Figure 1.11 Organizer Dialog Box

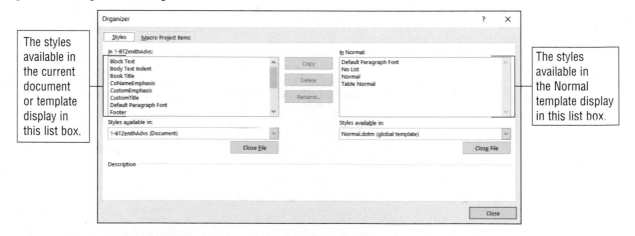

The styles available in the current document or template display in this list box.

The styles available in the Normal template display in this list box.

Activity 3f Copying Styles Between Templates at the Organizer Dialog Box

Part 6 of 6

1. The templates **1-BTTemplate** and **1-BTListTableTemplate** both contain styles for formatting Bayside Travel documents. Copy the Bayside Travel styles in **1-BTListTableTemplate** to **1-BTTemplate** by completing the following steps:
   a. Press Ctrl + N to display a blank document.
   b. Display the Styles task pane.

c. Click the Manage Styles button at the bottom of the Styles task pane.

d. At the Manage Styles dialog box, click the Import/Export button in the lower left corner.

e. At the Organizer dialog box, click the Close File button below the left list box.

f. Click the Open File button (previously the Close File button).

g. At the Open dialog box, navigate to your WL3C1 folder and then double-click *1-BTListTableTemplate* in the Content pane.

h. Click the Close File button below the right list box.

i. Click the Open File button (previously the Close File button).

j. At the Open dialog box, navigate to your WL3C1 folder and then double-click *1-BTTemplate* in the Content pane.

k. Click the *BTTable* style in the left list box.

l. Click the Copy button between the two list boxes.

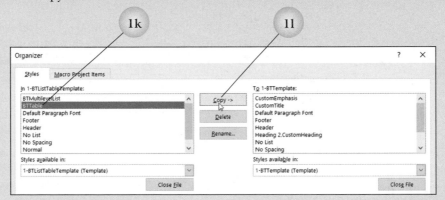

m. Click the *BTMultilevelList* style in the left list box.

n. Click the Copy button between the two list boxes.

o. Click the Close button to close the Organizer dialog box.

p. If a message displays asking if you want to save the changes made to **1-BTTemplate**, click the Save button.

2. Open a document based on **1-BTTemplate** by completing the following steps:

   a. Click the File Explorer icon.

   b. Navigate to your WL3C1 folder.

   c. Double-click *1-BTTemplate*.

3. Insert a document into the existing document by completing the following steps:

   a. Click the Insert tab.

   b. Click the Object button arrow and then click *Text from File* at the drop-down list.

   c. Navigate to your WL3C1 folder and then double-click *BTEastAdventures*.

4. Apply the following styles to the document:

   a. Apply the CustomTitle style to the title *Eastern Adventures*.

   b. Apply the CustomHeading style to the two headings in the document.

   c. Apply the BTTable style to the two tables in the document.

5. Save the document and name it **1-BTEastAdventures**. If a message displays asking if you want to save the changes to the document template, click Yes.

6. Print and then close **1-BTEastAdventures**.

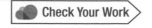

Chapter Summary

- A style is a set of formatting instructions that can be applied to text. Word provides a number of predesigned styles and groups them into style sets. Styles are available in style sets in the Styles group on the Home tab.

- Apply a style by clicking the style in the Styles group or by clicking the More Styles button and then clicking the style at the drop-down gallery. The Styles task pane provides another method for applying a style. Display the task pane by clicking the Styles group task pane.

- A style can be created based on existing formatting or style formatting or by modifying a predesigned style. A new style can also be created without first applying formatting to text.

- Create a new style at the Create New Style from Formatting dialog box. Display this dialog box by clicking the More Styles button in the Styles group on the Home tab and then clicking *Create a Style* at the drop-down gallery.

- Use options at the expanded Create New Style from Formatting dialog box to name the style and specify the style type and style formatting.

- Assign a keyboard shortcut to a style with options at the Customize Keyboard dialog box. Display this dialog box by clicking the Format button at the expanded Create New Style from Formatting dialog box and then clicking *Shortcut key* at the drop-down list.

- Modify a predesigned style by right-clicking the style in the Styles group and then clicking *Modify* at the shortcut menu. Type a name for the style at the Modify Style dialog box, make the formatting changes, and then click OK.

- To make the styles in a document available for future documents, save the document as a template. Do this by displaying the Save As dialog box, changing the *Save as type* option to *Word Template*, and then clicking the Save button.

- Open a document based on a template saved in the default folder, Custom Office Templates, by clicking the File tab and then clicking the *New* option. At the New backstage area, click the *Personal* option and then click the template thumbnail.

- Open a document based on a template that is saved to a location other than the default folder, Custom Office Templates, by opening the template using File Explorer.

- Display all available styles with options at the Style Pane Options dialog box. Display the dialog box by clicking the Styles group task pane launcher or by displaying the Styles task pane using the keyboard shortcut Alt + Ctrl + Shift + S and then clicking the Options button in the lower right corner.

- Reveal style formatting by hovering the mouse pointer over a style in the Styles task pane, by inserting a check mark in the *Show Preview* check box in the Styles task pane, or by pressing Shift + F1 to turn on the display of the Reveal Formatting task pane.

- Save styles in a custom style set by clicking the Design tab, clicking the More Style Sets button in the Document Formatting group, and then clicking *Save as a New Style Set* at the drop-down gallery. At the Save as a New Style Set dialog box, type a name for the new style set and then click the Save button. The custom style set will be available for all future documents based on the Normal template.

- Change default settings by choosing a style set, theme, theme colors, theme fonts, theme effects, and/or paragraph spacing and then clicking the Set as Default button in the Document Formatting group on the Design tab.

- Delete a custom style set by clicking the More Style Sets button in the Document Formatting group on the Design tab, right-clicking the custom style set, and then clicking *Delete* at the shortcut menu.

- Create a multilevel list style at the Define New List Style dialog box. Display this dialog box by clicking the Multilevel List button in the Paragraph group on the Home tab and then clicking *Define New Style List*.

- A multilevel list style can also be created at the Create New Style from Formatting dialog box with the *Style type* option changed to *List*. Specify formatting for each level in the list.

- A multilevel list style displays in the *List Styles* section of the Multilevel List button drop-down list.

- To save a style in a template, open a document based on the template, create the style, and then click the *New documents based on this template* option at the Create New Style dialog box.

- Create a table style at the Create New Style from Formatting dialog box with *Table* selected in the *Style type* option box. Specify formatting for the entire table or specific parts of the table.

- A custom table style displays in the Table Styles group on the Table Tools Design tab.

- Modify a multilevel list style by clicking the Multilevel List button, right-clicking the style, and then clicking *Modify* at the shortcut menu. This displays the Modify Style dialog box with options for specifying changes to the style.

- Modify a table style by clicking in a table, clicking the Table Tools Design tab, right-clicking the table style, and then clicking *Modify Table Style* at the shortcut menu. This displays the Modify Style dialog box with options for specifying changes to the style.

- Use the Style Inspector task pane to investigate the styles applied to text in a document. Display the Style Inspector task pane by displaying the Styles task pane and then clicking the Style Inspector button at the bottom of the task pane.

- The Manage Styles dialog box provides one location for managing all styles. Display this dialog box by clicking the Manage Styles button at the bottom of the Styles task pane or by clicking the Paragraph Spacing button in the Document Formatting group on the Design tab and then clicking *Custom Paragraph Spacing* at the drop-down gallery.

- Copy styles from one template or document to another with options at the Organizer dialog box. Display this dialog box by clicking the Import/Export button in the bottom left corner of the Manage Styles dialog box. Styles can also be deleted and renamed at the Organizer dialog box.

Commands Review

FEATURE	RIBBON TAB, GROUP	BUTTON, OPTION	KEYBOARD SHORTCUT
Create New Style from Formatting dialog box	Home, Styles	⬇, *Create a Style*	
Manage Styles dialog box	Home, Styles OR Design, Document Formatting	◰, A✓	
Organizer dialog box	Home, Styles	◰, A✓, Import/Export... OR ✎, *Custom Paragraph Spacing*	
Reveal Formatting task pane			Shift + F1
Style Inspector task pane	Home, Styles	◰, A🔍	
Style Pane Options dialog box	Home, Styles	◰, Options	
Styles task pane	Home, Styles	◰	Alt + Ctrl + Shift + S

Performance Objectives

Upon successful completion of Chapter 2, you will be able to:

1 Input text during a merge

2 Insert fields in a main document

3 Merge a main document with other data sources, including a Word document, an Excel worksheet, and an Access database table

4 Sort records in a data source file

5 Select records in a data source file

6 Find records in a data source file

Use Word's Mail Merge feature to create documents with standard text and variable information. A merge generally requires two files: the data source file and the main document. The main document contains the standard text along with fields that identify where variable information is inserted during the merge. The data source file contains the variable information that will be inserted in the main document during the merge. In addition to a data source file, a Fill-in field can be inserted in a main document that allows for keyboard input of variable information during the merge. In this chapter, you will learn how to insert a Fill-in field in a main document as well as a Merge Record # field and an If...Then...Else field. You will also learn how to merge a main document with other data sources and how to sort, select, and find records in a data source file.

Data Files

Before beginning chapter work, copy the WL3C2 folder to your storage medium and then make WL3C2 the active folder.

The online course includes additional training and assessment resources.

Merging with Fields

The Mail Merge feature provides a number of methods for inserting fields into a main document. Click the Rules button in the Write & Insert Fields group on the Mailings tab and a drop-down list displays with merge fields. Click the *Fill-in* field to insert a field where specific information is inserted at the keyboard during a merge. Click the *Merge Record #* field to insert a record number in each merged document, and click the *If...Then...Else...* field to insert a field that compares two values and inserts one set of text or another depending on result of the comparison.

Inputting Text during a Merge

Inputting Text during a Merge

In some situations, keeping all the variable information in a data source file may not be necessary. For example, variable information that changes on a regular basis might include a customer's monthly balance, a product price, and so on. Insert a Fill-in field in the main document so that when the main document is merged with the data source file, variable information can be inserted in the document using the keyboard.

Rules

Insert a Fill-in field in a main document by clicking the Rules button in the Write & Insert Fields group on the Mailings tab and then clicking *Fill-in* at the drop-down list. This displays the Insert Word Field: Fill-in dialog box, shown in Figure 2.1. At this dialog box, type a brief instruction for what type of information should be entered at the keyboard and then click OK. At the Microsoft Word dialog box with the typed message in the upper left corner, type the text to display in the document and then click OK. After the Fill-in field or fields are added, save the main document in the normal manner. A document can contain any number of fill-in fields.

Quick Steps

Insert Fill-In Field in Main Document
1. Click Mailings tab.
2. Click Rules button.
3. Click *Fill-in*.
4. Type prompt text.
5. Click OK.
6. Type text to display in document.
7. Click OK.

Figure 2.1 Insert Word Field: Fill-in Dialog Box

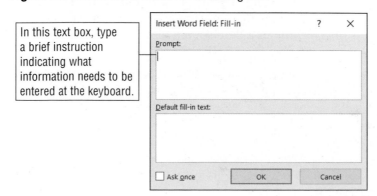

In this text box, type a brief instruction indicating what information needs to be entered at the keyboard.

When the main document is merged with the data source file, the first record is merged with the main document and the Microsoft Word dialog box displays with the typed message in the upper left corner. Type the specified information for the first record in the data source file and then click OK. Word displays the dialog box again. Type the specified information for the second record in the data source file and then click OK. Continue in this manner until the information has been entered for each record in the data source file. Word then completes the merge.

Activity 1 Adding Fill-in Fields to a Main Document   Part 1 of 1

1. Open **MFundsMD** and then save it with the name **2-MFundsMD**.
2. Specify **MFundsDS** as the data source file by completing the following steps:
   a. Click the Mailings tab.
   b. Click the Select Recipients button and then click *Use an Existing List* at the drop-down list.
   c. At the Select Data Source dialog box, navigate to your WL3C2 folder and then double-click the data source file *MFundsDS*.
3. Select the text *(representative's name)* in the second paragraph and then insert a Fill-in field by completing the following steps:
   a. If necessary, click the Mailings tab.
   b. Click the Rules button in the Write & Insert Fields group and then click *Fill-in* at the drop-down list.
   c. At the Insert Word Field: Fill-in dialog box, type Insert rep name in the *Prompt* text box and then click OK.
   d. At the Microsoft Word dialog box with *Insert rep name* in the upper left corner, type (representative's name) and then click OK.

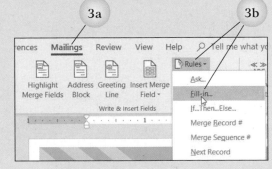

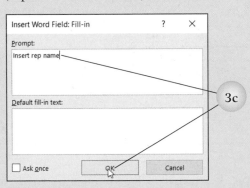

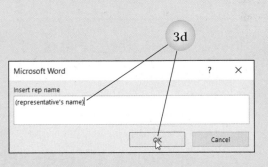

4. Select the text (phone number) in the second paragraph and then complete steps similar to those in Step 3 to insert a Fill-in field, except type Insert phone number in the *Prompt* text box at the Insert Word Field: Fill-in dialog box and type (phone number) at the Microsoft Word dialog box.
5. Save **2-MFundsMD**.

6. Merge the main document with the data source file by completing the following steps:
   a. Click the Finish & Merge button and then click *Edit Individual Documents* at the drop-down list.
   b. At the Merge to New Document dialog box, make sure *All* is selected and then click OK.
   c. When Word merges the main document with the first record, a dialog box displays with the instruction *Insert rep name* and the text *(representative's name)* selected. At this dialog box, type Marilyn Smythe and then click OK.

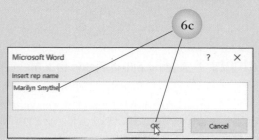

   d. At the dialog box with the message *Insert phone number* and *(phone number)* selected, type (646) 555-8944 and then click OK.
   e. At the dialog box with the instruction *Insert rep name*, type Anthony Mason (over *Marilyn Smythe*) and then click OK.
   f. At the dialog box with the instruction *Insert phone number*, type (646) 555-8901 (over the previous number) and then click OK.
   g. At the dialog box with the instruction *Insert rep name*, type Faith Ostrom (over *Anthony Mason*) and then click OK.
   h. At the dialog box with the instruction *Insert phone number*, type (646) 555-8967 (over the previous number) and then click OK.
   i. At the dialog box with the instruction *Insert rep name*, type Thomas Rivers (over *Faith Ostrom*) and then click OK.
   j. At the dialog box with the instruction *Insert phone number*, type (646) 555-0793 (over the previous number) and then click OK.
7. Save the merged document and name it **2-MFundsLtrs**.
8. Print and then close **2-MFundsLtrs**.
9. Save and then close **2-MFundsMD**.

 Check Your Work

---

Activity 2 Insert Merge Fields in a Main Document   1 Part

You will insert an If...Then...Else... field and a Merge Record # field in a City of Edgewood main document and then merge it with a data source file.

Inserting a Merge Record # Field

Quick Steps

Insert Record Number Field
1. In main document, click Mailings tab.
2. Click Rules button.
3. Click *Merge Record #*.

After merging a small number of records, determining if all the records were merged and printed is easy. When merging a large number of records in a data source file, consider inserting a Merge Record # field to ensure that each document merges and prints. This field will insert a record number in each merged document. To insert a Merge Record # field, click the Rules button in the Write & Insert Fields group on the Mailings tab and then click *Merge Record #* at the drop-down list. This inserts the field «*Merge Record #*» in the document.

Tutorial

Inserting an If...
Then...Else... Field

Quick Steps

**Insert If...Then...
Else... Field**

1. In main document,
   click Mailings tab.
2. Click Rules button.
3. Click If...Then...
   Else....
4. Click *Field name*
   option box arrow.
5. Click field at drop-
   down list.
6. If necessary, specify
   compare value.
7. Type text in *Insert this
   text* text box if field
   entry is matched.
8. Type text in *Otherwise
   insert this text* text
   box if field entry is
   not matched.
9. Click OK.

Hint Alt + F9
displays or hides fields
in a document.

Inserting an If...Then...Else... Field

Use an If...Then...Else... field to tell Word to compare two values and then, depending on what is determined, enter one set of text or the other. Click *If... Then...Else...* at the Rules button drop-down list and the Insert Word Field: IF dialog box appears, as shown in Figure 2.2.

Specify the field Word will use in the comparison by clicking the *Field name* option box arrow and then clicking the field at the drop-down list. The drop-down list shows all the fields specified in the data source file. Use the *Comparison* option to identify how Word is to compare values. By default, *Equal to* displays in the *Comparison* option box. Click the *Comparison* option box arrow and a drop-down list displays with a variety of value options, such as *Not equal to, Less than, Greater than*, and so on. In the *Compare to* text box, type the specific field value Word is to use. For example, to include a statement in a letter for all customers with the zip code *98405*, click the *Field name* option box arrow and then click *ZIP_Code* at the drop-down list. Type the zip code in the *Compare to* text box.

After specifying the field name and field entry, provide the text that should be inserted if the field entry is matched by typing it in the text box labeled *Insert this text*. In the text box labeled *Otherwise insert this text*, type the text that should be inserted if the field entry is not matched. The text box *Otherwise insert this text* can be left empty. This tells Word not to insert any text if the specific entry value is not matched.

By default, an If...Then...Else... field does not display in the document. To make the field visible, press Alt + F9. To turn off the display, press Alt + F9 again. Turning on the display of field codes also expands other merge codes.

Figure 2.2 Insert Word Field: IF Dialog Box

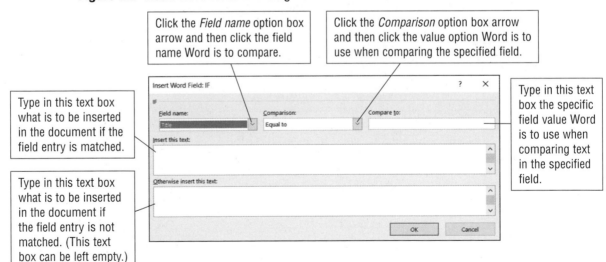

Click the *Field name* option box arrow and then click the field name Word is to compare.

Click the *Comparison* option box arrow and then click the value option Word is to use when comparing the specified field.

Type in this text box what is to be inserted in the document if the field entry is matched.

Type in this text box what is to be inserted in the document if the field entry is not matched. (This text box can be left empty.)

Type in this text box the specific field value Word is to use when comparing text in the specified field.

1. Open **CofEMD** and then save it with the name **2-CofEMD**.
2. Specify **CofEDS** as the data source file by completing the following steps:
   a. Click the Mailings tab.
   b. Click the Select Recipients button and then click *Use an Existing List* at the drop-down list.
   c. At the Select Data Source dialog box, navigate to your WL3C2 folder and then double-click the data source file *CofEDS*.
3. Insert an If...Then...Else... field that tells Word to add text if the membership is equal to *Platinum* by completing the following steps:
   a. Position the insertion point right of the period after the word *pledge* that ends the second paragraph and then press the spacebar.
   b. If necessary, click the Mailings tab.
   c. Click the Rules button in the Write & Insert Fields group and then click *If...Then...Else...* at the drop-down list.

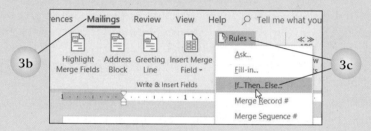

   d. At the Insert Word Field: IF dialog box, click the *Field name* option box arrow and then click *Membership* at the drop-down list. (Scroll down the list box to see this field.)
   e. Click in the *Compare to* text box and then type Platinum.
   f. Click in the *Insert this text* text box and then type We hope you will continue your Platinum membership and enjoy the benefits of supporting your local community.
   g. Click OK to close the dialog box.

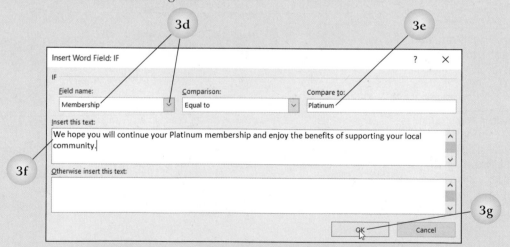

   h. View the If...Then...Else... field code (and expand the other merge codes) by pressing Alt + F9.
   i. After viewing the expanded fields, press Alt + F9 again to turn off the display.
4. Replace the letters *XX* near the bottom of the letter with your initials and then change the file name after your initials to **2-CofEMD**.

5. Insert a Merge Record # field by completing the following steps:
   a. Position the insertion point immediately right of the letters *MD* in the document name **2-CofEMD**.
   b. Type a hyphen.
   c. Click the Rules button in the Write & Insert Fields group and then click *Merge Record #* at the drop-down list.
6. Save **2-CofEMD**.
7. Merge the main document with the data source file by completing the following steps:
   a. Click the Finish & Merge button and then click *Edit Individual Documents* at the drop-down list.
   b. At the Merge to New Document dialog box, make sure *All* is selected and then click OK.
8. Save the merged document with the name **2-CofELetters**.
9. Print and then close **2-CofELetters**.
10. Save and then close **2-CofEMD**.

Check Your Work

Activity 3 Merge Data Source Files with a Travel Letter   3 Parts

You will merge a Bayside Travel main document with different data source files, including a Word table, an Excel worksheet, and an Access database table.

Tutorial

Merging a Main
Document with
Other Data Source
Files

Merging with Other Data Source Files

Word saves a data source file as an Access database with the *.mdb* file extension and uses the Access database when merging with a main document. A main document can also be merged with other data source files, such as a Word document containing data in a table, an Excel worksheet, an Access database table, and an Outlook contacts list. Select the data source file—such as a Word document, Excel worksheet, or Access database table—in the same manner as selecting a data source file with the *.mdb* file extension.

Activity 3a Merging a Main Document with a Word Table Data Source File   Part 1 of 3

1. Open **BTTourLtr** and then save it with the name **2-BTTourLtrMD**.
2. Open **BTClientTable** from your WL3C2 folder. Notice that the document, which will be used as a data source file, contains only a table with data in columns and rows. After viewing the document, close it.
3. Identify **BTClientTable** as the data source file by completing the following steps:
   a. Click the Mailings tab.
   b. Click the Select Recipients button and then click *Use an Existing List* at the drop-down list.
   c. At the Select Data Source dialog box, navigate to your WL3C2 folder and then double-click *BTClientTable*.
4. Press the Down Arrow key four times and then click the Address Block button in the Write & Insert Fields group.
5. At the Insert Address Block dialog box, click OK.
6. Press the Enter key two times.

7. Insert the greeting line fields by completing the following steps:
   a. Click the Greeting Line button in the Write & Insert Fields group.
   b. At the Insert Greeting Line dialog box, click the option box arrow for the option box containing the comma (the box right of the box containing *Mr. Randall*).
   c. At the drop-down list, click the colon.
   d. Click OK to close the Insert Greeting Line dialog box.
8. Scroll to the end of the letter and then replace the *XX* with your initials.
9. Merge the document by clicking the Finish & Merge button and then clicking *Edit Individual Documents* at the drop-down list. At the Merge to New Document dialog box, click OK.
10. Save the merged letters with the name **2-BTTourMergedLtrs**.
11. Print the first two pages (letters) of the document and then close it.
12. Save and then close **2-BTTourLtrMD**.

If the fields in a data source file do not match the fields in the address block, use options at the Match Fields dialog box to match the field names. Display the Match Fields dialog box by clicking the Match Fields button in the Write & Insert group or by clicking the Match Fields button in the Insert Address Block dialog box or the Greeting Line dialog box. To match the fields, click the option box arrow at the right side of the field to be matched and then click the field at the drop-down list of fields in the data source file.

For example, in Activity 3b, you will use an Excel worksheet as a data source file. One of the fields, *MailingAddress*, does not have a match in the address block, so you will use the Match Fields button to match the *Address 1* field in the address block to the *MailingAddress* field in the Excel worksheet.

Activity 3b Merging a Main Document with an Excel Worksheet Data Source File Part 2 of 3

1. Open **BTTourLtr** and then save it with the name **2-BTMD**.
2. Identify an Excel worksheet as the data source file by completing the following steps:
   a. Click the Mailings tab.
   b. Click the Select Recipients button and then click *Use an Existing List* at the drop-down list.
   c. At the Select Data Source dialog box, navigate to your WL3C2 folder and then double-click the Excel file **BTClientsExcel**.
   d. At the Select Table dialog box, click OK.

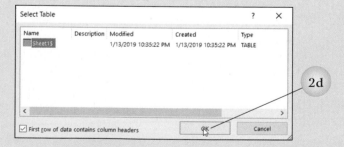

3. Press the Down Arrow key four times and then insert the address block by completing the following steps:
   a. Click the Address Block button.
   b. At the Insert Address Block dialog box, click the Match Fields button.

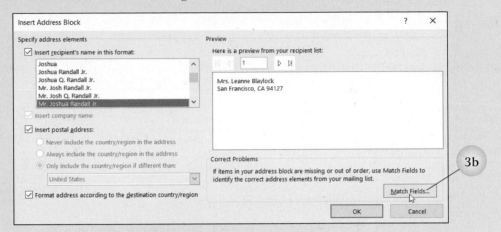

c. At the Match Fields dialog box, click the *Address 1* field option box arrow and then click *MailingAddress* at the drop-down list.
   d. Click OK to close the Match Fields dialog box.
   e. Click OK to close the Insert Address Block dialog box.
4. Press the Enter key two times.
5. Insert the greeting line fields by completing the following steps:
   a. Click the Greeting Line button.
   b. At the Insert Greeting Line dialog box, click the option box arrow to the right of the option box containing the comma.
   c. At the drop-down list, click the colon.
   d. Click OK to close the Insert Greeting Line dialog box.

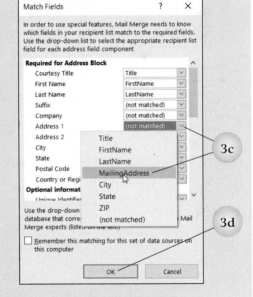

6. Scroll to the end of the letter and then replace the *XX* with your initials.
7. Merge the document by clicking the Finish & Merge button and then clicking *Edit Individual Documents* at the drop-down list. At the Merge to New Document dialog box, click OK.
8. Save the merged letters with the name **2-BTExcelMergedLtrs**.
9. Print the first two pages (letters) of the document and then close it.
10. Save and then close **2-BTMD**.

In addition to a Word table or Excel worksheet, an Access database table can be used as a data source file. To choose an Access database table, display the Select Data Source dialog box, navigate to the folder, and then double-click the Access database file. At the Select Table dialog box, select the specific table and then click OK.

Activity 3c Merging a Main Document with an Access Database Table Data Source File   Part 3 of 3

1. Open **BTTourLtr** and then save it with the name **2-BTLtrMD**.
2. Identify an Access table as the data source file by completing the following steps:
   a. Click the Mailings tab.
   b. Click the Select Recipients button and then click *Use an Existing List* at the drop-down list.
   c. At the Select Data Source dialog box, navigate to your WL3C2 folder and then double-click the Access database **BaysideTravel**.
   d. At the Select Table dialog box, click the *Clients* table and then click OK.

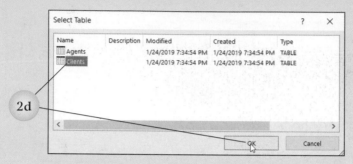

3. Press the Down Arrow key four times.
4. Click the Address Block button and then click OK at the Insert Address Block dialog box.
5. Press the Enter key two times.
6. Insert the greeting line fields by completing the following steps:
   a. Click the Greeting Line button.
   b. At the Insert Greeting Line dialog box, click the option box arrow to the right of the option box containing the comma.
   c. At the drop-down list, click the colon.
   d. Click OK to close the Insert Greeting Line dialog box.
7. Scroll to the end of the letter and then replace the *XX* with your initials.
8. Merge the document by clicking the Finish & Merge button and then clicking *Edit Individual Documents* at the drop-down list. At the Merge to New Document dialog box, click OK.
9. Save the merged letters with the name **2-BTAccessMergedLtrs**.
10. Print the first two pages (letters) of the document and then close it.
11. Save and then close **2-BTLtrMD**.

You will sort data in a data source file and create a labels main document. You will select and merge records and find specific records in a data source file.

Sorting, Selecting, and Finding Records in a Data Source File

If an activity requires sorting or selecting data and merging documents, consider the order in which the merged documents are to be printed or which records are to be merged and then sort and select the data before merging.

Tutorial

Sorting Records in a Data Source File

Select Recipients

Edit Recipient List

Sorting Records in a Data Source File

To sort records in a data source file, click the Mailings tab, click the Select Recipients button, and then click *Use an Existing List*. At the Select Data Source dialog box, navigate to the folder containing the data source file and then double-click the file. Click the Edit Recipient List button in the Start Mail Merge group on the Mailings tab and the Mail Merge Recipients dialog box displays, similar to the one shown in Figure 2.3.

Figure 2.3 Mail Merge Recipients Dialog Box

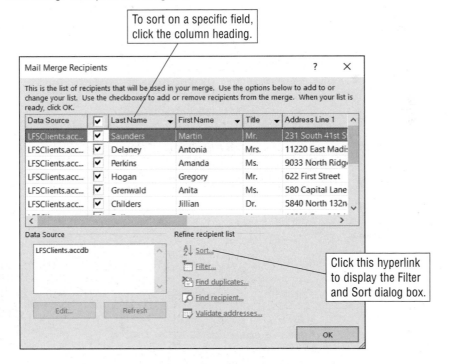

Quick Steps

Sort Records in Data Source File

1. Click Mailings tab.
2. Click Select Recipients button.
3. Click *Use an Existing List*.
4. Double-click file.
5. Click Edit Recipient List button.
6. At Mail Merge Recipients dialog box, sort by specific field by clicking field column heading.
7. Click OK.

Click the column heading to sort data in a specific column in ascending order. To perform an additional sort, click the down arrow at the right side of the column heading and then click the sort order. Another method for performing an additional sort is to click the <u>Sort</u> hyperlink in the *Refine recipient list* section of the Mail Merge Recipients dialog box. Clicking this hyperlink displays the Filter and Sort dialog box with the Sort Records tab selected, as shown in Figure 2.4. The options at this dialog box are similar to the options available at the Sort Text (and Sort) dialog box.

Figure 2.4 Filter and Sort Dialog Box with the Sort Records Tab Selected

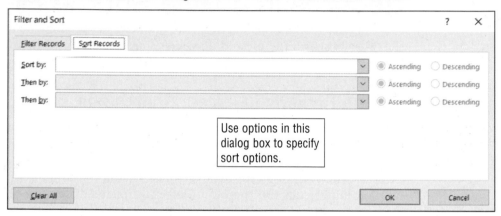

Activity 4a Sorting Data in a Data Source File

Part 1 of 4

1. At a blank document, click the Mailings tab, click the Start Mail Merge button in the Start Mail Merge group, and then click *Labels* at the drop-down list.
2. At the Label Options dialog box, click the *Label vendors* option box arrow and then click *Avery US Letter* at the drop-down list.
3. Scroll down the *Product number* list box, click *5160 Address Labels*, and then click OK.

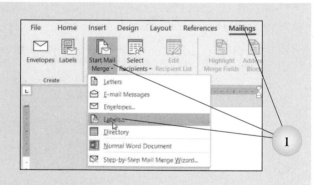

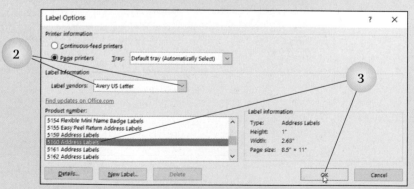

4. Click the Select Recipients button and then click *Use an Existing List* at the drop-down list.

5. At the Select Data Source dialog box, navigate to your WL3C2 folder and then double-click the Access data source file **LFSClients**.
6. Click the Edit Recipient List button in the Start Mail Merge group on the Mailings tab.
7. At the Mail Merge Recipients dialog box, click the *Last Name* column heading. (This sorts the last names in ascending alphabetical order.)
8. Scroll right to display the *City* field and then click the *City* column heading.
9. Sort records by zip code and then by last name by completing the following steps:

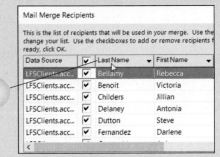

a. Click the <u>Sort</u> hyperlink in the *Refine recipient list* section of the Mail Merge Recipients dialog box.

b. At the Filter and Sort dialog box with the Sort Records tab selected, click the *Sort by* option box arrow and then click *ZIP Code* at the drop-down list. (You will need to scroll down the list to display the *ZIP Code* field.)
c. Make sure *Last Name* displays in the *Then by* option box.
d. Click OK to close the Filter and Sort dialog box.

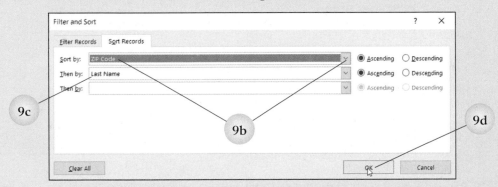

e. Click OK to close the Mail Merge Recipients dialog box.
10. At the labels document, click the Address Block button.
11. At the Insert Address Block dialog box, click OK.
12. Click the Update Labels button in the Write & Insert Fields group.
13. Click the Finish & Merge button and then click *Edit Individual Documents* at the drop-down list.
14. At the Merge to New Document dialog box, make sure *All* is selected and then click OK.
15. Press Ctrl + A to select the entire document and then click the *No Spacing* style in the Styles group on the Home tab.
16. Save the merged labels and name the document **2-Lbls01**.
17. Print and then close **2-Lbls01**.
18. Close the labels main document without saving it.

Check Your Work

Tutorial

Selecting Specific
Records for
Merging

Selecting Records in a Data Source File

If a data source file contains numerous records, specific records can be selected from the data source file and then merged with a main document. For example, records with a specific zip code or city can be selected from a data source file. One method for selecting records is to display the Mail Merge Recipients dialog box and then insert or remove check marks from specific records.

💡 **Hint** Including or excluding certain records from a merge is referred to as *filtering.*

Using check boxes to select specific records is useful in a data source file containing a limited number of records; however, it may not be practical in a data source file containing many records. In a large data source file, use options at the Filter and Sort dialog box with the Filter Records tab selected, as shown in Figure 2.5. To display this dialog box, click the <u>Filter</u> hyperlink in the *Refine recipient list* section of the Mail Merge Recipients dialog box.

When a field is selected from the *Field* drop-down list at the Filter and Sort dialog box, Word automatically inserts *Equal to* in the *Comparison* option box but other comparisons can be made. Clicking the *Comparison* option box arrow displays a drop-down list with these additional options: *Not equal to, Less than, Greater than, Less than or equal, Greater than or equal, Is blank,* and *Is not blank.* Use one of these options to create a select equation.

Figure 2.5 Filter and Sort Dialog Box with the Filter Records Tab Selected

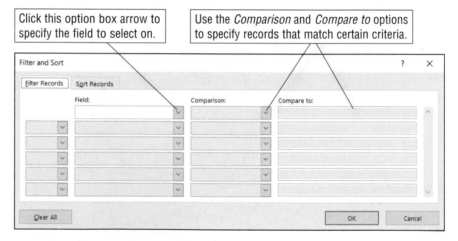

Activity 4b Selecting Records in a Data Source File

Part 2 of 4

1. At a blank document, click the Mailings tab, click the Start Mail Merge button, and then click *Labels* at the drop-down list.
2. At the Label Options dialog box, make sure *Avery US Letter* displays in the *Label vendors* option box and *5160 Address Labels* displays in the *Product number* list box and then click OK.
3. Click the Select Recipients button and then click *Use an Existing List* at the drop-down list.
4. At the Select Data Source dialog box, navigate to your WL3C2 folder and then double-click the Access database file named ***LFSClients.***
5. Click the Edit Recipient List button.

6. At the Mail Merge Recipients dialog box, click the Filter hyperlink in the *Refine recipient list* section.

7. At the Filter and Sort dialog box with the Filter Records tab selected, click the *Field* option box arrow and then click *ZIP Code* at the drop-down list. (You will need to scroll down the list to display *ZIP Code*. When *ZIP Code* is inserted in the *Field* option box, *Equal to* is inserted in the *Comparison* option box, and the insertion point is positioned in the *Compare to* text box.)

8. Type 21000 in the *Compare to* text box.

9. Click the *Comparison* option box arrow and then click *Greater than* at the drop-down list.

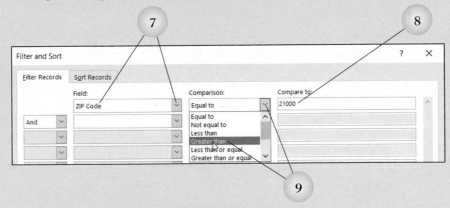

10. Click OK to close the Filter and Sort dialog box.
11. Click OK to close the Mail Merge Recipients dialog box.
12. At the labels document, click the Address Block button and then click OK at the Insert Address Block dialog box.
13. Click the Update Labels button.
14. Click the Finish & Merge button and then click *Edit Individual Documents* at the drop-down list.
15. At the Merge to New Document dialog box, make sure *All* is selected and then click OK.
16. Press Ctrl + A to select the entire document and then click the *No Spacing* style in the Styles group on the Home tab.
17. Save the merged labels and name the document **2-Lbls02**.
18. Print and then close **2-Lbls02**.
19. Close the labels main document without saving it.

When a field is selected from the *Field* option box, Word automatically inserts *And* in the first box at the left side of the dialog box but this can be changed to *Or* if necessary. With the *And* and *Or* options, more than one condition for selecting records can be specified. For example, in Activity 4c, all the records of clients living in the cities Rosedale or Towson will be selected. If the data source file contained another field, such as a specific financial plan for each customer, all the customers living in these two cities that subscribe to a specific financial plan could be selected. In this situation, the *And* option would be used.

To clear the current options at the Filter and Sort dialog box with the Filter Records tab selected, click the Clear All button. This clears all the text from the text boxes and leaves the dialog box on the screen. Click the Cancel button to close the Filter and Sort dialog box without specifying any records.

Activity 4c Selecting Records with Specific Cities in a Data Source File

1. At a blank document, click the Mailings tab, click the Start Mail Merge button, and then click *Labels* at the drop-down list.
2. At the Label Options dialog box, make sure *Avery US Letter* displays in the *Label vendors* option box and *5160 Address Labels* displays in the *Product number* list box and then click OK.
3. Click the Select Recipients button and then click *Use an Existing List* at the drop-down list.
4. At the Select Data Source dialog box, navigate to your WL3C2 folder and then double-click the Access database file named ***LFSClients***.
5. Click the Edit Recipient List button.
6. At the Mail Merge Recipients dialog box, click the <u>Filter</u> hyperlink in the *Refine recipient list* section.
7. At the Filter and Sort dialog box with the Filter Records tab selected, click the *Field* option box arrow and then click *City* at the drop-down list. (You will need to scroll down the list to see this field.)
8. Type Rosedale in the *Compare to* text box.
9. Click the option box arrow for the option box containing the word *And* (at the left side of the dialog box) and then click *Or* at the drop-down list.
10. Click the second *Field* option box arrow and then click *City* at the drop-down list. (You will need to scroll down the list to see this field.)
11. With the insertion point positioned in the second *Compare to* text box (the one below the box containing *Rosedale*), type Towson.
12. Click OK to close the Filter and Sort dialog box.

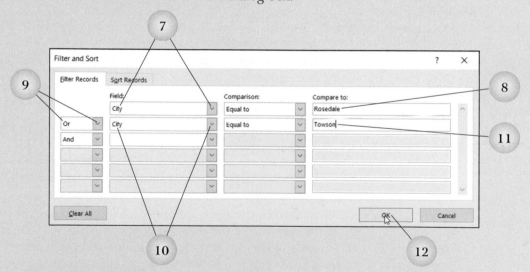

13. Click OK to close the Mail Merge Recipients dialog box.
14. At the labels document, click the Address Block button and then click OK at the Insert Address Block dialog box.
15. Click the Update Labels button.
16. Click the Finish & Merge button and then click *Edit Individual Documents* at the drop-down list.
17. At the Merge to New Document dialog box, make sure *All* is selected and then click OK.

18. Press Ctrl + A to select the entire document and then click the *No Spacing* style in the Styles group on the Home tab.
19. Save the merged labels and name the document **2-Lbls03**.
20. Print and then close **2-Lbls03**.
21. Save the labels main document and name it **2-LblsMD**.

 Tutorial

Finding Records in a Data Source File

Finding Records in a Data Source File

The Find duplicates and Find recipient hyperlinks in the *Refine recipient list* section of the Mail Merge Recipients dialog box can be useful for finding records in an extensive data source file. Use the Find duplicates hyperlink to locate duplicate records that appear in the data source file. Use the Find recipient hyperlink to find a record or records that meet a specific criterion. The Validate addresses hyperlink in the *Refine recipient list* section is available only if address validation software has been installed.

Click the Find duplicates hyperlink and any duplicate records display in the Find Duplicates dialog box. At this dialog box, remove the check mark from the check box for the duplicate record that should not be included in the merge. To find a specific record in a data source file, click the Find recipient hyperlink. At the Find Entry dialog box, type the text to find and then click the Find Next button. Continue clicking the Find Next button until a message displays indicating that there are no more entries that contain the text. By default, Word searches for the specified text in all the fields of all the records in the data source file. The search can be limited by clicking the *This field* option box arrow and then clicking the specific field. Type the text to find in the *Find* text box and then click OK.

Activity 4d Finding Records in a Data Source File

Part 4 of 4

1. With **2-LblsMD** open, remove the filter by completing the following steps:
   a. With the Mailings tab active, click the Edit Recipient List button.
   b. At the Mail Merge Recipients dialog box, click the Filter hyperlink in the *Refine recipient list* section.
   c. At the Filter and Sort dialog box, click the Clear All button.
   d. Click OK to close the Filter and Sort dialog box.
   e. At the Mail Merge Recipients dialog box, click the Find duplicates hyperlink in the *Refine recipient list* section.
   f. At the Find Duplicates dialog box, which indicates that there are no duplicate items, click OK.

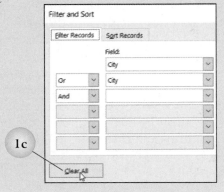

1c

2. Find all the records containing the zip code *20376* by completing the following steps:
   a. At the Mail Merge Recipients dialog box, click the <u>Find recipient</u> hyperlink in the *Refine recipient list* section.
   b. At the Find Entry dialog box, type 20376 in the *Find* text box.
   c. Click the *This field* option box arrow and then click *ZIP Code* at the drop-down list. (You will need to scroll down the list to display this field.)
   d. Click the Find Next button.

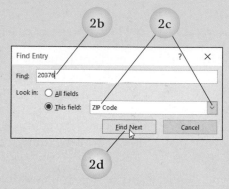

   e. When the first record is selected containing the zip code *20376*, click the Find Next button.
   f. When the second record is selected containing the zip code *20376*, click the Find Next button.
   g. At the message indicating that there are no more entries that contain the text you typed, click OK.
   h. Click the Cancel button to close the Find Entry dialog box.
3. Select and then merge records of those clients with a zip code of *20376* by completing the following steps:
   a. At the Mail Merge Recipients dialog box, click the <u>Filter</u> hyperlink in the *Refine recipient list* section of the dialog box.
   b. At the Filter and Sort dialog box, click the *Field* option box arrow and then click *ZIP Code* at the drop-down list. (You will need to scroll down the list to see this field.)
   c. Type 20376 in the *Compare to* text box.
   d. Click OK to close the Filter and Sort dialog box.
   e. Click OK to close the Mail Merge Recipients dialog box.
4. At the label document, click the Finish & Merge button and then click *Edit Individual Documents* at the drop-down list.
5. At the Merge to New Document dialog box, make sure that *All* is selected and then click OK.
6. Press Ctrl + A to select the entire document and then click the *No Spacing* style in the Styles group on the Home tab.
7. Save the merged labels and name the document **2-Lbls04**.
8. Print and then close **2-Lbls04**.
9. Save and then close **2-LblsMD**.

Check Your Work

Chapter Summary

- Use the Fill-in field in a main document to insert variable information at the keyboard during a merge. Insert a Fill-in field by clicking the Rules button in the Write & Insert Fields group on the Mailings tab and then clicking *Fill-in* at the drop-down list.

- Insert a Merge Record # field in a main document to insert a record number in each merged document. Insert the field with the Rules button in the Write & Insert Fields group on the Mailings tab.

- Use an If...Then...Else field to compare two values and then, depending on what is determined, enter one set of text or another. Insert the field with the Rules button in the Write & Insert Fields group on the Mailings tab.

- A main document can be merged with data source files, such as a Word document containing a table, an Excel worksheet, a table in an Access database, or an Outlook contacts list.

- If the fields in a data source file do not match the fields used in the address block, use options at the Match Fields dialog box to match the field names.

- Sort records in a data source file at the Mail Merge Recipients dialog box. Sort by clicking the column heading or using options at the Filter and Sort dialog box with the Sort Records tab selected.

- Select specific records in a data source file with options at the Filter and Sort dialog box with the Filter Records tab selected.

- Use the *Comparison* option box at the Filter and Sort dialog box to refine a search for records that meet specific criteria.

- Use the Find duplicates hyperlink in the *Refine recipient list* section of the Mail Merge Recipients dialog box to find duplicate records in a data source file. Use the Find recipient hyperlink to search for records that meet a specific criterion.

Commands Review

FEATURE	RIBBON TAB, GROUP	BUTTON, OPTION
Fill-in merge field	Mailings, Write & Insert Fields	, *Fill-in*
Filter and Sort dialog box with Filter Records tab selected	Mailings, Start Mail Merge	, Filter
Filter and Sort dialog box with Sort Records tab selected	Mailings, Start Mail Merge	, Sort
insert merge fields	Mailings, Write & Insert Fields	
Insert Word Field: IF dialog box	Mailings, Write & Insert Fields	, *If...Then...Else*
Mail Merge Recipients dialog box	Mailings, Start Mail Merge	
Match Fields dialog box	Mailings, Write & Insert Fields	
Merge Record # field	Mailings, Write & Insert Fields	, *Merge Record #*

Word

Managing Macros

Performance Objectives

Upon successful completion of Chapter 3, you will be able to:

1 Record, run, and delete macros

2 Assign a macro to a keyboard command

3 Assign a macro to the Quick Access Toolbar

4 Run a macro automatically

5 Specify macro security settings

6 Save a macro-enabled document and template

7 Copy macros between documents and templates

8 Record and run a macro with a Fill-in field

9 Edit a macro

10 Record and store a macro in the default template

A macro is a time-saving tool that allows many editing and formatting tasks to be performed automatically. Working with macros involves two steps: recording and running a macro. In this chapter, you will learn how to record and run a macro in a document, assign a keyboard command to a macro, assign a macro to the Quick Access Toolbar, and record a macro with a Fill-in field. You will also learn how to specify macro security settings, save a macro-enabled document and template, copy macros between documents and templates, insert a Fill-in field in a macro, edit a macro, and record and store a macro in Normal.dotm.

When working with various types of documents and templates, file extensions are helpful for identifying the document or template. For example, in this chapter, you will save a macro-enabled document and template. File extensions identify that the document or template is macro enabled. In the first activity, you will be instructed to turn on the display of file extensions using File Explorer.

 Data Files

Before beginning chapter work, copy the WL3C3 folder to your storage medium and then make WL3C3 the active folder.

The online course includes additional training and assessment resources.

Tutorial

Recording and Running a Macro

Recording and Running a Macro

Macros allow users to save time when formatting and editing a document by automating frequently performed tasks. Each macro is a series of prerecorded steps grouped into a single command. The word *macro* was coined by computer programmers for a collection of commands used to make a large programming job easier and thus save time. Two basic steps are involved in working with macros: recording a macro and running a macro. When recording a macro, all the keys pressed and dialog boxes displayed are recorded and become part of the macro. After a macro is recorded, running it carries out the recorded actions.

Recording a Macro

Recording a macro involves turning on the macro recorder, performing the steps to be recorded, and then turning off the recorder. Both the View tab and the Developer tab contain buttons for recording a macro. If the Developer tab does not appear on the ribbon, display this tab by opening the Word Options dialog box with *Customize Ribbon* selected in the left panel, inserting a check mark in the *Developer* check box in the list box at the right, and then clicking OK to close the dialog box.

Record Macro

Macros

Quick Steps

Record Macro
1. Click Developer tab.
2. Click Record Macro button.
OR
1. Click View tab.
2. Click Macros button arrow.
3. Click *Record Macro*.
4. Make changes at dialog box.
5. Click OK.
6. Complete steps.
7. Click Stop Recording button.
OR
7. Click macro icon on Status bar.

Stop Recording

Three options are available to begin recording a macro: Click the Record Macro button in the Code group on the Developer tab; click the View tab, click the Macros button arrow in the Macros group, and then click *Record Macro* at the drop-down list; or click the macro icon on the Status bar. Any of these methods displays the Record Macro dialog box shown in Figure 3.1.

At the Record Macro dialog box, type a name for the macro in the *Macro name* text box. A macro name must begin with a letter and can contain only letters and numbers. Specify where to store a macro with the *Store macro in* option box at the Record Macro dialog box. Type a description of the macro in the *Description* text box at the dialog box. A macro description can contain a maximum of 255 characters and may include spaces. After typing the macro name, specifying where to store the macro, and typing a description of the macro, click OK to close the Record Macro dialog box.

At the open document, a macro icon displays near the left side of the Status bar and the mouse displays with a cassette icon () attached. In the document, perform the actions to be recorded. A macro can record mouse clicks and key presses. However, if part of the macro is selecting text, use the keyboard to select text because a macro cannot record selections made by the mouse. When all the steps have been completed, click the Stop Recording button (previously the Record Macro button) in the Code group on the Developer tab or click the macro icon near the left side of the Status bar.

Figure 3.1 Record Macro Dialog Box

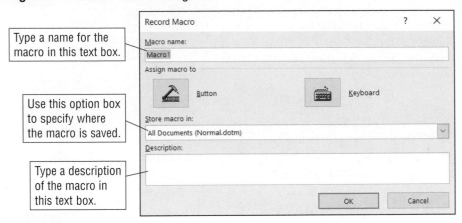

Type a name for the macro in this text box.

Use this option box to specify where the macro is saved.

Type a description of the macro in this text box.

Saving a Macro-Enabled Template

Quick Steps

Use File Explorer to Open Document Based on Template
1. Click File Explorer icon on taskbar.
2. Navigate to folder containing template.
3. Double-click template.

By default, a template is saved to the Custom Office Templates folder. A document can be opened based on a template saved in that folder by displaying the New backstage area, clicking the *Personal* option, and then clicking the template thumbnail. For the macro activities in this chapter, you will record macros in personal templates that you save to your WL3C3 folder. The macros you record will be available only in your templates. Since you will save your templates to a location other than the Custom Office Templates folder, you will not be able to open documents based on your templates at the New backstage area. Instead, you will need to use File Explorer to open documents based on your templates.

To save a macro-enabled template to a location other than the Custom Office Templates folder, display the Save As dialog box, type a name for the template, and then change the *Save as type* option to *Word Macro-Enabled Template (*.dotm)*. Navigate to the folder where the template is to be saved and then click the Save button.

Activity 1a Recording Macros

Part 1 of 4

1. Turn on the display of file extensions by completing the following steps:
   a. Click the File Explorer icon on the taskbar.
   b. At the window that displays, click the View tab.
   c. Click the *File name extensions* check box in the Show/hide group to insert a check mark.

1b   1c

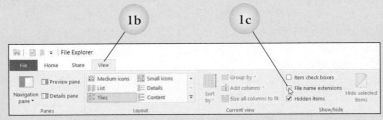

   d. Close File Explorer by clicking the Close button at the upper right corner of the dialog box.

2. Turn on the display of the Developer tab by completing the following steps. (Skip to Step 3 if the Developer tab is already visible.)

   a. Click the File tab and then click *Options*.

   b. At the Word Options dialog box, click *Customize Ribbon* in the left panel.

   c. In the list box at the right side of the dialog box, click the *Developer* check box to insert a check mark.

   d. Click OK to close the dialog box.

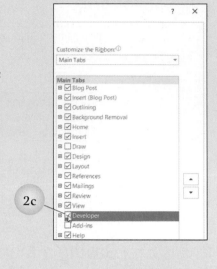

3. Open **Macros.docx** from your WL3C3 folder and then save it as a macro-enabled template by completing the following steps:

   a. Press the F12 function key to display the Save As dialog box.

   b. Type 3-MacrosTemplate in the *File name* text box.

   c. Click the *Save as type* option and then click *Word Macro-Enabled Template (*.dotm)*.

   d. Navigate to your WL3C3 folder.

   e. Click the Save button.

4. Record a macro that selects text, indents a paragraph of text, and then applies italic formatting by completing the following steps:

   a. Position the insertion point at the left margin of the paragraph that begins with *This is text to use for creating a macro*.

   b. Click the Developer tab.

   c. Click the Record Macro button in the Code group.

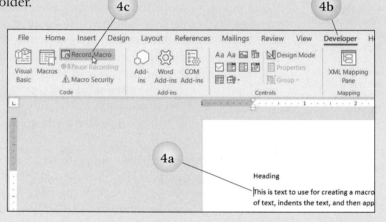

   d. At the Record Macro dialog box, type IndentItalics in the *Macro name* text box.

   e. Click the *Store macro in* option box and then click *Documents Based On 3-MacrosTemplate.dotm* at the drop-down list.

   f. Click inside the *Description* text box and then type Select text, indent text, and apply italic formatting.

   g. Click OK.

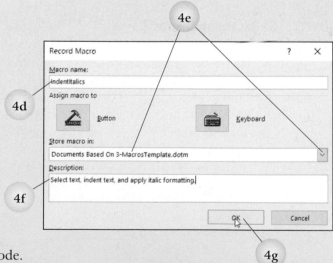

   h. At the document, press the F8 function key to turn on Extend mode.

   i. Press and hold down the Shift key and the Ctrl key, press the Down Arrow key, and then release the Shift and Ctrl keys. (Shift + Ctrl + Down Arrow is the keyboard shortcut to select a paragraph.)

   j. Click the Home tab.

k. Click the Paragraph group dialog box launcher.
   l. At the Paragraph dialog box, click the *Left* measurement box up arrow until *0.5"* displays.
   m. Click the *Right* measurement box up arrow until *0.5"* displays.
   n. Click OK.
   o. Press Ctrl + I to apply italic formatting.
   p. Press the Esc key and then press the Left Arrow key. (This deselects the text.)
   q. Click the macro icon on the Status bar to turn off the macro recording.

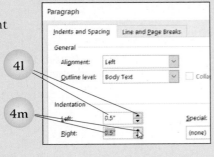

5. Record a macro that applies formatting to a heading by completing the following steps:
   a. Move the insertion point to the beginning of the text *Heading*.
   b. Click the macro icon on the Status bar.
   c. At the Record Macro dialog box, type Heading in the *Macro name* text box.
   d. Click the *Store macro in* option box and then click *Documents Based On 3-MacrosTemplate.dotm* at the drop-down list.
   e. Click inside the *Description* text box and then type Select text, change font size, turn on bold and italic, and insert bottom border line.
   f. Click OK.
   g. At the document, press the F8 function key and then press the End key.
   h. Click the Home tab.
   i. Click the Bold button in the Font group.
   j. Click the Italic button in the Font group.
   k. Click the *Font Size* option box arrow in the Font group and then click *12* at the drop-down gallery.
   l. Click the Borders button arrow in the Paragraph group and then click *Bottom Border* at the drop-down list.
   m. Press the Home key. (This moves the insertion point back to the beginning of the heading and deselects the text.)
   n. Click the macro icon on the Status bar to turn off the macro recording.
6. Select and then delete the text in the template.
7. Save and then close **3-MacrosTemplate.dotm**.

Running a Macro

Q̌uick Steps

Run Macro
1. Click Developer tab.
2. Click Macros button.
3. At Macros dialog box, double-click macro in list box.
OR
1. Click View tab.
2. Click Macros button.
3. At Macros dialog box, double-click macro in list box.

To run a recorded macro, click the Macros button in the Code group on the Developer tab, click the Macros button on the View tab, or use the keyboard shortcut Alt + F8. This displays the Macros dialog box, shown in Figure 3.2. At this dialog box, double-click a macro in the list box or click a macro and then click the Run button.

Figure 3.2 Macros Dialog Box

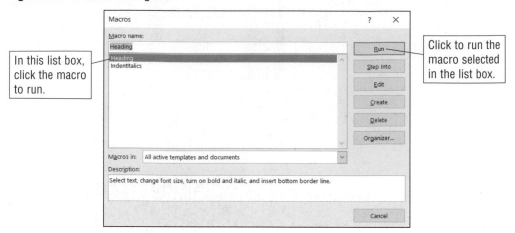

In this list box, click the macro to run.

Click to run the macro selected in the list box.

Activity 1b Running Macros

1. Use File Explorer to open a document based on **3-MacrosTemplate.dotm**, saved in your WL3C3 folder. (If a yellow message bar displays, click the Enable Content button.)
2. Insert **WriteResumes.docx** from your WL3C3 folder into the open document using the *Text from File* option at the Object button arrow drop-down list on the Insert tab.
3. Press Ctrl + Home to move the insertion point to the beginning of the heading *Resume Strategies* and then run the Heading macro by completing the following steps:
   a. Click the View tab.
   b. Click the Macros button in the Macros group.

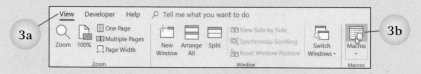

   c. At the Macros dialog box, click the *Macros in* option box and then click *3-MacrosTemplate.dotm (template)* at the drop-down list.
   d. Click *Heading* in the list box.
   e. Click the Run button.

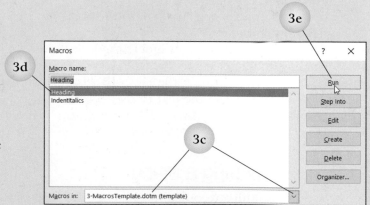

4. Complete steps similar to those in Step 3 to run the macro for the two other headings in the document: *Writing Style* and *Phrases to Avoid*.
5. Move the insertion point to the beginning of the paragraph below *First Person* (begins with *Manage 22-person team*) and then complete the following steps to run the IndentItalics macro:
   a. Click the Developer tab.
   b. Click the Macros button in the Code group.
   c. At the Macros dialog box, double-click *IndentItalics* in the list box.

6. Complete steps similar to those in Step 5 to run the IndentItalics macro for the paragraph below *Third Person* (begins with *Ms. Sanderson manages*), the paragraph that begins *Responsible for all marketing and special events*, and the paragraph that begins *Orchestrated a series of marketing and special-event programs*.
7. Save the document and name it **3-WriteResumes**.
8. Print and then close **3-WriteResumes.docx**.

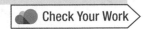 Check Your Work

Pausing and Resuming a Macro

Pause Recording

When recording a macro, the recording can be suspended temporarily to perform actions that should not be included. To pause the recording of a macro, click the Pause Recording button in the Code group on the Developer tab or click the Macros button arrow on the View tab and then click *Pause Recording* at the drop-down list. To resume recording the macro, click the Resume Recorder button (previously the Pause Recording button).

Deleting a Macro

If a macro is no longer needed, delete it. To delete a macro, display the Macros dialog box, click the macro name in the list box, and then click the Delete button. At the confirmation message, click Yes. Click the Close button to close the Macros dialog box.

Activity 1c Deleting a Macro   Part 3 of 4

1. Delete the IndentItalics macro by completing the following steps:
   a. Open **3-MacrosTemplate.dotm** from your WL3C3 folder. (You are opening the template and not a document based on the template. If a yellow message bar displays, click the Enable Content button.)
   b. Click the Developer tab and then click the Macros button in the Code group.
   c. At the Macros dialog box, make sure *3-MacrosTemplate.dotm (template)* displays in the *Macros in* option box.
   d. Click *IndentItalics* in the list box.
   e. Click the Delete button.

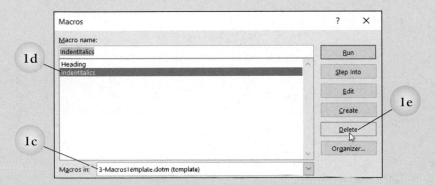

   f. At the message asking if you want to delete the macro, click Yes.
   g. Click the Close button to close the Macros dialog box.
2. Save and then close **3-MacrosTemplate.dotm**.

 Tutorial

Assigning a Macro
to a Keyboard
Command

Assigning a Macro to a Keyboard Command

Consider assigning regularly used macros to keyboard commands. To run a macro that has been assigned to a keyboard command, simply press the assigned keys. A macro can be assigned to a keyboard command with the following combinations:

Alt + letter
Ctrl + letter
Alt + Ctrl + letter
Alt + Shift + letter
Ctrl + Shift + letter
Alt + Ctrl + Shift + letter

Word already uses many combinations for Word functions. For example, pressing Alt + Ctrl + C inserts the copyright symbol (©).

Assign a macro to a keyboard command at the Customize Keyboard dialog box, shown in Figure 3.3. Specify the keyboard command by pressing the keys, such as Alt + D. The keyboard command entered displays in the *Press new shortcut key* text box. Word inserts the message *Currently assigned to* below the *Current keys* list box. If the keyboard command is already assigned to a command, the command is listed after the *Currently assigned to* message. If Word has not used the keyboard command, *[unassigned]* displays after the *Currently assigned to* message. When assigning a keyboard command to a macro, use an unassigned keyboard command.

In Activity 1d, you will record a macro and then assign it to a keyboard command. When you delete a macro, the keyboard command is no longer assigned to that action. This allows using the key combination again.

Figure 3.3 Customize Keyboard Dialog Box

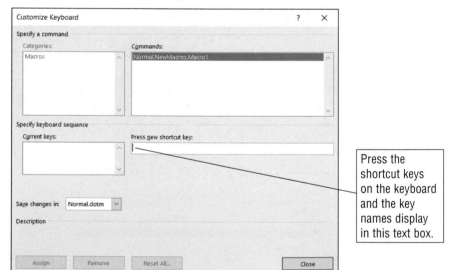

Press the shortcut keys on the keyboard and the key names display in this text box.

1. Open **3-MacrosTemplate.dotm**. (If necessary, click the Enable Content button.)
2. Record a macro named *Font* that selects text and applies font formatting and assign it to the keyboard command Alt + Ctrl + A by completing the following steps:
   a. Click the Developer tab and then click the Record Macro button in the Code group.
   b. At the Record Macro dialog box, type Font in the *Macro name* text box.
   c. Click the *Store macro in* option box arrow and then click *Documents Based On 3-MacrosTemplate.dotm* at the drop-down list.
   d. Click inside the *Description* text box and then type Select text and change the font and font color.
   e. Click the Keyboard button.

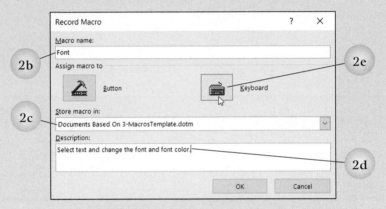

   f. At the Customize Keyboard dialog box with the insertion point positioned in the *Press new shortcut key* text box, press Alt + Ctrl + A.
   g. Check to make sure *[unassigned]* displays after *Currently assigned to*.
   h. Click the Assign button.
   i. Click the Close button.

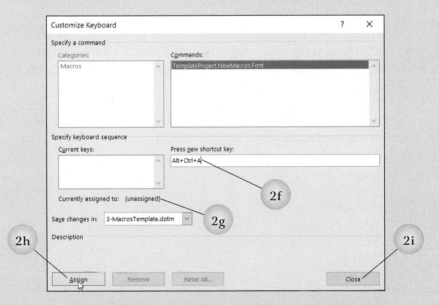

   j. At the document, click the Home tab.
   k. Press Ctrl + A.

    l. Click the Font group dialog box launcher.

    m. At the Font dialog box, click *Cambria* in the *Font* list box and click the *Dark Blue* font color (ninth option in the *Standard Colors* section).

    n. Click OK to close the Font dialog box.

    o. At the document, press the Down Arrow on the keyboard.

    p. Click the macro icon on the Status bar to turn off the macro recording.

3. Save and then close **3-MacrosTemplate.dotm**.

4. Use File Explorer to open a document based on **3-MacrosTemplate.dotm**, saved in your WL3C3 folder. (If a yellow message bar displays, click the Enable Content button.)

5. Insert **GSHLtr.docx** into the open document. (Use the Object button arrow on the Insert tab.)

6. Run the Font macro by pressing Alt + Ctrl + A.

7. Run the Heading macro for the heading *Procedural* and the heading *Teaching*.

8. Save the document and name it **3-GSHLtr**.

9. Print and then close **3-GSHLtr.docx**.

 Check Your Work

---

Activity 2 Record and Run a Macro to Format a Table of Contents   1 Part

You will create a macro that sets tabs and then assign the macro to the Quick Access Toolbar. You will then run the macro to format text in a table of contents.

 Tutorial

Assigning a Macro to the Quick Access Toolbar

Quick Steps

Assign Macro to Quick Access Toolbar
1. Click View tab.
2. Click Macros button arrow.
3. Click *Record Macro.*
4. Type macro name.
5. Click Button button.
6. Click macro name in left list box.
7. Click Add button.
8. Click Modify button.
9. Click icon.
10. Click OK.
11. Click OK.

Assigning a Macro to the Quick Access Toolbar

If a macro is used on a regular basis, consider assigning it to the Quick Access Toolbar so that it can be run with the click of a button. To assign a macro to the toolbar, click the Button button at the Record Macro dialog box. This displays the Word Options dialog box with the *Quick Access Toolbar* option selected in the left panel. Click the macro name in the left list box and then click the Add button between the two list boxes. This adds the macro name to the right list box.

Specify a button icon by clicking the Modify button, clicking an icon at the Modify Button dialog box, and then clicking OK. Click OK to close the Word Options dialog box and a Macro button is inserted on the Quick Access Toolbar. To remove a Macro button from the Quick Access Toolbar, right-click the button on the toolbar and then click *Remove from Quick Access Toolbar* at the shortcut menu.

1. Open **3-MacrosTemplate.dotm**.
2. Create a macro and assign it to the Quick Access Toolbar by completing the following steps:
   a. Click the View tab.
   b. Click the Macros button arrow and then click *Record Macro* at the drop-down list.
   c. At the Record Macro dialog box, type Tabs in the *Macro name* text box.
   d. Click the *Store macro in* option box arrow and then click *Documents Based On 3-MacrosTemplate.dotm* at the drop-down list.
   e. Click in the *Description* text box and then type Set left tabs at 0.5 and 1.0 and a right tab with leaders at 5.5.
   f. Click the Button button.
   g. At the Word Options dialog box, click the macro *TemplateProject.NewMacros.Tabs* in the left list box.
   h. Click the Add button.

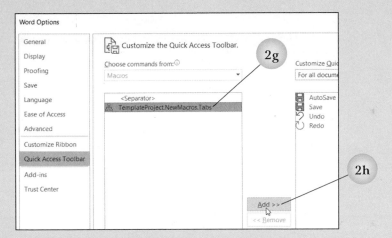

   i. Click the Modify button at the lower right corner of the dialog box.
   j. At the Modify Button dialog box, click the fourth button from the left in the top row.
   k. Click OK to close the Modify Button dialog box.
   l. Click OK to close the Word Options dialog box.
   m. At the blank document, click the Home tab and then click the Paragraph group dialog box launcher.
   n. At the Paragraph dialog box, click the Tabs button in the lower left corner of the dialog box.
   o. At the Tabs dialog box, type 0.5 and then click the Set button.
   p. Type 1 and then click the Set button.
   q. Type 5.5, click the *Right* option in the *Alignment* section, click *2 ....* in the *Leader* section, and then click the Set button.
   r. Click OK to close the dialog box.
   s. At the blank document, click the macro icon on the Status bar to turn off the macro recording.

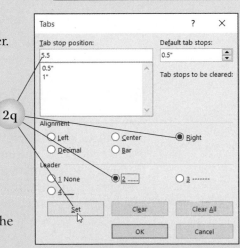

3. Press Ctrl + Q to remove the tab formatting that was applied to the document when you created the Tabs macro.
4. Save and then close **3-MacrosTemplate.dotm**.
5. Use File Explorer to open a document based on **3-MacrosTemplate.dotm**.
6. Insert **ConceptsTofC.docx** from your WL3C3 folder into the current document. (Do this with the Object button arrow on the Insert tab.)
7. Select the text from *Computer Hardware* to the end of the document.
8. Apply the Tabs macro by clicking the Macros button on the Quick Access Toolbar. (If you hover the mouse pointer over the button, the ScreenTip displays with *TemplateProject.NewMacros.Tabs*.)

9. Save the document and name it **3-ConceptsTofC**.
10. Remove the Macro button from the Quick Access Toolbar by right-clicking the button and then clicking *Remove from Quick Access Toolbar* at the shortcut menu.

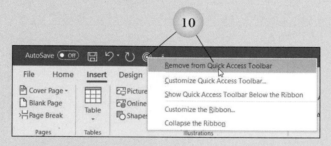

11. Print and then close **3-ConceptsTofC.docx**.

 Check Your Work

---

Activity 3 Record and Run an Automatic Macro and a Heading Macro in a Resume
1 Part

You will record a macro that changes the margins and applies a theme and style set and that runs automatically when a new document is opened. You will then open a document based on a template that runs the automatic macro, insert a resume document into the open document, and then run the Heading macro for each heading.

Running a Macro Automatically

A macro can be created that starts automatically when a certain action is performed, such as opening or closing a document or closing Word. To use a macro that starts automatically, the macro must contain one of the names listed in Table 3.1. To create a macro that runs automatically, display the Record Macro dialog box, type the macro name from the list in Table 3.1 in the *Macro name* text box, and then click OK. Complete the steps for the macro and then end the recording.

Table 3.1 Automatic Macros

Automatic Macro Name	Action
AutoExec	Runs when Word is opened
AutoOpen	Runs when a document is opened
AutoNew	Runs when a new document is opened
AutoClose	Runs when a document is closed
AutoExit	Runs when Word is closed

Activity 3 Recording Macros and Running Macros Automatically

1. Open **3-MacrosTemplate.dotm**.
2. Create a macro that changes the margins and applies a theme and style set and that runs automatically when a new document is opened by completing the following steps:
   a. Click the View tab.
   b. Click the Macros button arrow and then click *Record Macro* at the drop-down list.

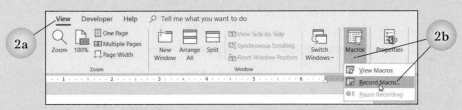

   c. At the Record Macro dialog box, type AutoNew in the *Macro name* text box.
   d. Click the *Store macro in* option box arrow and then click *Documents Based On 3-MacrosTemplate.dotm* at the drop-down list.
   e. Click inside the *Description* text box and then type Runs automatically when a new document is opened, changes the margins, and applies a theme and style set.
   f. Click OK.
   g. Click the Layout tab, click the Margins button, and then click the *Moderate* option.
   h. Click the Design tab, click the Themes button, and then click the *Retrospect* theme.
   i. Click the *Basic (Simple)* option (third option from the left) in the Style Sets gallery in the Document Formatting group.
   j. Click the macro icon on the Status bar to turn off the macro recording.
3. Save and then close **3-MacrosTemplate.dotm**.

4. Use File Explorer to open a document based on **3-MacrosTemplate.dotm**. (The AutoNew macro ran automatically and changed the margins and applied the Retrospect theme and Basic (Simple) style set.)

5. Insert **ResumeStandards.docx** from your WL3C3 folder into the current document. (Do this with the Object button arrow on the Insert tab.)

6. Position the insertion point at the beginning of the heading *Type Standards* and then run the Heading macro.

7. Position the insertion point at the beginning of the heading *Page Standards* and then run the Heading macro.

8. Save the document and name it **3-ResumeStandards**.

9. Print and then close **3-ResumeStandards.docx**.

10. Open **3-MacrosTemplate.dotm**.

11. Delete the AutoNew macro by completing the following steps:
    a. Click the View tab and then click the Macros button.
    b. At the Macros dialog box, click the *Macros in* option box arrow and then click *3-MacrosTemplate.dotm (template)* at the drop-down list.
    c. Make sure *AutoNew* is selected in the *Macro name* list box and then click the Delete button.

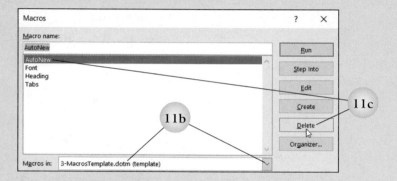

    d. At the message asking if you want to delete the macro, click Yes.
    e. Click the Close button to close the Macros dialog box.

12. Save and then close **3-MacrosTemplate.dotm**.

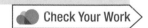 Check Your Work

---

Activity 4 Manage Macros and Record and Run a Macro with Fill-in Fields   3 Parts

You will change macro security settings, copy macros, and save a macro-enabled document. You will also record and run a macro with Fill-in fields in a legal document.

Specifying Macro Security Settings

Some macros pose a security risk because they have the potential to introduce and spread viruses on a computer or network. For this reason, Microsoft Word provides macro security settings to specify what actions occur with macros in a

 Macro Security

document. To display the macro security settings, click the Macro Security button in the Code group on the Developer tab. This displays the Trust Center dialog box with *Macro Settings* selected in the left panel, as shown in Figure 3.4. Another method for displaying the Trust Center dialog box is to click the File tab and then click *Options*. At the Word Options dialog box, click *Trust Center* in the left panel and then click the Trust Center Settings button.

Choose the first option, *Disable all macros without notification*, and all macros and security alerts are disabled. The second option, *Disable all macros with notification,* is the default setting. At this setting, a security alert appears if a macro is present that asks if the macro should be enabled. Choose the third option, *Disable all macros except digitally signed macros,* and a digitally signed macro by a trusted publisher will automatically run. (However, a digitally signed macro will still need to be enabled for a publisher that is not trusted.) The last option, *Enable all macros (not recommended; potentially dangerous code can run),* allows all macros to run but, as the option states, this is not recommended.

Changes made to the macro security settings in Word only apply to Word. The macro security settings do not change in the other programs in the Office suite.

Saving a Macro-Enabled Document

The macros in the activities in this chapter have been saved in a macro-enabled template in your WL3C3 folder. Save a macro-enabled document in a similar manner as a macro-enabled template. To do this, display the Save As dialog box and then change the *Save as type* option to *Word Macro-Enabled Document (*.docm).* Navigate to the desired folder and then click the Save button.

Figure 3.4 Trust Center Dialog Box

Trust Center	? X
Trusted Publishers	**Macro Settings**
Trusted Locations	○ Disable all macros without notification
Trusted Documents	◉ Disable all macros with notification
Trusted Add-in Catalogs	○ Disable all macros except digitally signed macros
Add-ins	○ Enable all macros (not recommended; potentially dangerous code can run)
ActiveX Settings	**Developer Macro Settings**
Macro Settings	☐ Trust access to the VBA project object model
Protected View	
Message Bar	Choose an option in this section to specify the macro security setting.
File Block Settings	
Privacy Options	
	OK Cancel

Copying Macros between Documents and Templates

Macros saved in a template or document can be copied to other templates or documents at the Organizer dialog box with the Macro Project Items tab selected. Display this dialog box by clicking the Macros button in the Code group on the Developer tab and then clicking the Organizer button at the Macros dialog box. The Macros dialog box can also be displayed by clicking the Macros button in the Macros group on the View tab.

Macros created in a document or template are saved in the NewMacros project. At the Organizer dialog box with the Macro Project Items tab selected, copy the NewMacros project from a document or template to another document or template. To copy the NewMacros project, click *NewMacros* in the list box at the left or right and then click the Copy button between the two list boxes.

By default, the Organizer dialog box displays the NewMacros project for the open document or template in the list box at the left and the NewMacros project for Normal.dotm in the list box at the right. Choose a different document or template by clicking the Close File button. This changes the Close File button to the Open File button. Choose a different document or template by clicking the Open File button. At the Open dialog box, navigate to the folder containing the document or template and then double-click the document or template.

The Organizer dialog box contains buttons for renaming and deleting macro projects. To rename the NewMacros project, click *NewMacros* in the list box and then click the Rename button between the two list boxes. At the Rename dialog box, type the new name and then press the Enter key. Delete a macro project by clicking the project name in the list box and then clicking the Delete button between the two list boxes.

Activity 4a Changing Macro Security Settings, Copying Macros, and Saving a Macro-Enabled Document

Part 1 of 3

1. Press Ctrl + N to open a blank document.
2. Change the macro security settings by completing the following steps:
   a. Click the Developer tab and then click the Macro Security button in the Code group.
   b. At the Trust Center dialog box, click the *Enable all macros (not recommended; potentially dangerous code can run)* option.

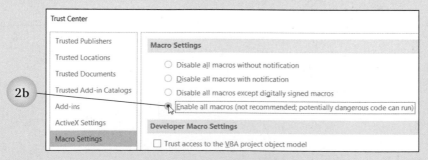

   c. Click OK.
3. Save the document as a macro-enabled document in your WL3C3 folder by completing the following steps:
   a. Press the F12 function key to display the Save As dialog box.

b. Type 3-LegalMacros in the *File name* text box.
c. Click the *Save as type* option box and then click *Word Macro-Enabled Document (*.docm)* at the drop-down list.

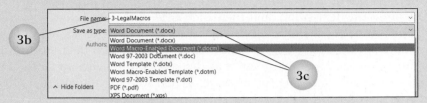

d. Navigate to your WL3C3 folder.
e. Click the Save button.
4. Your WL3C3 folder contains a macro-enabled document named **MacroDocument.docm** that contains two macros. Copy the macros from **MacroDocument.docm** to the current document by completing the following steps:
   a. Make sure the Developer tab is active and then click the Macros button in the Code group.
   b. At the Macros dialog box, click the Organizer button.
   c. At the Organizer dialog box with the Macro Project Items tab selected, click the Close File button below the right list box.
   d. Click the Open File button (previously the Close File button).
   e. At the Open dialog box, click the option box that displays right of the *File name* text box and then click *All Files (*.*)* at the drop-down list.
   f. Navigate to your WL3C3 folder and then double-click ***MacroDocument.docm***.
   g. At the Organizer dialog box with *NewMacros* selected in the list box at the right, click the Copy button between the list boxes. (This copies the *NewMacros* project to the left list box.)
   h. Click the Close button to close the Organizer dialog box.

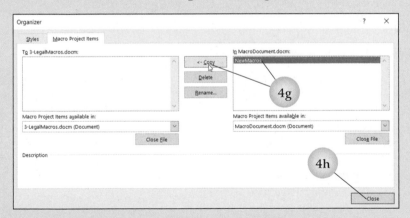

5. Save **3-LegalMacros.docm**.
6. Since this document contains macros that will be used in other documents, you decide to save it as a macro-enabled template by completing the following steps:
   a. Press the F12 function key to display the Save As dialog box.
   b. Type 3-LegalMacrosTemplate in the *File name* text box.
   c. Click the *Save as type* option box and then click *Word Macro-Enabled Template (*.dotm)* at the drop-down list.
   d. Navigate to your WL3C3 folder.
   e. Click the Save button.
7. Keep the template open for the next activity.

Tutorial

Recording a Macro
with a Fill-in Field

 Quick Parts

Recording a Macro with a Fill-in Field

A macro can be recorded that requires input from the keyboard using the Fill-in field. To insert a Fill-in field in a macro, begin recording the macro. At the point when the Fill-in field is to be inserted, click the Insert tab, click the Quick Parts button in the Text group, and then click *Field* at the drop-down list. At the Field dialog box with *(All)* selected in the *Categories* list box, as shown in Figure 3.5, scroll down the *Field names* list and then click the *Fill-in* field. Add information telling the user what text to enter at the keyboard by clicking in the *Prompt* text box and then typing the message. When running the macro, type the text specified by the prompt message.

Figure 3.5 Field Dialog Box

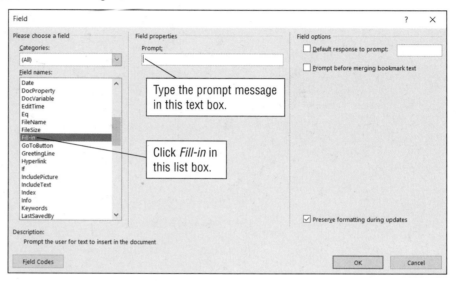

Activity 4b Recording a Macro with Fill-in Fields

1. With **3-LegalMacrosTemplate.dotm** open, begin recording a macro by clicking the macro icon on the Status bar.
2. At the Record Macro dialog box, type Notary in the *Macro name* text box.
3. Click the *Store macro in* option box arrow and then click *Documents Based On 3-LegalMacrosTemplate.dotm* at the drop-down list.
4. Click in the *Description* text box and then type Notary signature information.
5. Click the Keyboard button.
6. At the Customize Keyboard dialog box with the insertion point positioned in the *Press new shortcut key* text box, press Alt + Shift + S.
7. Click the Assign button.
8. Click the Close button.

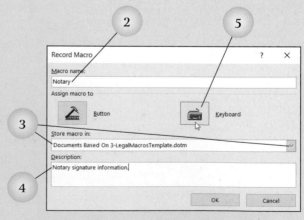

9. At the document, click the Home tab and then click the *No Spacing* style in the Styles group.
10. Set three left tabs by completing the following steps:
    a. Make sure the alignment button above the vertical ruler displays with the left tab symbol.
    b. Click the 0.5-inch mark on the horizontal ruler.
    c. Click the 2-inch mark on the horizontal ruler.
    d. Click the 2.5-inch mark on the horizontal ruler.
11. Type the text shown in Figure 3.6 up to *(name of person)*. (Do not type the text *(name of person)*.)
12. Insert a Fill-in field by completing the following steps:
    a. Click the Insert tab.
    b. Click the Quick Parts button in the Text group and then click *Field* at the drop-down list.
    c. At the Field dialog box with *(All)* selected in the *Categories* list box, scroll down the list and then click *Fill-in*.
    d. Click in the *Prompt* text box and then type Type name of person signing.
    e. Click OK.

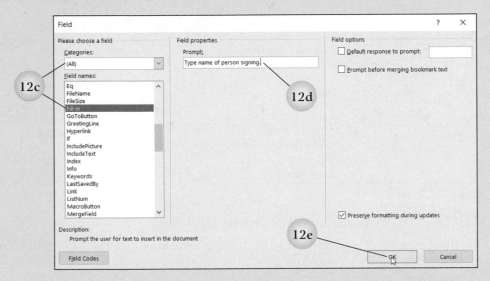

    f. At the Microsoft Word dialog box, type (name of person) in the text box and then click OK.

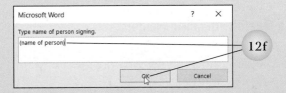

13. Continue typing the notary signature information shown in Figure 3.6 up to the text *(day)* and then complete steps similar to those in Step 12 to insert a Fill-in field that prompts the operator to type the current day.
14. Continue typing the notary signature information shown in Figure 3.6 up to the text *(month)* and then complete steps similar to those in Step 12 to insert a Fill-in field that prompts the operator to type the current month.

15. Continue typing the notary signature information shown in Figure 3.6 up to the text *(expiration date)* and then complete steps similar to those in Step 12 to insert a Fill-in field that prompts the operator to type the expiration date.
16. After inserting the expiration date information, press the Enter key.
17. End the recording by clicking the macro icon on the Status bar.
18. Click the Save button on the Quick Access Toolbar to save the template.
19. Press Ctrl + A to select the entire template and then press the Delete key. (The template should not contain any text.)
20. Save and then close **3-LegalMacrosTemplate.dotm**.

Check Your Work

Figure 3.6 Activity 4b

STATE OF CALIFORNIA   )
) ss.
COUNTY OF LOS ANGELES   )

      On this day personally appeared before me (name of person), known to me to be the individual described in and who executed the aforesaid instrument, and acknowledged that he/she signed as his/her free and voluntary act and deed for the uses and purposes therein mentioned.
      Given under my hand and official seal this (day) day of (month), 2021.

_____
NOTARY PUBLIC in and for the State of California
My appointment expires (expiration date)

Running a Macro with a Fill-in Field

Run a macro with a Fill-in field and the macro will run to the location of the first Fill-in field and then stop and insert the prompt that was entered when the macro was recorded. Type the required information and then click OK and the macro will run to the next Fill-in field. When text for the last Fill-in field has been entered, the macro finishes running.

Activity 4c Running a Macro with Fill-in Fields   Part 3 of 3

1. Use File Explorer to open a document based on **3-LegalMacrosTemplate.dotm**. (If necessary, click the Enable Content button.)
2. Use the Object button arrow on the Insert tab to insert **Affidavit.docx** from your WL3C3 folder into the current document.
3. Position the insertion point at the beginning of the title *AFFIDAVIT OF TRUST* and then run the Title macro. (This is one of the macros that was copied to the legal template in Activity 4a.)

4. Select the numbered paragraphs of text (paragraphs 1 through 6) and then run the Indent macro. (This was the other macro that was copied to the legal template in Activity 4a.)
5. Complete the following finds and replaces:
   a. Find all occurrences of *NAME* and replace them with *LOREN HOUSTON*. (Be sure to replace only the occurrences of *NAME* in all uppercase letters.) **Hint: Expand the Find and Replace dialog box and insert a check mark in the** Match case *check box.*
   b. Find the one occurrence of *ADDRESS* and replace it with *102 Marine Drive, Los Angeles, CA.* (Be sure to replace only the occurrence of *ADDRESS* in all uppercase letters.)
6. Press Ctrl + End to move the insertion point to the end of the document and then run the Notary macro by completing the following steps:
   a. Press Alt + Shift + S.
   b. When the macro stops and prompts you for the name of a person, type LOREN HOUSTON and then click OK.
   c. When the macro stops and prompts you for the day, type 9th and then click OK.
   d. When the macro stops and prompts you for the month, type March and then click OK.
   e. When the macro stops and prompts you for the expiration date, type 12/31/2023 and then click OK.
7. Save the document and name it **3-Affidavit**.
8. Print and then close **3-Affidavit.docx**.
9. At a blank screen, change the macro security settings by completing the following steps:
   a. Click the Developer tab and then click the Macro Security button in the Code group.
   b. At the Trust Center dialog box, click the *Disable all macros with notification* option.
   c. Click OK.

Check Your Work

Activity 5 Edit a Macro
1 Part

You will edit a macro in a template and then open a document based on the template, insert a file in the document, and then run macros.

Editing a Macro

The steps in a macro are recorded using the programming language Visual Basic for Applications, which is generally shortened to VBA. Recording macros in Word does not require an understanding of VBA, but if a macro needs to be edited, having some knowledge of VBA will be helpful. Some basic or minor edits can be made to a macro with minimal knowledge of VBA.

To edit a macro, display the Macros dialog box, click the macro name in the list box, and then click the Edit button. This opens the VBA window with the lines of programming code. Other methods for opening the VBA window include clicking the Visual Basic button in the Code group on the Developer tab or using the keyboard shortcut Alt + F11. Figure 3.7 shows the VBA window for the Heading macro in 3-PhotoMacros.dotm.

 Visual Basic

Some of the lines of code for the Heading macro identify formatting applied by the macro, including bold, italic, and font size formatting. Basic editing in this macro might include deleting a line of code that applies specific formatting or changing the number for the font size. In Activity 5, you will edit the Heading macro by deleting the line of code that applies italic formatting.

Figure 3.7 Heading Macro in VBA Window

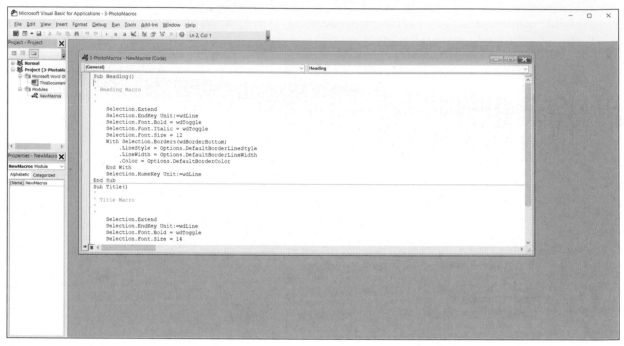

Activity 5 Editing a Macro

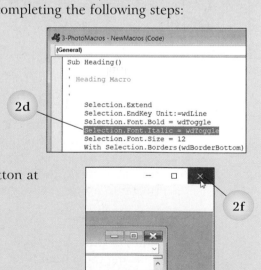

Part 1 of 1

1. Open **PhotoMacros.dotm** and then save it with the name **3-PhotoMacros**. (Make sure it is saved as a macro-enabled template with the .dotm file extension.)
2. Edit the Heading macro saved in the template by completing the following steps:
   a. Click the Developer tab.
   b. Click the Macros button.
   c. At the Macros dialog box, with *Heading* selected in the *Macro name* list box, click the Edit button.
   d. At the VBA window, select the line of code *Selection.Font.Italic = wdToggle*.
   e. Press the Delete key. (This removes the line of code that applies italic formatting.)
   f. Close the VBA window by clicking the Close button at the upper right corner of the screen.
3. Save and then close **3-PhotoMacros.dotm**.
4. Use File Explorer to open a document based on **3-PhotoMacros.dotm**.

5. Use the Object button arrow on the Insert tab to insert **Photography.docx** from your WL3C3 folder into the current document.
6. Position the insertion point at the beginning of the heading *Camera Basics* and then run the Heading macro.
7. Position the insertion point at the beginning of the heading *Pixels* and then run the Heading macro.
8. Position the insertion point at the beginning of the heading *White Balance* and then run the Heading macro.
9. Save the document and name it **3-Photography**.
10. Print and then close **3-Photography.docx**.

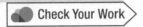 Check Your Work

---

Activity 6 Storing a Macro in Normal.dotm   1 Part

You will record and store a macro in the default template, Normal.dotm, and then run the macro in a travel document.

Storing a Macro in Normal.dotm

In this chapter, macros have been stored in personal templates. If a template or document is not specified with the *Store macro in* option at the Record Macros dialog box, a recorded macro is stored in the template Normal.dotm, which is the default template. Macros stored in Normal.dotm are available in all documents based on that template.

In a public setting, such as a school, storing macros in Normal.dotm may be restricted. Activity 6 includes steps for storing a macro in the Normal.dotm template. Macros from other users may also be stored in the template, so you will need to include your initials in a macro name to distinguish it from macros stored by others. If you are restricted from storing a macro in Normal.dotm, you will not be able to complete Activity 6.

Activity 6 Storing a Macro in and Running a Macro from Normal.dotm   Part 1 of 1

1. Press Ctrl + N to open a blank document.
2. Record a macro named XXXQuote (type your initials in place of the XXX) that is stored in the Normal.dotm template and applies the following paragraph formatting:
   • center alignment
   • left and right indents of 0.5 inch
   • top border line and bottom border line
   • Blue, Accent 5, Lighter 80% (ninth column, second row in the *Theme Colors* section) paragraph shading
3. After recording the macro, close the document without saving it.
4. Open **BTAdventure.docx** and then save it with the name **3-BTAdventure**.

5. Run the XXXQuote (where your initials appear in place of the *XXX*) for the quote at the beginning of the document. (At the Macros dialog box, change the *Macros in* option to *Normal.dotm (global template)*.)
6. Save, print, and then close **3-BTAdventure.docx**.
7. Press Ctrl + N to open a blank document.
8. Display the Macros dialog box and make sure your XXXQuote macro displays in the list box.
9. Press Alt + Print Screen to make a screen capture of the dialog box. (Depending on your keyboard, you may need to press Alt + FN + Print Screen.)
10. Close the dialog box.
11. Press Ctrl + V to paste the screen capture of the Macros dialog box into the current document.
12. Save the document and name it **3-MacrosDialogBox**.
13. Print and then close **3-MacrosDialogBox.docx**.
14. Delete your XXXQuote macro.

 Check Your Work

Chapter Summary

- A macro is a time-saving tool that allows many editing and formatting tasks to be performed automatically. Working with macros involves two steps: recording and running a macro.

- Both the View tab and the Developer tab contain buttons for recording a macro. Display the Developer tab by inserting a check mark in the *Developer* check box at the Word Options dialog box with *Customize Ribbon* selected in the left panel.

- One method for turning on and off the recording of a macro is to click the macro icon on the Status bar.

- Name, specify a template for, and type a description of a macro at the Record Macro dialog box. Display the dialog box by clicking the Record Macro button on the Developer tab, by clicking the Macros button arrow on the View tab and then clicking *Record Macro* at the drop-down list, or by clicking the macro icon on the Status bar.

- Save a template as macro enabled at the Save As dialog box by changing the *Save as type* option to *Word Macro-Enabled Template (*.dotm)*. By default, a template is saved to the Custom Office Templates folder. Use File Explorer to open a document based on a template saved in another location.

- Run a macro by displaying the Macros dialog box and then double-clicking the macro name or clicking the name and then clicking the Run button.

- Temporarily suspend the recording of a macro by clicking the Pause Recording button in the Code group on the Developer tab.

- Delete a macro by displaying the Macros dialog box, clicking the macro name, and then clicking the Delete button.

- Assign a macro to a keyboard command at the Customize Keyboard dialog box. To run a macro that has been assigned a keyboard command, press the keys assigned to the macro.

- Assign a regularly used macro to the Quick Access Toolbar using the Button button at the Record Macro dialog box.

- A macro can be recorded that start automatically when Word is opened, when a document is opened, when new document is opened, when a document is closed, or when Word is closed.

- Specify macro security settings at the Trust Center with *Macro Settings* selected in the left panel. Display the Trust Center by clicking the Macro Security button in the Code group on the Developer tab.

- Save a document as a macro-enabled document by changing the *Save as type* option at the Save As dialog box to *Word Macro-Enabled Document (*.docm)*.

- Macros saved in a template or document can be copied to other templates or documents at the Organizer dialog box with the Macro Project Items tab selected. Display this dialog box by clicking the Organizer button at the Macros dialog box.

- A macro can be recorded that requires input from the keyboard when running the macro. When recording a macro, use the Fill-in field at the location that keyboard entry is required. The Fill-in field is available at the Field dialog box with *(All)* selected in the *Categories* list box.

- When running a macro with a Fill-in field, the macro runs to the location of the field, stops, and inserts the prompt entered when the macro was recorded. Type the required information and then click OK.

- The steps of a macro are recorded using Visual Basic for Applications (VBA). To edit a macro, click the Edit button at the Macros dialog box and then make edits at the VBA window.

- If a template or document is not specified with the *Store macro in* option at the Record Macros dialog box, a recorded macro is stored in the template Normal.dotm, which is the default template.

Commands Review

FEATURE	RIBBON TAB, GROUP/OPTION	BUTTON	KEYBOARD SHORTCUT
Field dialog box	Insert, Text	, *Field*	
Macros dialog box	Developer, Code OR View, Macros		Alt + F8
Organizer dialog box	Developer, Code OR View, Macros	, Organizer...	
Pause macro recording	Developer, Code OR View, Macros		
Record Macro dialog box	Developer, Code OR View, Macros		
Run macro	Developer, Code OR View, Macros		
Stop macro recording	Developer, Code OR View, Macros		
Trust Center dialog box	Developer, Code		
VBA window	Developer, Code		Alt + F11

Microsoft®

Word

Creating Forms

Performance Objectives

Upon successful completion of Chapter 4, you will be able to:

1 Design and create a form and save it as a template

2 Insert content controls in a form

3 Define a group and edit text and content controls in Design mode

4 Open and fill in a form based on a template

5 Edit a form template

6 Insert and edit placeholder text

7 Create a form using a table

8 Restrict editing of a template

9 Insert picture, date picker, drop-down list, combo box, and check box content controls

10 Specify and customize properties for content controls

11 Edit a protected form template

12 Create a form with legacy tools

13 Print a form

14 Customize form field options

Many businesses have preprinted forms that respondents fill in by hand or with a computer. Using these forms involves a printing cost and requires space for storage. With Word, you can create your own forms and eliminate the need to buy and store preprinted forms. Word includes content controls and legacy tools that can be used to create forms. In this chapter, you will learn how to create forms, how to restrict editing in a form, and how to create a document based on a form.

 Data Files

Before beginning chapter work, copy the WL3C4 folder to your storage medium and then make WL3C4 the active folder.

The online course includes additional training and assessment resources.

Activity 1 Creating a Mailing List Form for a Travel Company   4 Parts

You will create a mailing list template for Terra Travel Services, insert plain text controls in the template, group the text and content controls, and then prepare a mailing list form based on the template.

Tutorial

Creating a Form and Defining a Group with Content Controls

Creating and Using a Form

In Word, the term *form* refers to a protected document that includes user-defined sections into which a user (respondent) enters information. These user-defined sections are made up of content controls. Content controls limit response options to ensure the collection of specific data.

The Developer tab, shown in Figure 4.1, contains options for inserting content controls. The Developer tab also contains options for creating forms with legacy tools, which were available in previous versions of Word.

Designing a Form

Designing a form involves two goals: gathering all the information necessary to meet a specific objective and gathering information that is useful and accurate. Thus, the first step in designing a form is to determine its purpose. To do so, make a list of all the information needed to meet the purpose of the form. Be careful not to include unnecessary or redundant information, which will clutter the appearance of the form and frustrate the respondents that complete it.

The next step is to plan the layout of the form. The simplest way to design a form is to find an existing form that requests similar information or serves a similar purpose and then mimic it. Finding a similar form is not always easy, however, and in many cases, a form may need to be designed from scratch. When starting from scratch, first sketch out the form. This will provide a guide to follow when creating the form in Word. Here are some other points to consider when designing a form:

- Group like items in the form. This makes it easy for users to provide complete and accurate information.

- Place the most important information at the top of the form to increase the likelihood of obtaining it. Many respondents fail to complete a form entirely before submitting it.

Figure 4.1 Developer Tab

- Leave plenty of space for respondent input. The respondent may become frustrated if a field does not contain enough space for the data to be entered.
- Use fonts, colors, lines, and graphics purposefully and sparingly. Overusing such design elements tends to clutter a form and make it difficult to read.
- Separate sections of the form using white space, lines, and shading. Each section should be clearly defined.

Creating a Form Template

A form is created as a template, so a respondent who fills it in is working in a copy of the form, rather than the original. That way, a form can be used again and again without changing the original. When a form is created from a form template, information can be typed only in the content controls that are designated when the form was created.

Figure 4.2 shows an example of a form template created with content controls. (This form will be created in Activity 1a.) A form can contain content controls for text, such as the *First Name:*, *Last Name:*, *Address:*, and so on. A form can also contain drop-down lists, dates, and pictures.

Quick Steps
Save Form as Template
1. Open blank document.
2. Display Save As dialog box.
3. Change *Save as type* option to *Word Template*.
4. Click Save button.

Create a new form template by opening an existing document or a blank document, displaying the Save As dialog box, changing the *Save as type* option to *Word Template*, and then clicking the Save button. This saves the template in the Custom Office Templates folder in the Documents folder on the computer's hard drive. To use the template, display the New backstage area, click the *Personal* option, and then click the template thumbnail.

If you are working on a computer in a public environment, consider saving a template to your WL3C4 folder instead of the default folder. When the template is saved in a location other than the default folder, use File Explorer to open a document based on the template.

Figure 4.2 Activity 1a

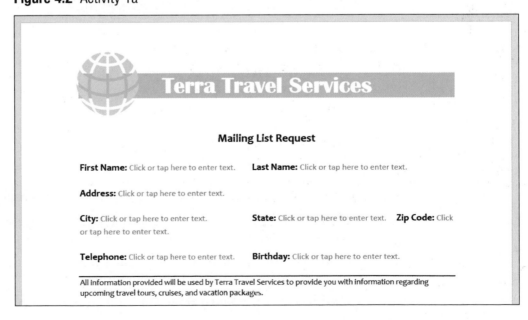

Another option for managing templates is to change the default location that templates are saved from the Custom Office Templates folder to another location, such as a disk drive. To change the default location for templates, display the Word Options dialog box, click *Save* in the left panel, and then specify the folder or drive in which to save templates with the *Default personal templates location* option. The folder or drive specified at this option will be the folder or drive that displays when the *Personal* option is clicked at the New backstage area. The activities in this chapter are based on the assumption that you are saving templates to your WL3C4 folder and using File Explorer to open documents based on your templates.

Displaying the Developer Tab

A number of buttons for creating a form are available in the Controls group on the Developer tab. To display the Developer tab on the ribbon, click the File tab and then click *Options*. At the Word Options dialog box, click *Customize Ribbon* in the left panel. In the list box at the right, click the Developer tab check box to insert a check mark and then click OK to close the dialog box. The Developer tab is positioned right of the View tab.

Inserting Content Controls

The Controls group on the Developer tab contains a number of buttons for inserting content controls in a form. Table 4.1 describes eight of them. Insert a content control by clicking the specific button in the Controls group. Several content controls, such as the plain text content control, include default placeholder text, such as *Click or tap here to enter text*. When filling in a form, the respondent clicks the placeholder text and then types the requested information.

Table 4.1 Content Control Buttons

Content Control Button	Description
Rich Text Content Control	Used to contain custom formatted text or another item, such as another content control or a table or image
Plain Text Content Control	Used to contain plain text; cannot contain another item, such as another content control or a table or image
Picture Content Control	Used to hold an image
Building Block Gallery Content Control	Used to insert a placeholder from which the respondent can select a building block from a specified gallery
Check Box Content Control	Used to insert a check box that can indicate on or off, depending on whether the respondent inserts a check mark in the check box
Combo Box Content Control	Used to create a list of values from which the respondent can select; also allows the respondent to enter other values
Drop Down List Content Control	Used to create a drop-down list of values from which the respondent can select; does not allow other values to be entered
Date Picker Content Control	Used to insert a calendar from which the respondent picks a date

Defining a Group

Quick Steps

Define Group
1. Select text and content controls.
2. Click Developer tab.
3. Click Group button.
4. Click *Group* option.

 Group

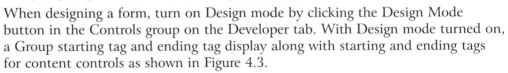 Design Mode

Use the Group button on the Developer tab to define a group, which is a protected region in a form that cannot be edited or deleted by a respondent. A group can contain text, tables, graphics, and content controls. When a group is defined, the respondent can enter information in the content controls but cannot edit the other text or items in the group. To define a group, select the text and content controls, click the Group button in the Controls group on the Developer tab, and then click the *Group* option at the drop-down list.

Displaying a Form in Design Mode

When designing a form, turn on Design mode by clicking the Design Mode button in the Controls group on the Developer tab. With Design mode turned on, a Group starting tag and ending tag display along with starting and ending tags for content controls as shown in Figure 4.3.

Figure 4.3 Form in Design Mode

1. When working with templates, displaying file extensions is helpful to easily identify the type of file. Turn on the display of file extensions by completing the following steps:
   a. Click the File Explorer icon on the taskbar.
   b. Click the View tab.
   c. Click the *File name extensions* check box to insert a check mark.
   d. Close File Explorer.
2. Display the Developer tab by completing the following steps (skip the steps if the Developer tab displays on the ribbon):
   a. Click the File tab and then click *Options*.
   b. At the Word Options dialog box, click *Customize Ribbon* in the left panel.
   c. In the list box at the right, click the *Developer* check box to insert a check mark.

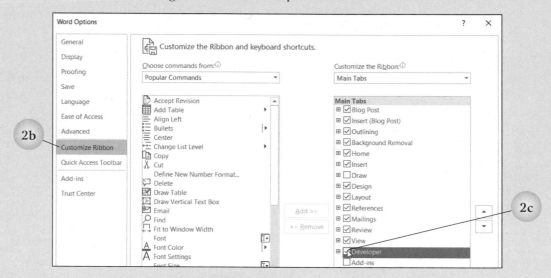

   d. Click OK to close the dialog box.
3. Create the form shown in Figure 4.2 (on page 87). To begin, create a template with an existing document by completing the following steps:
   a. Open **TTSLtrhd.docx** from your WL3C4 folder.
   b. Press the F12 function key to display the Save As dialog box.
   c. At the Save As dialog box, type 4-MailingListTemplate in the *File name* text box.
   d. Click the *Save as type* option box and then click *Word Template (*.dotx)* at the drop-down list.
   e. Navigate to your WL3C4 folder.
   f. Click the Save button.
4. At the template, begin creating the form by completing the following steps:
   a. Click the Layout tab and then click two times on the *Spacing After* measurement box down arrow in the Paragraph group. (This displays *0 pt* in the measurement box.)
   b. Click the Home tab, turn on bold formatting, and then change the font to Candara and the font size to 14 points.
   c. Click the Center button in the Paragraph group, type Mailing List Request, and then press the Enter key two times.
   d. Click the Align Left button in the Paragraph group and then change the font size to 12 points.
   e. Set left tabs at the 3-inch mark and 4.5-inch mark on the horizontal ruler.
   f. Type First Name: and then turn off bold formatting.
   g. Press the spacebar.

5. Insert a plain text content control by completing the following steps:
   a. Click the Developer tab.
   b. Click the Plain Text Content Control button in the Controls group.
   c. Press the Right Arrow key to deselect the content control.

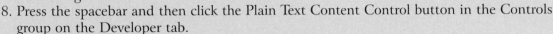

6. Press the Tab key to move the insertion point to the tab at the 3-inch mark.
7. Turn on bold formatting, type Last Name:, and then turn off bold formatting.
8. Press the spacebar and then click the Plain Text Content Control button in the Controls group on the Developer tab.
9. Press the Right Arrow key to deselect the content control.
10. Press the Enter key two times.
11. Continue typing the text and inserting content controls to create the form shown in Figure 4.2 (on page 87). Remember to turn off bold formatting before inserting the plain text content control. (When you enter the line that contains *City:*, *State:*, and *Zip Code:*, press the Tab key to align each item at the correct tab setting. As you type, content controls and text appear crowded and wrap to the next line. The content controls will not print when you create a document from this template.)
12. Position the insertion point one double space below the last line of the form.
13. Insert the horizontal line by pressing Shift + - (the hyphen key) three times and then pressing the Enter key. (AutoFormat will automatically change the hyphens into a vertical line.)
14. Change the font to 10-point Candara and then type the paragraph of text below the horizontal line, as shown in Figure 4.2.
15. Turn on Design mode by clicking the Developer tab and then clicking the Design Mode button in the Controls group.
16. Group the text and content controls by completing the following steps:

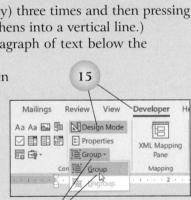

   a. Press Ctrl + A to select all the text and content controls in the document (excluding the header and footer).
   b. Click the Group button in the Controls group and then click *Group* at the drop-down list.
17. Save and then close **4-MailingListTemplate.dotx**.

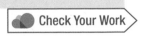

Filling in a Form with Content Controls

Opening and Filling in a Form Document

After a form template has been created, grouped, and saved, it can be used to create a personalized form document. Open a document based on a template saved to the default Custom Office Templates folder by displaying the New backstage area, clicking the *Personal* option, and then clicking the thumbnail representing the template. To open a template saved in a location other than the default folder, open File Explorer, navigate to the folder containing the template, and then double-click the template. This opens a document based on the template.

When a document based on a form template is opened, the insertion point is positioned at the beginning of the document. Click in the placeholder text in the first content control to make it active and then type the required text. Press the Tab key to select the placeholder text in the next content control or press Shift + Tab to select the placeholder text in the preceding content control.

Activity 1b Filling in a Mailing List Form

Part 2 of 4

1. Create a form document from the template **4-MailingListTemplate.dotx** by completing the following steps:
   a. Click the File Explorer icon on the taskbar.
   b. Navigate to your WL3C4 folder.
   c. Double-click **4-MailingListTemplate.dotx**.
   d. If necessary, click the Enable Contents button.
2. Click in the placeholder text for the first content control (the one that displays after *First Name:*) and then type Ava.
3. Press the Tab key to advance to the next content control and continue entering the information as shown in Figure 4.4. Make sure bold formatting is applied to the labels but not the text that is typed in the content controls.
4. Save the document and name it **4-JacksonML**.
5. Print and then close **4-JacksonML.docx**.

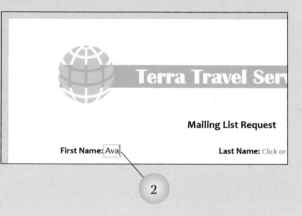

Check Your Work

Figure 4.4 Activity 1b

Mailing List Request

First Name: Ava   Last Name: Jackson

Address: 3458 Peachtree Lane

City: Atlanta   State: GA   Zip Code: 30322

Telephone: 404-555-3412   Birthday: January 15

All information provided will be used by Terra Travel Services to provide you with information regarding upcoming travel tours, cruises, and vacation packages.

Editing Grouped Data

Quick Steps

Edit Grouped Data
1. Open form template.
2. Click Developer tab.
3. Click Design Mode button.
4. Edit text and/or content controls.

When a group has been defined in a form template, the text and content controls in the group can be edited if Design mode is turned on. With Design mode turned off, the placeholder text can be edited but the other text in the group cannot be edited.

Activity 1c Editing a Mailing List Form Template   Part 3 of 4

1. Open **4-MailingListTemplate.dotx** from your WL3C4 folder.
2. Turn on Design mode by clicking the Developer tab and then clicking the Design Mode button in the Controls group.
3. Delete, edit, and insert a content control as shown in Figure 4.5 by completing the following steps:
   a. Select the word *Birthday*, the colon, and the plain text content control placeholder text *Click or tap here to enter text.* and then press the Delete key.
   b. Select the word *Telephone* and then type Home Phone.
   c. Move the insertion point right of the *Home Phone:* plain text content control.
   d. Press the Tab key.
   e. Turn on bold formatting, type Cell Phone:, turn off bold formatting, and then press the spacebar.

Home Phone: Click or tap here to enter text.   **Cell Phone:**

All information provided will be used by Terra Travel Services to provide you with information regarding upcoming travel tours, cruises, and vacation packages. Group

3e

   f. Click the Plain Text Content Control button.
   g. Move the insertion point so it is positioned right of the ending tag for the plain text content control after *Cell Phone:*.
   h. Press the Enter key two times.
   i. Turn on bold formatting, type Email Address:, turn off bold formatting, and then press the spacebar.
   j. Click the Plain Text Content Control button.
4. Turn off Design mode by clicking the Design Mode button.
5. Save and then close **4-MailingListTemplate.dotx**.

Check Your Work

Figure 4.5 Activity 1c

Activity 1d Filling in the Edited Mailing List Form

1. Use File Explorer to open a document based on **4-MailingListTemplate.dotx**.
2. Type the following text in the specified content controls:

   First Name: Caleb
   Last Name: Ellison
   Address: 12302 132nd Street East
   City: Decatur
   State: GA
   Zip Code: 30015
   Home Phone: 678-555-9447
   Cell Phone: 678-555-1140
   Email Address: cellison@ppi-edu.net

3. Save the document in your WL3C4 folder and name it **4-EllisonML**.
4. Print and then close **3-EllisonML.docx**.

Check Your Work

You will open a fax document, save it as a template, insert content controls, protect the template, and restrict editing to filling in the form.

Inserting Specific Placeholder Text

Providing specific placeholder text for respondents who are filling in a form can aid in obtaining accurate information. When creating a form, type text in a content control placeholder that provides specific directions to respondents on what information to enter. To insert specific instructional text, click the Plain Text Content Control button in the Controls group on the Developer tab and then type the instructional text. Or type the instructional text at the location the content control will be inserted, select the text, and then click the Plain Text Content Control button. To edit placeholder text in an existing form template, open the template, turn on Design mode, select the placeholder text, and then type the specific instructional text.

Creating a Form Using a Table

The Tables feature in Word is an efficient tool for designing and creating forms. Using a table, a framework for the form can be created that provides spaces to enter data fields. Using a table also allows for easy alignment and placement of the elements of the form.

Activity 2a **Inserting Specific Placeholder Text in Content Controls in a Fax Template** **Part 1 of 2**

1. Open **TTSFax.docx** and then save it as a template by completing the following steps:
   a. Press the F12 function key to display the Save As dialog box.
   b. At the Save As dialog box, type 4-FaxTemplate in the *File name* text box.
   c. Click the *Save as type* option and then click *Word Template (*.dotx)* at the drop-down list.
   d. Navigate to your WL3C4 folder.
   e. Click the Save button.
2. Insert a plain text content control and then type specific placeholder text by completing the following steps:
   a. Click the Developer tab.
   b. Click in the *To:* text box and position the insertion point one space right of the colon.
   c. Click the Plain Text Content Control button in the Controls group.
   d. Type Receiver's name.

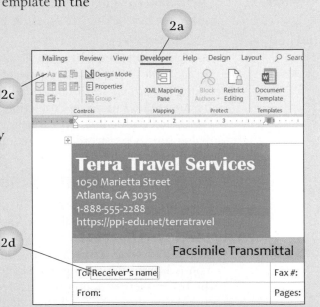

3. Complete steps similar to those in Step 2 to insert the plain text content controls and placeholder text in the *Fax #:*, *From:*, *Pages:*, and *Notes:* cells, as shown in Figure 4.6. (You will insert a field for the date in the next activity.)
4. Click the Save button on the Quick Access Toolbar to save the template.

Check Your Work

Figure 4.6 Activity 2a

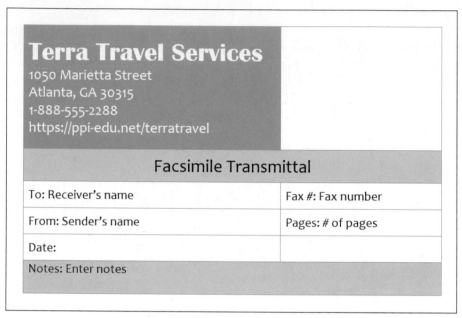

Terra Travel Services
1050 Marietta Street
Atlanta, GA 30315
1-888-555-2288
https://ppi-edu.net/terratravel

Facsimile Transmittal	
To: Receiver's name	Fax #: Fax number
From: Sender's name	Pages: # of pages
Date:	
Notes: Enter notes	

 Tutorial

Protecting a Form Template

 Restrict Editing

Protecting a Template

A form template can be restricted so that it cannot be edited. Restrict a template from editing at the Restrict Editing task pane, shown in Figure 4.7. Display this task pane by clicking the Restrict Editing button in the Protect group on the Developer tab.

At the Restrict Editing task pane, click in the *Allow only this type of editing in the document* check box to insert a check mark. Click the option box arrow in the *Editing restrictions* section and then click *Filling in forms* at the drop-down list. Click the Yes, Start Enforcing Protection button in the task pane. At the Start Enforcing Protection dialog box, type a password, confirm the password, and then close the dialog box. A password is not required to protect a form.

Inserting a Picture Content Control

Picture Content Control

A picture content control can be inserted in a template that displays an image, drawing, shape, chart, table, or SmartArt graphic. Insert an image or other visual element in a form using the Picture Content Control button in the Controls group on the Developer tab. Click this button and a picture frame containing a picture icon is inserted at the location of the insertion point. Click the picture icon and the Insert Picture dialog box displays. At this dialog box, navigate to the folder containing the image and then double-click the image file; the image fills the picture content control.

Figure 4.7 Restrict Editing Task Pane

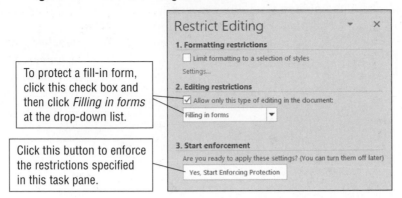

To protect a fill-in form, click this check box and then click *Filling in forms* at the drop-down list.

Click this button to enforce the restrictions specified in this task pane.

Inserting a Date Picker Content Control

A date picker content control can be inserted in a template that displays a calendar when the respondent clicks the arrow at the right side of the control. The respondent can navigate to the month and year and then click the date or insert the current date by clicking the Today button. To insert a date picker content control, click the Date Picker Content Control button in the Controls group on the Developer tab.

 Date Picker Content Control

Activity 2b **Inserting Picture and Date Picker Content Controls, Restricting Editing, and Filling in the Fax Form**   Part 2 of 2

1. With **4-FaxTemplate.dotx** open, insert a picture content control by completing the following steps:
   a. Click in the cell at the right in the top row.
   b. Click the Developer tab.
   c. Click the Picture Content Control button in the Controls group.
   d. Click the picture icon in the middle of the picture content control in the cell.
   e. At the Insert Pictures window, click the *From a File* option, navigate to your WL3C4 folder, and then double-click ***TTSGlobe.jpg***.
2. Insert a date picker content control by completing the following steps:
   a. Click in the *Date:* cell and then position the insertion point one space right of the colon.
   b. Click the Date Picker Content Control button in the Controls group.

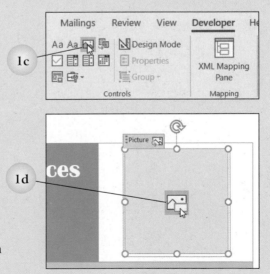

3. Protect the template by completing the following steps:
   a. Click the Restrict Editing button in the Protect group.
   b. Click the *Allow only this type of editing in the document* check box in the Restrict Editing task pane.
   c. Click the option box arrow in the *Editing restrictions* section of the task pane and then click *Filling in forms* at the drop-down list.
   d. Click the Yes, Start Enforcing Protection button.

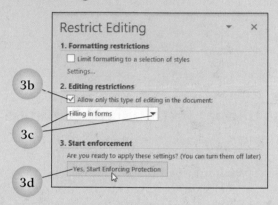

   e. At the Start Enforcing Protection dialog box, click OK. (Creating a password is optional.)
   f. Click the Close button at the upper right corner of the Restrict Editing task pane to close the task pane.
4. Save and then close **4-FaxTemplate.dotx**.
5. Use File Explorer to open a document based on **4-FaxTemplate.dotx**.
6. Click in the text *To:*. (This selects the *To:* placeholder text *Receiver's name*.)
7. Type Max Lopez and then press the Tab key.
8. Type 770-555-9876 and then press the Tab key.
9. Type Amelia Landers and then press the Tab key.
10. Type 3 including cover and then press the Tab key.
11. With the *Date:* content control text selected, click the arrow at the right side of the content control, click the Today button below the calendar, and then press the Tab key.

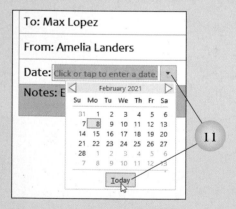

12. Type Please review the two draft contract documents and make a note of any legal revisions that need to be made. I would like to meet with you next week to finalize these contracts.
13. Save the document in your WL3C4 folder and name it **4-TTSFax**.
14. Print and then close **4-TTSFax.docx**.

Check Your Work

Inserting a Drop-Down List Content Control

The designer of a form may want respondents to choose an item from a drop-down list of items, rather than type data in a content control. To make only specific items available, insert a drop-down list content control. To do so, click the Drop-Down List Content Control button in the Controls group on the Developer tab.

Inserting a Combo Box Content Control

Like a drop-down list content control, a combo box content control can be inserted in a form to allow the respondent to choose an item from a drop-down list. While a drop-down list content control limits the respondent to choosing an item from a drop-down list, a combo box content control allows the respondent to enter data in the content control other than items from the drop-down list. Click the Combo Box Content Control button in the Controls group to insert the content control.

Inserting a Check Box Content Control

When check boxes are inserted in a form, the respondent can be asked to insert *X*s to indicate choices. For example, check boxes can be inserted for yes and no responses. To insert a check box, click the Check Box Content Control button in the Controls group on the Developer tab. When filling in the form, the respondent clicks in the check box to insert an *X*.

Setting Content Control Properties

A content control can be customized with options at a properties dialog box. The options at the dialog box vary depending on the selected content control. For example, a list of items can be added for a drop-down list or combo box content control, a picture content control can be locked, and formatting can be specified for inserting a date with a date picker content control.

Specifying Drop-Down List Content Control Properties

Quick Steps

Specify Drop-Down List Content Control Properties

1. Select drop-down list content control.
2. Click Developer tab.
3. Click Properties button.
4. Click Add button.
5. Type choice.
6. Click OK.
7. Continue clicking Add button and typing choices.
8. Click OK to close Content Control Properties dialog box.

 Properties

To create a list of items from which the respondent will choose, select the drop-down list or combo box content control and then click the Properties button in the Controls group on the Developer tab. Clicking a drop-down list content control will display the Content Control Properties dialog box, shown in Figure 4.8. Each content control includes properties that can be changed with options at the dialog box. The content of the dialog box varies depending on the control selected.

To add drop-down list choices, click the Add button in the dialog box. At the Add Choice dialog box, type the first choice in the *Display Name* text box and then click OK. At the Content Control Properties dialog box, click the Add button and then continue until all the choices are entered.

Create a title for the content control with the *Title* option in the Content Control Properties dialog box. Type the title text in the *Title* text box and it displays in the content control tab at the template. Having a content control title is not necessary but can provide additional information for the person filling in the form.

A drop-down list item can be modified by clicking the item in the *Drop-Down List Properties* section and then clicking the Modify button. The position of an item in the list can also be changed by selecting the item and then clicking the Move Up or Move Down button. To remove an item from the list, select the item and then click the Remove button.

To fill in a form with a drop-down list, select the drop-down list or combo box content control, click the arrow at the right side of the content control, and then click an item. Another method is to press and hold down the Alt key, press the Down Arrow key until the item is selected, and then press the Enter key.

Figure 4.8 Content Control Properties Dialog Box for a Drop-Down List Content Control

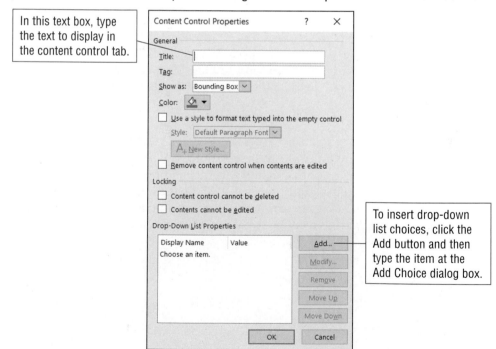

In this text box, type the text to display in the content control tab.

To insert drop-down list choices, click the Add button and then type the item at the Add Choice dialog box.

1. Open **TTSSurvey.docx** and then save it as a template in your WL3C4 folder and name it **4-TTSSurveyTemplate**.
2. Click in the cell immediately right of the cell containing the text *On average, how many times a year do you travel for vacation?* and then insert a drop-down list by completing the following steps:

   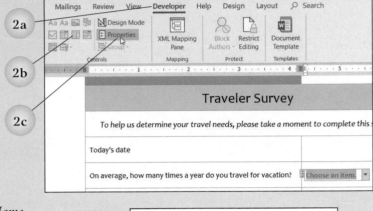

   a. Click the Developer tab.
   b. Click the Drop-Down List Content Control button in the Controls group.
   c. With the content control selected, click the Properties button in the Controls group.
   d. At the Content Control Properties dialog box, click the Add button.
   e. At the Add Choice dialog box, type 0 in the *Display Name* text box and then click OK.
   f. Complete steps similar to those in Steps 2d and 2e to expand the drop-down list, typing the following additional choices:

      1
      2
      3 or more

   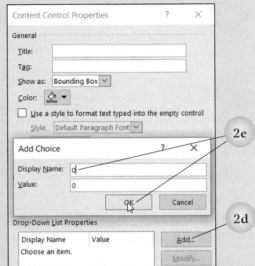

3. Click in the *Title* text box and then type Frequency.

   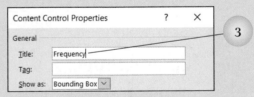

4. Click OK to close the Content Control Properties dialog box.
5. Click in the cell immediately right of the cell containing the text *What type of vacation travel most interests you?* and then insert a combo box drop-down list by completing the following steps:
   a. Click the Combo Box Content Control button in the Controls group.
   b. With the content control selected, click the Properties button in the Controls group.
   c. At the Content Control Properties dialog box, click the Add button.
   d. At the Add Choice dialog box, type All-inclusive resort in the *Display Name* text box and then click OK.
   e. Complete steps similar to those in Steps 5c and 5d to expand the drop-down list, typing the following additional choices:

      Cruise
      Guided tour
      Eco-tour

6. Click in the *Title* text box and then type Vacation preference.
7. Click OK to close the Content Control Properties dialog box.
8. Click in the cell immediately right of the cell containing the text *Would you like one of our travel consultants to contact you with information about vacation packages?* and then insert text and check boxes by completing the following steps:
   a. Click the Check Box Content Control button in the Controls group.
   b. Press the Right Arrow key two times. (This moves the insertion point right of the check box content control.)
   c. Press the spacebar and then type Yes.
   d. Press Ctrl + Tab two times. (This moves the insertion point to a tab position within the cell.)
   e. Click the Check Box Content Control button.
   f. Press the Right Arrow key two times.
   g. Press the spacebar and then type No.

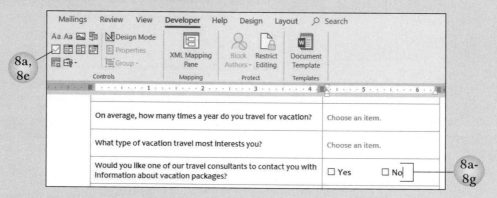

9. Click in the cell immediately right of the cell containing the text *Are you interested in receiving our monthly travel brochure?* and then complete Steps 8a through 8g to insert check boxes and text in the cell.
10. Click the Save button on the Quick Access Toolbar to save the template.

Check Your Work

Customizing Picture Content Control Properties

Quick Steps

Lock Picture Content Control
1. Select picture content control.
2. Click Developer tab.
3. Click Properties button.
4. Insert check mark in *Contents cannot be edited* check box.
5. Click OK.

When using a picture control in a form template, consider locking the picture. With the picture locked, the insertion point does not stop at the picture content control when the respondent presses the Tab key to move to the next data field. To lock a picture, select the picture content control and then click the Properties button in the Controls group on the Developer tab. At the Content Control Properties dialog box, shown in Figure 4.9, insert a check mark in the *Contents cannot be edited* check box. To specify that the picture content control cannot be deleted, insert a check mark in the *Content control cannot be deleted* check box.

Figure 4.9 Content Control Properties Dialog Box for a Picture Content Control

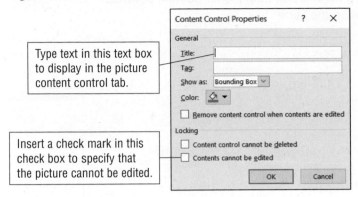

Type text in this text box to display in the picture content control tab.

Insert a check mark in this check box to specify that the picture cannot be edited.

Customizing Date Picker Content Control Properties

The date picker content control has a default format of *m/d/yyyy* for inserting the date. This date format can be customized with options at the Content Control Properties dialog box, shown in Figure 4.10. Choose the date format in the list box in the *Date Picker Properties* section of the dialog box and then click OK.

Figure 4.10 Content Control Properties Dialog Box for a Date Picker Content Control

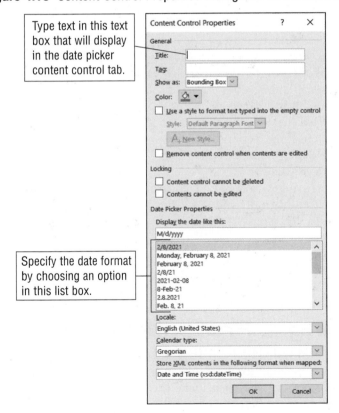

Type text in this text box that will display in the date picker content control tab.

Specify the date format by choosing an option in this list box.

1. With **4-TTSSurveyTemplate.dotx** open, insert a picture content control and lock the control by completing the following steps:
   a. Click in the cell at the right in the top row of the table.
   b. Click the Developer tab.
   c. Click the Picture Content Control button in the Controls group.
   d. Click the picture icon in the middle of the picture content control in the cell.
   e. At the Insert Pictures window, click the *From a File* option, navigate to your WL3C4 folder, and then double-click **TTSGlobe.jpg**.
   f. Click the Properties button in the Controls group.
   g. At the Content Control Properties dialog box, type Terra Image in the *Title* text box.
   h. Click the *Contents cannot be edited* check box to insert a check mark.
   i. Click OK to close the dialog box.
2. Insert a date picker content control and customize the control by completing the following steps:
   a. Click in the cell immediately right of the cell containing the text *Today's date*.
   b. Click the Date Picker Content Control button in the Controls group.
   c. Click the Properties button in the Controls group.
   d. Type Date in the *Title* text box.
   e. In the *Date Picker Properties* section of the Content Control Properties dialog box, click the third option from the top in the list box.
   f. Click OK to close the dialog box.
3. Protect the template to allow only filling in the form. (Refer to Activity 2b, Step 3.) Close the Restrict Editing task pane.
4. Save **4-TTSSurveyTemplate.dotx**.

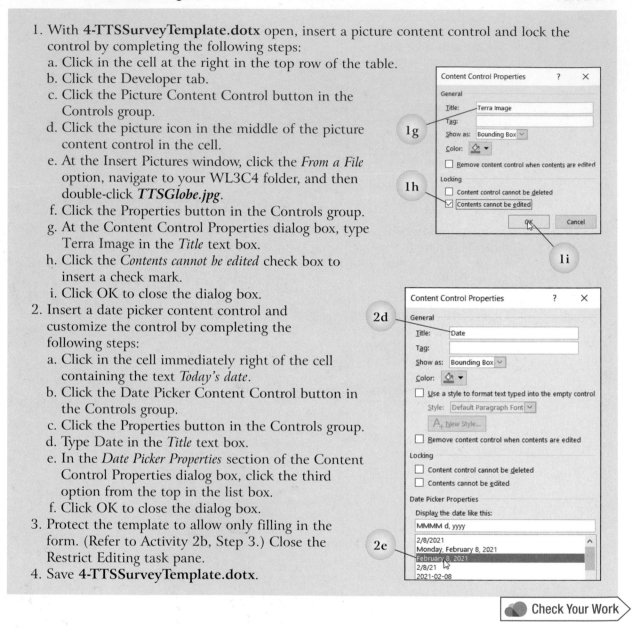

> **Check Your Work**

> Tutorial

Editing a Form Template

Editing a Protected Form Template

When a form template is created and then protected, the text in the template cannot be changed. To make a change to a form template, open the template, turn off the protection, and then make the changes. After making the changes, protect the template again before saving it.

To turn off the protection of a form template, click the Restrict Editing button in the Protect group on the Developer tab. At the Restrict Editing task pane, click the Stop Protection button. If the form template was protected with a password, enter the password and then click OK. Make the changes to the form template and then protect it again by clicking the Yes, Start Enforcing Protection button and then clicking OK at the Start Enforcing Protection dialog box.

1. With **4-TTSSurveyTemplate.dotx** open, turn off protection by completing the following steps:
   a. Click the Developer tab.
   b. Click the Restrict Editing button in the Protect group.
   c. At the Restrict Editing task pane, click the Stop Protection button at the bottom of the task pane.

2. Insert text and a content control object in the last cell by completing the following steps:
   a. Click in the last cell. (The cell is shaded.)
   b. Type Notes: and then press the spacebar.
   c. Type the text Type additional ideas or comments here.
   d. Select *Type additional ideas or comments here.* and then click the Plain Text Content Control button in the Controls group.

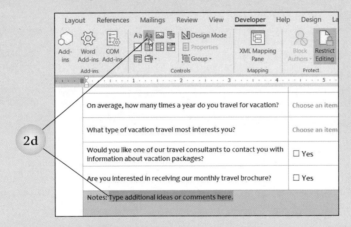

3. Protect the form template again by completing the following steps:
   a. Click the Yes, Start Enforcing Protection button.
   b. Click OK at the Start Enforcing Protection dialog box.
   c. Close the Restrict Editing task pane.
4. Save and then close **4-TTSSurveyTemplate.dotx**.
5. Use File Explorer to open a document based on **4-TTSSurveyTemplate.dotx**. (Refer to Figure 4.11, which shows the filled-in form.)
6. With the *Date:* content control text selected, click the arrow at the right side of the content control and then click the Today button below the calendar.
7. Press the Tab key. (This selects the drop-down list content control in the cell immediately right of the cell containing the text *On average, how many times a year do you travel for vacation?*)
8. Choose an option from the drop-down list by clicking the drop-down list content control down arrow and then clicking *2*.
9. Press the Tab key to select the combo box content control.

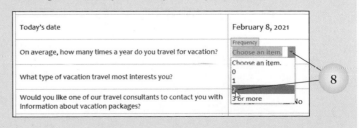

10. Instead of choosing an item from the drop-down list, type Disney vacation. (With a combo box content control, you can type in your own entry.)
11. Click the *Yes* check box in the cell right of the cell containing the text *Would you like one of our travel consultants to contact you with information about vacation packages?* (Refer to Figure 4.11.)
12. Click the *No* check box in the cell right of the cell containing the text *Are you interested in receiving our monthly travel brochure?*
13. With the *Notes:* plain text content control placeholder text selected, type We are interested in a family vacation to Disneyland in the summer of 2022.
14. Save the document in your WL3C4 folder and name it **4-TTSSurvey**.
15. Print and then close **4-TTSSurvey.docx**.

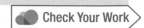 Check Your Work

Figure 4.11 Activity 3c

Terra Travel Services

1050 Marietta Street
Atlanta, GA 30315
1-888-555-2288
https://ppi-edu.net/terratravel

Travel the world
with
Terra Travel
Services

Traveler Survey

To help us determine your travel needs, please take a moment to complete this survey.

Today's date	February 8, 2021
On average, how many times a year do you travel for vacation?	2
What type of vacation travel most interests you?	Disney vacation
Would you like one of our travel consultants to contact you with information about vacation packages?	☒ Yes ☐ No
Are you interested in receiving our monthly travel brochure?	☐ Yes ☒ No

Notes: We are interested in a family vacation to Disneyland in the summer of 2022.

Activity 4 **Create and Fill in an Insurance Application Form**   **4 Parts**

You will insert form fields in an insurance application form, save the form as a template, open a document based on the template, and then insert data in the form fields.

Creating a Form
with Legacy Tools

Creating a Form with Legacy Tools

Legacy tools are tools for developing forms that were available in previous versions of Word. One advantage to legacy tools is that they are compatible with all versions of Word for Windows and Word for Mac while content controls are not supported in Word for Windows 2003 and earlier versions or Word for Mac 2011 or earlier. Legacy tools also include ActiveX controls, which can be used to create interactive documents such as online forms. (The malicious use of ActiveX controls became a widespread problem so they are less commonly used today.)

Legacy form fields are available from the Legacy Tools button drop-down list. Display this list by clicking the Legacy Tools button in the Controls group on the Developer tab. The drop-down list includes three form field buttons: the Text Form Field button, the Check Box Form Field button, and the Drop-Down Form Field button. The Legacy Tools button drop-down list contains three additional buttons: the Insert Frame button, the Form Field Shading button, and the Reset Form Fields button. The Legacy Tools buttons are described in Table 4.2.

Inserting a Text Form Field

Quick Steps

Insert Text Form Field
1. Click Developer tab.
2. Click Legacy Tools button.
3. Click Text Form Field button.

The text form field in the Legacy Tools button drop-down list is similar to the plain text content control. To insert a text form field, position the insertion point in the desired location, click the Legacy Tools button in the Controls group on the Developer tab, and then click the Text Form Field button. This inserts a gray shaded box in the form, which is where the respondent enters data when filling in the form. (The shading does not print when the form is printed.) The gray

[abl] Text Form Field

Table 4.2 Legacy Tools Buttons

Legacy Tools Button	Description
Text Form Field	Used to contain text that cannot be formatted by the respondent
Check Box Form Field	Used to insert a check box that indicates on or off, true or false, or yes or no, depending on whether the respondent inserts a check mark in the check box
Drop-Down Form Field	Used to create a drop-down list of values from which the respondent chooses
Insert Frame	Used to insert a frame around content and hold static data
Form Field Shading	Used to turn on or off the form field shading
Reset Form Fields	Used to clear all entries from the form

Form Field Shading

shading can be turned off by clicking the Form Field Shading button in the Legacy Tools button drop-down list. If the gray shading is turned off, click the button again to turn it back on.

Activity 4a Creating an Application Form Template

1. Open **LAApp01.docx** and then save it as a template in your WL3C4 folder and name it **4-LAApp01Form**.
2. Insert a text form field by completing the following steps. (Figure 4.12 shows the filled-in form.)
   a. Click the Developer tab.
   b. Position the insertion point one space right of the colon after the field label *Name:* below the heading *FIRST APPLICANT*.
   c. Click the Legacy Tools button in the Controls group on the Developer tab and then click the Text Form Field button.

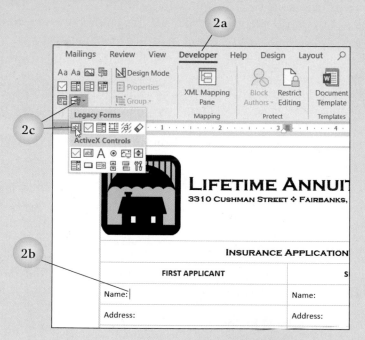

3. Complete steps similar to those in Steps 2b and 2c to insert a text form field one space right of the colon in each of the following field labels in the *FIRST APPLICANT* and *SECOND APPLICANT* sections: *Name:, Address:, Date of Birth:,* and *Occupation:*.
4. Click the Save button on the Quick Access Toolbar to save the template.

 Check Your Work

Figure 4.12 Insurance Application Form Created in Activity 4

LIFETIME ANNUITY COMPANY
3310 CUSHMAN STREET ❖ FAIRBANKS, AK 99705 ❖ 907-555-8875

INSURANCE APPLICATION

FIRST APPLICANT	SECOND APPLICANT
Name: Sara Trevier	Name: Chris Trevier
Address: 1762 32nd Street, Fairbanks, AK 99702	Address: 1762 32nd Street, Fairbanks, AK 99702
Date of Birth: 03/28/1978	Date of Birth: 10/02/1977
Occupation: Engineer Technician	Occupation: Police Officer

1. During the past three years, have you for any reason consulted a doctor or been hospitalized?

First Applicant: Yes ☐ No ☒	Second Applicant: Yes ☐ No ☒

2. Have you ever been treated for or advised that you have any of the following: heart, lung, kidney, or liver disorder; high blood pressure; drug abuse, including alcohol; cancer or tumor; diabetes; or any disorder of your immune system?

First Applicant: Yes ☒ No ☐	Second Applicant: Yes ☐ No ☒

3. During the past three years, have you for any reason been denied life insurance by any other insurance company?

First Applicant: Yes ☐ No ☒	Second Applicant: Yes ☐ No ☒

FIRST APPLICANT'S SIGNATURE	SECOND APPLICANT'S SIGNATURE

Inserting a Check Box Form Field

Quick Steps

Insert Check Box Form Field
1. Click Developer tab.
2. Click Legacy Tools button.
3. Click Check Box Form Field button.

☑ Check Box Form Field

When a check box form field is inserted in a form, the respondent can insert an *X* in it or leave it blank when filling in the form. Check boxes are useful in forms for indicating yes and no and for inserting options that the respondent can select by inserting check marks. To insert a check box form field, click the Legacy Tools button in the Controls group on the Developer tab and then click the Check Box Form Field button at the drop-down list.

1. With **4-LAApp01Form.dotx** open, insert a check box form field by completing the following steps:
   a. Position the insertion point two spaces right of the *Yes* with the heading *First Applicant* below the first question.
   b. Make sure the Developer tab is active.
   c. Click the Legacy Tools button in the Controls group.
   d. Click the Check Box Form Field button at the drop-down list.

2. Complete steps similar to those in Steps 1c and 1d to insert the remaining check boxes for the *Yes* and *No* responses for both the *First Applicant* and *Second Applicant* sections below questions 1, 2, and 3 (refer to Figure 4.12 on page 109).

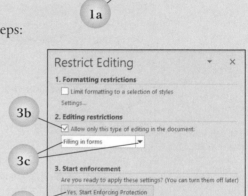

3. Protect the template by completing the following steps:
   a. Click the Restrict Editing button.
   b. Click the *Allow only this type of editing in the document* check box in the Restrict Editing task pane to insert a check mark.
   c. Click the option box arrow in the *Editing restrictions* section of the task pane and then click *Filling in forms* at the drop-down list.
   d. Click the Yes, Start Enforcing Protection button.
   e. At the Start Enforcing Protection dialog box, type your first name all lowercase letters in the *Enter new password (optional)* text box.
   f. Press the Tab key and then type your first name again (all lowercase letters).
   g. Click OK to close the Start Enforcing Protection dialog box.
   h. Click the Close button in the upper right corner of the Restrict Editing task pane to close the task pane.

4. Save and then close **4-LAApp01Form.dotx**.

 Check Your Work

---

 Tutorial

Filling in a Form
with Form Fields

Filling in a Form with Form Fields

Fill in a form with text and check box form fields in the same manner used to fill in a form with content controls. To fill in the form, open a document based on the template and then type the information in the form fields. Press the Tab key to move to the next field or press Shift + Tab to move to the previous field. Another option is to click in the form field and then type the information. To insert an X in a check box, press the spacebar or use the mouse to click in the check box.

1. Use File Explorer to open a document based on **4-LAApp01Form.dotx**.
2. With the insertion point positioned in the first form field after *Name:*, type Sara Trevier.
3. Press the Tab key to move to the next form field.
4. Fill in the remaining text and check box form fields as shown in Figure 4.12 (on page 109). Press the Tab key to move to the next form field or press Shift + Tab to move to the previous form field. To insert an *X* in a check box, make the check box active and then press the spacebar.
5. When the form is completed, save the document with the name **4-LATrevierApp**.
6. Print **4-LATrevierApp.docx**.

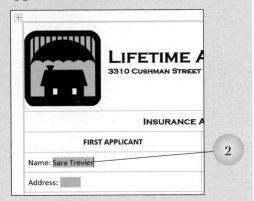

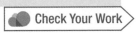

 Check Your Work

Printing a Form

After a form document has been filled in, it can be submitted electronically or it can be printed. The form can also be printed without the filled-in data, or only the data can be printed and not the entire form.

Quick Steps

Print Only Data in Form Document

1. Click File tab.
2. Click *Options*.
3. Click *Advanced*.
4. Click *Print only the data from a form* option.
5. Click OK.
6. Click File tab.
7. Click *Print*.
8. Click Print button.

Printing only the data is useful in a situation in which a preprinted form is used and inserted in the printer. Word will print the items of data in the same locations on the page as they appear in the form document. To print only the data in a form, display the Word Options dialog box and then click the *Advanced* option in the left panel. Scroll down the dialog box and then click the *Print only the data from a form* check box in the *When printing this document* section.

When you print the form data in Activity 4d, the table gridlines will print as well as the shading and image. If you do not want these elements to print, remove them from the form.

1. With **4-LATrevierApp.docx** open, print only the data by completing the following steps:
   a. Click the File tab and then click *Options*.
   b. At the Word Options dialog box, click *Advanced* in the left panel.
   c. Scroll down the dialog box to the *When printing this document* section and then click the *Print only the data from a form* check box.
   d. Click OK to close the Word Options dialog box.
   e. Click the File tab, click the *Print* option, and then click the Print button at the Print backstage area.

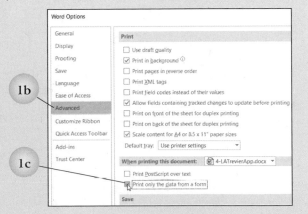

2. Remove the check mark from the *Print only the data from a form* check box by completing the following steps:
   a. Click the File tab and then click *Options*.
   b. At the Word Options dialog box, click *Advanced* in the left panel.
   c. Scroll down the dialog box to the *When printing this document* section and then click the *Print only the data from a form* check box to remove the check mark.
   d. Click OK to close the Word Options dialog box.
3. Save and then close **4-LATrevierApp.docx**.

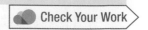 Check Your Work

---

Activity 5 Create and Fill in a Preferred Insurance Application Form 1 Part

You will insert form fields in a preferred insurance application form (including drop-down form fields), save the form as a template, and then open a document based on the template and insert data in the form fields.

 Tutorial

Customizing Form Field Options

Customizing Form Field Options

A text form field contains default settings and some of these defaults can be changed with options at the Text Form Field Options dialog box. Change default settings for a check box form field with options at the Check Box Form Field Options dialog box. Insert a drop-down list form field in a document with a button in the Legacy Tools button drop-down list. Insert a drop-down list form field and then change default settings with options at the Drop-Down Form Field Options dialog box, including typing the choices for the list.

Creating a Drop-Down List Form Field

 Drop-Down Form Field

To create a field that provides a number of options from which a respondent can choose when filling in the form, insert a drop-down list form field. To do this, click the Legacy Tools button in the Controls group on the Developer tab and then click the Drop-Down Form Field button. To insert the choices, click the Properties button in the Controls group. This displays the Drop-Down Form Field Options dialog box, shown in Figure 4.13.

Figure 4.13 Drop-Down Form Field Options Dialog Box

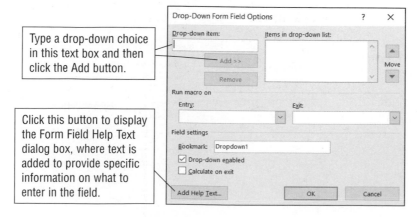

Type a drop-down choice in this text box and then click the Add button.

Click this button to display the Form Field Help Text dialog box, where text is added to provide specific information on what to enter in the field.

Quick Steps

Create Drop-Down Form Field
1. Click Developer tab.
2. Click Legacy Tools button.
3. Click Drop-Down Form Field button.
4. Click Properties button.
5. Type first list option.
6. Click Add button.
7. Continue typing choices and clicking Add button.
8. Click OK.

At the dialog box, type the first option in the *Drop-down item* text box and then click the Add button. This inserts the item in the *Items in drop-down list* list box. Continue in this manner until all the drop-down list items have been inserted. Remove a drop-down list item from the *Items in drop-down list* list box by clicking the item and then clicking the Remove button. When all the items have been entered in the list box, click OK to close the dialog box.

Specific information can be included in a form field to provide instructional text for a respondent who is filling in the form. To provide instructional text, click the Add Help Text button in the lower left corner of the Drop-Down Form Field Options dialog box. This displays the Form Field Help Text dialog box with the Status Bar tab selected, as shown in Figure 4.14. At the dialog box, click the *Type your own* option and then type the text that will display when the field is active. The typed text displays in the Status bar when the respondent is filling in the form.

To fill in a drop-down form field, click the form field down arrow at the right side of the field and then click an option at the drop-down list. The drop-down list can also be displayed by pressing the F4 function key or by pressing and holding down the Alt key and pressing the Down Arrow key.

Figure 4.14 Form Field Help Text Dialog Box

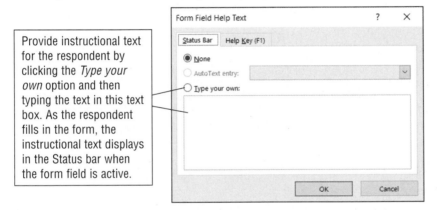

Provide instructional text for the respondent by clicking the *Type your own* option and then typing the text in this text box. As the respondent fills in the form, the instructional text displays in the Status bar when the form field is active.

Activity 5 Inserting Drop-Down Form Fields and Filling in a Form   Part 1 of 1

1. Open **LAApp02.docx** and then save the document as a template in your WL3C4 folder with the name **4-LAApp02Form**.
2. Insert a drop-down form field by completing the following steps. (Figure 4.15 on page 115 shows the filled-in form.)
   a. Position the insertion point one space right of the colon after *Nonprofit Employer*.
   b. Click the Developer tab.
   c. Click the Legacy Tools button in the Controls group and then click the Drop-Down Form Field button.

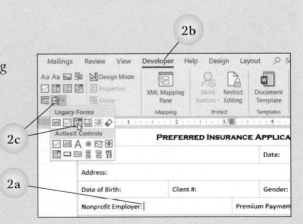

3. Insert the drop-down list choices and create instructional text by completing the following steps:

   a. With the insertion point positioned immediately right of the drop-down form field, click the Properties button.

   b. At the Drop-Down Form Field Options dialog box, type College in the *Drop-down item* text box.

   c. Click the Add button.

   d. Type Public school in the *Drop-down item* text box.

   e. Click the Add button.

   f. Type Private school in the *Drop-down item* text box.

   g. Click the Add button.

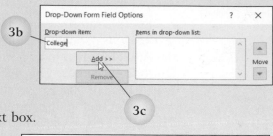

   h. Click the Add Help Text button in the lower left corner of the dialog box.

   i. At the Form Field Help Text dialog box with the Status Bar tab selected, click the *Type your own* option.

   j. In the text box, type the text Click the Nonprofit Employer form field down arrow and then click the employer at the drop-down list.

   k. Click OK to close the Form Field Help Text dialog box.

   l. Click OK to close the Drop-Down Form Field Options dialog box.

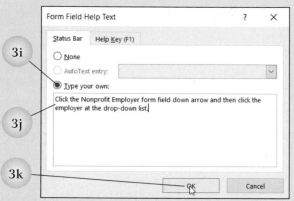

4. Insert a drop-down form field one space after the colon that follows *Premium Payments* and then complete steps similar to those in Step 3 to insert the following items at the Drop-Down Form Field Options dialog box: *Annually*, *Semiannually*, and *Quarterly*.

5. Insert text form fields (using the Text Form Field button from the Legacy Tools button drop-down list) one space following the colon after each of the following: *Name, Date, Address, Date of Birth,* and *Client #*.

6. Insert check box form fields (using the Check Box Form Field button in the Legacy Tools button drop-down list) two spaces right of *Female* and *Male* following *Gender* and right of *Yes* and *No* in the questions.

7. Protect the template to allow only filling in the form and use your last name (all lowercase letters) as the password. (Refer to Activity 4b, Step 3.)

8. Save and then close **4-LAApp02Form.dotx**.

9. Use File Explorer to open a document based on **4-LAApp02Form.dotx**.

10. At the document, enter the data in the form fields as shown in Figure 4.15. (To insert *Public school* in the *Nonprofit Employer* drop-down form field, click the *Nonprofit Employer* form field down arrow and then click *Public school* at the drop-down list. [Notice the instructional text in the Status bar.] Complete similar steps to insert *Quarterly* in the *Premium Payments* drop-down form field.)

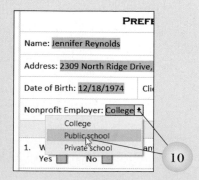

11. When the form is completed, save the document with the name **4-LAReynoldsApp**.

12. Print and then close **4-LAReynoldsApp.docx**.

Check Your Work

Figure 4.15 Preferred Insurance Application Form Created in Activity 5

LIFETIME ANNUITY COMPANY 3310 CUSHMAN STREET ❖ FAIRBANKS, AK 99705 ❖ 907-555-8875	
PREFERRED INSURANCE APPLICATION	
Name: Jennifer Reynolds	Date: 03/08/2021
Address: 2309 North Ridge Drive, Fairbanks, AK 99708	
Date of Birth: 12/18/1974 Client #: 210-322	Gender: Female ☒ Male ☐
Nonprofit Employer: Public school	Premium Payments: Quarterly
1. Will this insurance replace any existing insurance or annuity? Yes ☒ No ☐	
2. Within the past three years has your driver's license been suspended or revoked, or have you been convicted for driving under the influence of alcohol or drugs? Yes ☐ No ☒	
3. Do you have any intention of traveling or residing outside the United States or Canada within the next twelve months? Yes ☐ No ☒	
APPLICANT'S SIGNATURE:	DATE:

Activity 6 Create and Fill in an Application for Benefits Change Form — 2 Parts

You will insert form fields in an application for benefits change form, customize the form fields, save the form as a template, and then open a document based on the template and insert data in the form fields.

Customizing Check Box Form Field Options

Customize check box form field options at the Check Box Form Field Options dialog box, shown in Figure 4.16. Display this dialog box by inserting or selecting an existing check box form field and then clicking the Properties button in the Controls group on the Developer tab.

Figure 4.16 Check Box Form Field Options Dialog Box

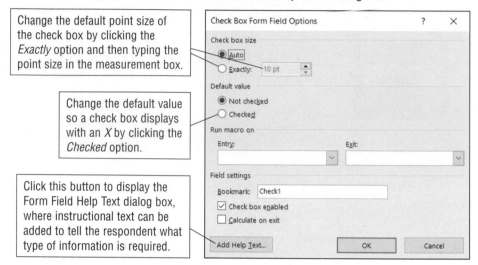

Change the default point size of the check box by clicking the *Exactly* option and then typing the point size in the measurement box.

Change the default value so a check box displays with an *X* by clicking the *Checked* option.

Click this button to display the Form Field Help Text dialog box, where instructional text can be added to tell the respondent what type of information is required.

By default, Word inserts a check box in a form template that is the same size as the adjacent text. To change the default point size, click the *Exactly* option and then type the point size in the measurement box or use the measurement box up or down arrow to increase or decrease the point size.

A check box form field is empty by default. This default can be changed so the check box displays with an *X* by clicking the *Checked* option in the *Default value* section of the dialog box.

Activity 6a Inserting and Customizing Check Box Form Fields

Part 1 of 2

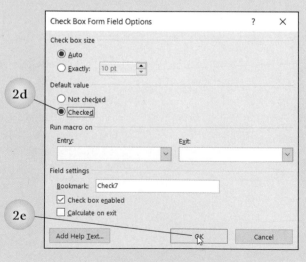

1. Open **LAApp03.docx** and then save the document as a template in your WL3C4 folder with the name **4-LAApp03Form**.
2. Insert a check box that contains a check mark by completing the following steps. (Figure 4.17 shows the filled-in form.)
   a. Position the insertion point two spaces right of the *Yes* below the *Are you currently working?* question.
   b. Click the Developer tab, click the Legacy Tools button in the Controls group, and then click the Check Box Form Field button at the drop-down list.
   c. With the insertion point positioned immediately right of the check box form field, click the Properties button.
   d. At the Check Box Form Field Options dialog box, click the *Checked* option in the *Default value* section.
   e. Click OK.

3. Complete steps similar to those in Step 2 to insert a check box that contains a check mark right of *Yes* below the *Do you work full time?* question.
4. Insert the remaining check boxes for questions 1, 2, and 3 (without check marks).
5. Insert a drop-down form field two spaces after the question mark that ends question 4 and insert the following items at the Drop-Down Form Field Options dialog box: *Standard, Premium, Gold,* and *Platinum.*
6. Insert a drop-down form field two spaces after the question mark that ends question 5 and insert the following items at the Drop-Down Form Field Options dialog box: *Standard, Premium, Gold,* and *Platinum.*
7. Save **4-LAApp03Form.dotx**.

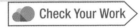

Figure 4.17 Application for Benefits Change Form Created in Activity 6

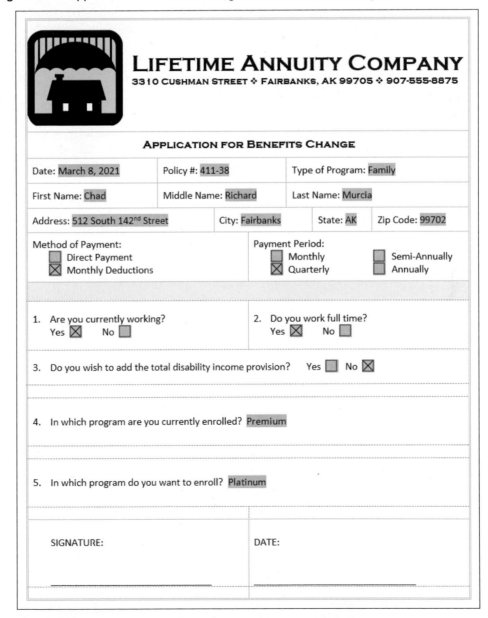

Customizing Text Form Fields

To change options for a text form field, select the form field (or position the insertion point immediately right of the form field) and then click the Properties button in the Controls group on the Developer tab. This displays the Text Form Field Options dialog box, shown in Figure 4.18.

Change the type of text to be inserted in the form field with the *Type* option at the Text Form Field Options dialog box. The default setting is *Regular text* and it can be changed to *Number*, *Date*, *Current date*, *Current time*, or *Calculation*. If the *Type* option is changed, Word displays an error message if the wrong type of information is entered in the form field. For example, if the *Type* option is changed to *Number*, a respondent filling in the form can only enter a number. If the respondent tries to enter something other than a number, Word displays an error message, selects the entry, and keeps the insertion point in the form field until a number is entered.

If a particular text form field generally requires the same information, type that text in the *Default text* text box and it will always display in the form field. When the form is filled in, the respondent can leave the default text in the form field or type over it. Use the *Maximum length* option at the dialog box to specify a maximum number of characters for the form field. This option has a default setting of *Unlimited*.

Apply formatting to text in a form field with options in the *Text format* option box. For example, to display text in all uppercase letters, click the *Text format* option box arrow and then click *Uppercase* at the drop-down list. When the respondent has typed text in the form field, that text is automatically converted to uppercase letters as soon as the respondent presses the Tab key or the Enter key. The *Text format* options vary depending on what is selected in the *Type* option box. Formatting can also be applied to a form field by selecting the form field, applying the formatting, and then using Format Painter to apply the same formatting to other form fields.

Figure 4.18 Text Form Field Options Dialog Box

Use the *Type* option to specify the type of information that can be entered in the form field. Click the option box arrow to display a drop-down list of options.

If the same information is generally required in a text form field, type the text in the *Default text* text box.

Use the *Maximum length* option box to specify the number of characters that can be entered in the text form field.

Click this button to display the Form Field Help Text dialog box, where instructional text can be added to tell the respondent what type of information is required.

1. With **4-LAApp03Form.dotx** open, create a custom text form field by completing the following steps:
   a. Position the insertion point one space right of the colon after *Type of Program*.
   b. Insert a text box form field by clicking the Legacy Tools button and then clicking the Text Form Field button at the drop-down list.
   c. Most employees are enrolled in a family insurance program. Reflect this by making *Family* the default setting for the text form field. To do this, make sure the insertion point is positioned immediately right of the text form field and then click the Properties button.
   d. At the Text Form Field Options dialog box, type Family in the *Default text* text box.
   e. Click OK to close the dialog box.

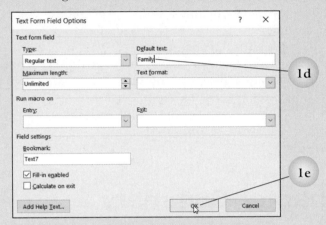

2. Create a custom text form field for the *State:* form field that specifies that the field must contain two uppercase letters by completing the following steps:
   a. Position the insertion point one space right of the colon after *State*.
   b. Insert a text box form field by clicking the Legacy Tools button and then clicking the Text Form Field button at the drop-down list.
   c. Click the Properties button.
   d. At the Text Form Field Options dialog box, click the *Maximum length* measurement box up arrow until *2* displays.
   e. Click the *Text format* option box arrow and then click *Uppercase* at the drop-down list.

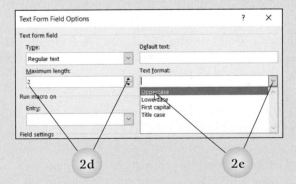

   f. Click OK to close the Text Form Field Options dialog box.
3. Complete steps similar to those in Step 2 to create a custom text form field for the *Zip Code* form field that specifies a maximum length of five characters.
4. Complete steps similar to those in Step 2 to create a custom text form field for the *Policy #* form field that specifies a maximum length of six characters.

5. Customize the text form field right of *Date* by completing the following steps:
   a. Click the text form field shaded box at the right of *Date*.
   b. Click the Properties button.
   c. At the Text Form Field Options dialog box, click the *Type* option box arrow and then click *Current date* at the drop-down list.
   d. Click the *Date format* option box arrow and then click the *MMMM d, yyyy* option at the drop-down list.
   e. Click OK to close the dialog box.
6. Protect the template to allow only filling in the form and use your initials (all uppercase letters) as the password.
7. Save and then close **4-LAApp03Form.dotx**.
8. Use File Explorer to open a document based on **4-LAApp03Form.dotx**.
9. Fill in the form as shown in Figure 4.17 (on page 117). (Type ak in the *State* data field and then press the Tab key; the text changes to uppercase letters.)
10. When the form is completed, save the document with the name **4-LAMurciaApp**.
11. Print and then close **4-LAMurciaApp.docx**.

Text Form Field Options dialog box

- Text form field
- Type: Current date
- Maximum length: Unlimited
- Run macro on
- Entry:
- Default date:
- Date format:
  - M/d/yyyy
  - dddd, MMMM d, yyyy
  - MMMM d, yyyy
  - M/d/yy
  - yyyy-MM-dd
  - d-MMM-yy
- Field settings

5c   5d

> Check Your Work

Chapter Summary

- In Word, a form is a protected document that includes user-defined sections into which a respondent enters information. These user-defined sections are made up of content controls.

- Designing a form includes gathering information that is useful and accurate and meets a specific objective. Determine the purpose of the form and then plan the layout of the form

- Design a form document based on a template and then build the structure of the form. Insert content controls in which information will be entered with the keyboard and save the form as a protected template.

- Save a form as a template at the Save As dialog box by changing the *Save as type* option to *Word Template (*.dotx)*.

- The Controls group on the Developer tab contains buttons for creating a form. Display this tab at the Word Options dialog box by clicking *Customize Ribbon* in the left panel, clicking the Developer tab check box in the list box at the right, and then clicking OK.

- Insert a content control for entering text in a form by clicking the Plain Text Content Control button in the Controls group on the Developer tab.

- Protect a region in a form from being edited by a respondent by defining a group. Define a group by selecting text and content controls, clicking the Group button in the Controls group on the Developer tab, and then clicking *Group* at the drop-down list.

- Turn Design mode on or off by clicking the Design Mode button in the Controls group on the Developer tab. To edit text or content controls within a group, Design mode must be turned on.

- Open a document based on a template saved to the default Custom Office Templates folder by clicking the *Personal* option at the New backstage area and then clicking the thumbnail representing the template. Use File Explorer to open a template saved in a location other than the default folder.

- Fill in a form document based on a template by clicking in the placeholder text for each content control and then typing the required text.

- Include instructional text in a plain text content control by inserting the content control and then typing the text. Or type the text where the content control will be inserted, select it, and then click the Plain Text Content Control button in the Controls group on the Developer tab.

- Consider using a table to provide the framework for a form allowing easy alignment and placement of elements.

- Use options at the Restrict Editing task pane to allow a respondent to enter information in a form but not edit the form. Display this task pane by clicking the Restrict Editing button in the Protect group on the Developer tab.

- In addition to a plain text content control, other types of content controls can be inserted in a form, including picture, date picker, drop-down list, combo box, and check box. Use buttons in the Controls group on the Developer tab to insert content controls.

- Click the Properties button in the Control group on the Developer tab to change the properties of the selected content control. This displays the Content Control Properties dialog box. The content of this dialog box varies depending on what content control is selected.

- Add drop-down list choices by clicking the Add button at the Content Control Properties dialog box, typing the first choice in the Add Choice dialog box, and then clicking OK. Continue in this manner until all the choices are entered.

- Lock a picture in a picture content control by inserting a check mark in the *Contents cannot be edited* check box at the Content Control Properties dialog box.

- Change the data picker content control formatting with options in the *Date Picker Properties* section of the Content Control Properties dialog box.

- To edit a protected form template, turn off protection at the Restrict Editing task pane, make the changes, and then protect the template again before saving it.

- The Legacy Tools button in the Controls group on the Developer tab contains buttons for inserting text, check box, and drop-down form fields in a form. Other Legacy Tools buttons include Insert Frame, Form Field Shading, and Reset Form Fields.

- A text form field is similar to a plain text content control. Insert a text form field by clicking the Legacy Tools button in the Controls group on the Developer tab and then clicking the Text Form Field button at the drop-down list.

- Insert a check box form field in a form in which the respondent is to choose an option by inserting an *X* in the check box.

- Fill in a form with text and check box form fields in the same manner used to fill in a form with content controls.

- Print a filled-in form in the normal manner, print the form without the data, or print only the data. To print only the data, display the Word Options dialog box, click the *Advanced* option in the left panel, scroll down the dialog box, and then insert a check mark in the *Print only the data from a form* check box in the *When printing this document* section.

- Create a drop-down list of choices from which the respondent can select by inserting a drop-down list form field and then typing the choices at the Drop-Down Form Field Options dialog box. Display this dialog box by inserting a drop-down form field and then clicking the Properties button in the Controls group on the Developer tab.
- To fill in a form with a drop-down form field, the respondent clicks the form field down arrow and then clicks an option at the drop-down list. Other ways to display the drop-down list are to press the F4 function key and to press and hold down the Alt key and then press the Down Arrow key.
- Customize check box form field options at the Check Box Form Field Options dialog box. Display this dialog box by inserting a check box form field and then clicking the Properties button in the Controls group on the Developer tab.
- Customize text form field options at the Text Form Field Options dialog box. Display this dialog box by inserting a text form field and then clicking the Properties button in the Controls group on the Developer tab.

Commands Review

FEATURE	RIBBON TAB, GROUP	BUTTON, OPTION
check box content control	Developer, Controls	
check box form field	Developer, Controls	
Check Box Form Field Options dialog box	Developer, Controls	
combo box content control	Developer, Controls	
date picker content control	Developer, Controls	
Drop-Down Form Field Options dialog box	Developer, Controls	
Define group	Developer, Controls	, Group
Design mode	Developer, Controls	
drop-down list content control	Developer, Controls	
drop-down list form field	Developer, Controls	
Legacy Tools button drop-down list	Developer, Controls	
picture content control	Developer, Controls	
plain text content control	Developer, Controls	
Restrict Editing task pane	Developer, Protect	
text form field	Developer, Controls	
Text Form Field Options dialog box	Developer, Controls	

Microsoft® Word Level 3

Unit 2

Customizing Word and Word Elements

CHAPTER

5

Creating a Table of Authorities and Index

Performance Objectives

Upon successful completion of Chapter 5, you will be able to:

1 Insert a table of authorities

2 Update or delete a table of authorities

3 Mark text for an index

4 Insert an index

5 Create a concordance file

6 Use a concordance file to create an index

7 Update or delete an index

In a legal brief or legal document, a *table of authorities* is a list of the cases, statutes, and secondary sources that are cited in the brief, along with the page numbers where each citation appears. In Word, citations can be marked for inclusion in a table of authorities and the table of authorities can be inserted and updated with buttons in the Captions group on the References tab. Many documents also contain an *index* that lists topics in alphabetical order, along with the page numbers on which they appear. Use buttons in the Index group on the References tab to mark text for an index and to insert and update the index. In this chapter, you will learn how to create and manage a table of authorities and an index.

 Data Files

Before beginning chapter work, copy the WL3C5 folder to your storage medium and then make WL3C5 the active folder.

The online course includes additional training and assessment resources.

Activity 1 **Insert a Table of Authorities in a Legal Brief** **1 Part**

You will open a legal brief, mark citations, and then insert a table of authorities.

Tutorial

Inserting and
Updating a Table of
Authorities

💡**Hint** A table of
authorities provides a
list of all the sources
cited in a legal
document.

Creating a Table of Authorities

A table of authorities lists citations that appear in a legal brief or other legal document along with the page numbers on which they appear. Word provides many common categories under which citations can be organized: *Cases*, *Statutes*, *Other Authorities*, *Rules*, *Treatises*, *Regulations*, and *Constitutional Provisions*. Within each category, Word alphabetizes the citations. Figure 5.1 shows an example of a table of authorities.

Creating a table of authorities requires thought and planning. Before marking any text in a legal document for inclusion in such a table, first determine what section headings to use and what listings to include within each section. When marking text for the table, find the first occurrence of each citation, mark it as a full citation with the complete name, and then specify a short citation. Once a full citation has been provided in a legal document, subsequent references within the same document can be referenced using a shorter form of the citation.

To mark a citation for a table of authorities, select the first occurrence of the citation, click the References tab, and then click the Mark Citation button in the Table of Authorities group or press Alt + Shift + I. At the Mark Citation dialog box, shown in Figure 5.2, edit and format the text in the *Selected text* text box as it should appear in the table of authorities. Edit and format the text in the *Short citation* text box so it matches the short citation Word should search for in the document. Click the *Category* option box and then, at the drop-down list, click the category that applies to the citation. Click the Mark button to mark the selected citation or click the Mark All button to mark all the long and short citations in the document that match those displayed in the Mark Citation dialog box.

Mark Citation

⚡**Quick Steps**

Mark Citation for Table of Authorities
1. Select first occurrence of citation.
2. Press Alt + Shift + I.
3. At Mark Citation dialog box, edit and format text.
4. Specify category.
5. Click Mark All button.

Insert Table of Authorities
1. Click References tab.
2. Click Insert Table of Authorities button.
3. Choose format.
4. Click OK.

Figure 5.1 Table of Authorities

TABLE OF AUTHORITIES

Cases

Mansfield v. Rydell, 72 Wn.2d 200, 433 P.2d 723 (2009) 3
State v. Fletcher, 73 Wn.2d 332, 124 P.2d 503 (2019) 5
Yang v. Buchwald, 21 Wn.2d 385, 233 P.2d 609 (2021) 7

Statutes

RCW 8.12.230(2) 4
RCW 6.23.590 7
RCW 5.23.103(3) 10

Figure 5.2 Mark Citation Dialog Box

Edit and format the text in this text box as it should appear in the table of authorities.

Edit and format the text in this text box so it matches the short citation that Word searches for in the document.

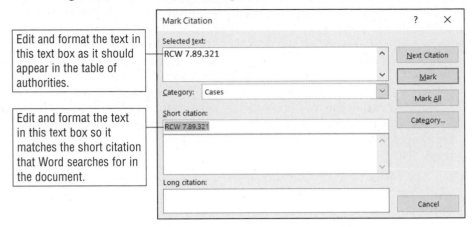

The Mark Citation dialog box remains open to mark other citations. Click the Next Citation button to find the next citation in the document. Word searches the document for the next occurrence of text commonly found in a citation, such as *in re* or *v*. Continue marking citations and, when finished, click the Close button to close the Mark Citation dialog box.

Inserting a Table of Authorities

After marking citations in a document, insert the table of authorities. A table of authorities is inserted in a document in a manner similar to a table of contents or figures. A table of authorities generally appears at the beginning of a document on a separate page. To insert a table of authorities in a document that contains text marked as citations, click the References tab and then click the Insert Table of Authorities button in the Table of Authorities group. This displays the Table of Authorities dialog box, shown in Figure 5.3. At this dialog box, make any necessary changes and then click OK to close the dialog box.

 Insert Table of Authorities

Hint Word inserts codes around marked citations that can be displayed by turning on the display of nonprinting characters.

Figure 5.3 Table of Authorities Dialog Box

Click this option box arrow to choose a leader style.

Click this option box arrow to display a drop-down list of table of authorities formatting styles.

Click this button to display the Style dialog box to select a level style and then modify the formatting of the level style.

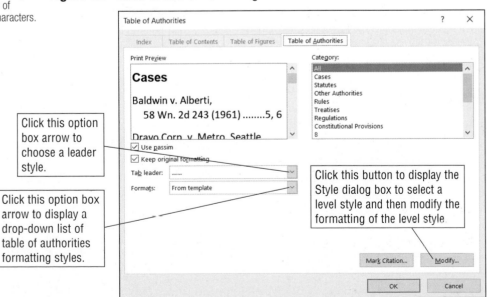

The Table of Authorities dialog box contains options for formatting a table of authorities. The *Use passim* check box contains a check box by default. This means that if a particular case or authority is cited five or more times throughout the document, Word will not repeat the full citation each time, but will insert the word *passim* (meaning "found throughout") for the second and subsequent citations. With the *Keep original formatting* check box active, Word retains the formatting of the citation as it appears in the document. Click the *Tab leader* option to change the leader character. When a table of authorities is inserted, Word includes a heading for each of the seven categories by default. To insert citations for only a specific category, select that category at the *Category* drop-down list.

The formatting of a heading level style for a table of authorities can be modified. To do this, click the Modify button in the Table of Authorities dialog box, click *Table of Authorities* in the *Styles* list box, and then click the Modify button. At the Modify Style dialog box, apply the desired formatting and then click OK.

Updating or Deleting a Table of Authorities

Quick Steps

Update Table of Authorities
1. Click in table of authorities.
2. Click References tab.
3. Click Update Table button in Table of Authorities group or press F9 function key.

 Update Table

If changes are made to a document after a table of authorities has been inserted, update the table. To do this, click anywhere in the table and then click the Update Table button in the Table of Authorities group or press the F9 function key. To edit a citation, edit it in the document and not in the table of authorities. If a citation is edited in the table of authorities, the changes will be lost the next time the table is updated. To delete a table of authorities, select the entire table using the mouse or keyboard and then press the Delete key.

Activity 1 Inserting a Table of Authorities

Part 1 of 1

1. Open **LarsenBrief** and then save it with the name **5-LarsenBrief**.
2. Mark *RCW 7.89.321* as a statute citation by completing the following steps:
   a. Select *RCW 7.89.321*. (This citation is located near the middle of the second page.) *Hint: Use the Find feature to help you locate this citation.*
   b. Click the References tab.
   c. Click the Mark Citation button in the Table of Authorities group.
   d. At the Mark Citation dialog box, click the *Category* option box arrow and then click *Statutes* at the drop-down list.
   e. Click the Mark All button. (This turns on the display of nonprinting characters.)
   f. Click the Close button to close the Mark Citation dialog box.

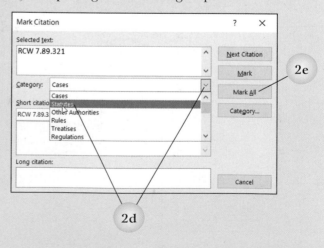

3. Complete steps similar to those in Step 2 to mark all instances of *RCW 7.53.443* as a statute citation. (This citation is located near the middle of the second page.)
4. Complete steps similar to those in Step 2 to mark all instances of *RCW 7.72A.432(2)* as a statute citation. (This citation is located near the bottom of the second page.)
5. Complete steps similar to those in Step 2 to mark all instances of *RCW 7.42A.429(1)* as a statute citation. (This citation is located near the bottom of the second page.)
6. Mark *State v. Connors, 73 W.2d 743, 430 P.2d 199 (1999)* as a case citation by completing the following steps:
   a. Select *State v. Connors, 73 W.2d 743, 430 P.2d 199 (1999)*. (This citation is located near the middle of the second page.) **Hint: Use the Find feature to help you locate this citation.**
   b. Press Alt + Shift + I.
   c. At the Mark Citation dialog box, type State v. Connors in the *Short citation* text box.
   d. Click the *Category* option box arrow and then click *Cases* at the drop-down list.
   e. Click the Mark All button.

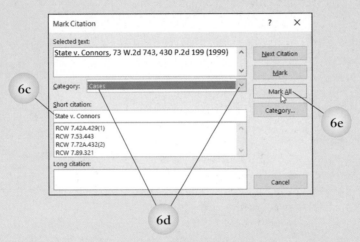

   f. Click the Close button to close the Mark Citation dialog box.
7. Complete steps similar to those in Step 6 to mark all instances of *State v. Bertelli, 63 W.2d 77, 542 P.2d 751 (2004)* as a case citation. Type State v. Bertelli as the short citation. (This citation is located near the middle of the second page.)
8. Complete steps similar to those in Step 6 to mark all instances of *State v. Landers, 103 W.2d 432, 893 P.2d 2 (2002)* as a case citation. Type State v. Landers as the short citation. (This citation is located near the bottom of the second page.)
9. Insert page numbers by completing the following steps:
   a. Position the insertion point at the beginning of the document and then press the Enter key.
   b. Position the insertion point immediately left of the first *S* in *STATEMENT OF CASE* and then insert a section break that begins a new page. (To insert a section break that begins a new page, click the Layout tab, click the Breaks button in the Page Setup group, and then click *Next Page* at the drop-down list.)
   c. With the insertion point positioned below the section break, click the Insert tab.
   d. Click the Page Number button in the Header & Footer group, point to *Bottom of Page*, and then click the *Plain Number 2* option.
   e. Click the Page Number button in the Header & Footer group on the Header & Footer Tools Design tab and then click *Format Page Numbers*.
   f. At the Page Number Format dialog box, click the *Start at* option to start numbering at page 1.
   g. Click OK to close the dialog box.

10. Double-click in the document to make it active and then complete the following steps:
    a. Press Ctrl + Home to move the insertion point to the beginning of the document.
    b. Make sure bold formatting and center alignment are active and then type TABLE OF AUTHORITIES.
    c. Press the Enter key, turn off bold formatting, and change to left alignment.
11. Modify and insert the table of authorities by completing the following steps:
    a. Click the References tab.
    b. Click the Insert Table of Authorities button in the Table of Authorities group.
    c. At the Table of Authorities dialog box, make sure *All* is selected in the *Category* list box and then click the Modify button.
    d. At the Style dialog box, click *Table of Authorities* in the *Styles* list box and then click the Modify button.
    e. At the Modify Style dialog box, click the Italic button.
    f. Click the *Font Color* option box arrow and then click *Dark Blue* (ninth option in the *Standard Colors* section).
    g. Click OK to close the Modify Style dialog box, click OK to close the Style dialog box, and then click OK to close the Table of Authorities dialog box.

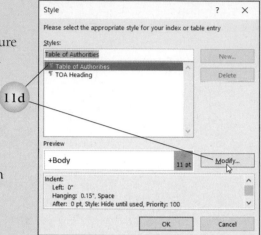

12. Apply different formatting to the table of authorities by completing the following steps:
    a. Click the Undo button on the Quick Access Toolbar to remove the table of authorities. (If this does not remove the table of authorities, select the *Cases* entries and *Statutes* entries and then press the Delete key.)
    b. Click the Insert Table of Authorities button.
    c. At the Table of Authorities dialog box, click the *Formats* option box arrow and then click *Distinctive* at the drop-down list.
    d. Click the *Tab leader* option box arrow and then click the hyphen symbols at the drop-down list (second option from the bottom of the list).
    e. Click OK to close the Table of Authorities dialog box.

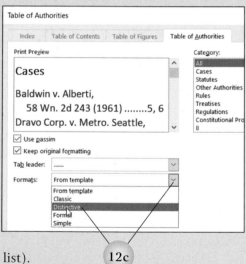

13. With the insertion point positioned in the table of authorities page, number the page with a lowercase roman numeral *i* by completing the following steps:
    a. Click the Insert tab.
    b. Click the Page Number button in the Header & Footer group and then click *Format Page Numbers* at the drop-down list.
    c. At the Page Number Format dialog box, click the *Number format* option box arrow and then click the *i, ii, iii* option.
    d. Click the *Start at* option to start numbering at page i.
    e. Click OK to close the dialog box.

14. Turn off the display of nonprinting characters.
15. Make sure the table of authorities displays the correct page numbers by selecting all the entries in the *Cases* section and the *Statutes* section and then clicking the Update Table button in the Table of Authorities group.
16. Save **5-LarsenBrief** and then print the table of authorities page.
17. Close **5-LarsenBrief**.

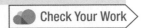

Activity 2 Create an Index for a Desktop Publishing Report   2 Parts

You will open a report containing information on desktop publishing, mark specific text for an index, and then insert the index in the document.

Creating an Index

An index is a list of the topics in a publication that includes the numbers of the pages where those topics are discussed. In Word, the process of creating an index is automated similarly to the process of creating a table of contents. When creating an index, single words and groups of words are marked to be included.

Creating an index takes careful thought and consideration. The author of the book, manuscript, or report must determine the main entries to be included, as well as the subentries to be added under the main entries. An index may include entries such as the main subject of a document, the main subjects of chapters and sections, variations of headings and subheadings, and abbreviations. Figure 5.4 shows an example of a portion of an index.

Figure 5.4 Example of Part of an Index

INDEX

A
Alignment, 12, 16
ASCII, 22, 24, 35
    data processing, 41
    word processing, 39

B
Backmatter, 120
    page numbering, 123
Balance, 67-69
Banners, 145

C
Callouts, 78
Captions, 156
Color, 192-195
      ink for offset printing, 193
      process color, 195

D
Databases, 124-129
    fields, 124
    records, 124
Directional flow, 70-71

Marking Text for an Index

A selected word or group of words can be marked for inclusion in an index. Before marking the text for an index, determine what main entries and subentries are to be included. Selected text is marked as an index entry at the Mark Index Entry dialog box.

To mark text for an index, select the word or group of words, click the References tab, and then click the Mark Entry button in the Index group. Another option is to use the keyboard shortcut Alt + Shift + X. At the Mark Index Entry dialog box, shown in Figure 5.5, the selected word or group of words appears in the *Main entry* text box. Click the Mark button to mark the word or groups of words and then click the Close button. Word automatically turns on the display of nonprinting characters and displays the index field code.

At the Mark Index Entry dialog box, if the selected word or group of words displayed in the *Main entry* text box is to be a main entry, leave it as displayed. However, if the selected text is to be a subentry, type the main entry in the *Main entry* text box, click in the *Subentry* text box, and then type the selected text. For example, suppose a publication includes the terms *Page layout* and *Portrait*. The group of words *Page layout* is to be marked as a main entry for the index and the word *Portrait* is to be marked as a subentry below *Page layout*. Marking these terms for use in an index would involve completing these steps:

1. Select *Page layout*.
2. Click the References tab and then click the Mark Entry button or press Alt + Shift + X.
3. At the Mark Index Entry dialog box, click the Mark button. (This turns on the display of nonprinting characters.)
4. With the Mark Index Entry dialog box still displayed, click in the document to make it active and then select the word *Portrait*.
5. Click the Mark Index Entry dialog box Title bar to make it active.
6. Select *Portrait* in the *Main entry* text box and then type Page layout.
7. Click in the *Subentry* text box and then type Portrait.
8. Click the Mark button.
9. Click the Close button.

Mark Entry

Quick Steps

Mark Text for Index
1. Select text.
2. Click References tab.
3. Click Mark Entry button.
4. Click Mark button.

💡 **Hint** You can also mark text for an index using the keyboard shortcut Alt + Shift + X.

Figure 5.5 Mark Index Entry Dialog Box

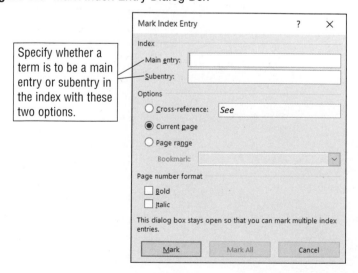

Specify whether a term is to be a main entry or subentry in the index with these two options.

The main entry and subentry do not have to be the same as the selected text. Select text for an index, type specific text to be displayed in the document in the *Main entry* or *Subentry* text box, and then click the Mark button. At the Mark Index Entry dialog box, bold and/or italic formatting can be applied to the page numbers that will appear in the index. In the *Page number format* section, click *Bold* and/or *Italic* to insert a check mark in the check box.

In the *Options* section of the Mark Index Entry dialog box, *Current page* is the default. At this setting, the current page number will be provided in the index for the main entry and/or subentry. Click the *Cross-reference* option to cross reference specific text. To do this, type the text to be used as a cross-reference for the index entry in the *Cross-reference* text box. For example, the word *Serif* can be marked and cross referenced to *Typefaces*.

Click the Mark All button at the Mark Index Entry dialog box to mark all occurrences of the term in the document as index entries. Word marks only those entries for which the uppercase and lowercase letters match the index entries.

Activity 2a Marking Text for an Index   Part 1 of 2

1. Open **DTP** and then save it with the name **5-DTP**.
2. Insert a page number at the bottom center of each page.
3. In the first paragraph, mark *software* for the index as a main entry and mark *word processing* as a subentry below *software* by completing the following steps:
   a. Select *software* (located in the second sentence of the first paragraph).
   b. Click the References tab and then click the Mark Entry button in the Index group.
   c. At the Mark Index Entry dialog box, click the Mark All button. (This turns on the display of nonprinting characters.)

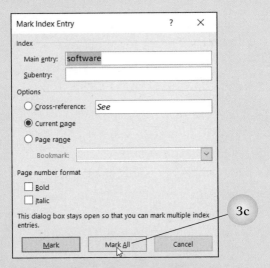

   d. With the Mark Index Entry dialog box still displayed, click in the document to make it active and then select *word processing* (located in the last sentence of the first paragraph). (You may want to drag the dialog box down the screen so more of the document text is visible.)
   e. Click the Title bar of the Mark Index Entry dialog box to make the dialog box active.

f. Select *word processing* in the *Main entry* text box and then type software.

g. Click in the *Subentry* text box and then type word processing.

h. Click the Mark All button.

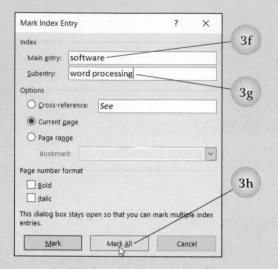

i. With the Mark Index Entry dialog box still displayed, complete steps similar to those in Steps 3d through 3h to select the first occurrence of each of the following words and then mark the word as a main entry or subentry for the index. (Click the Mark All button at the Mark Index Entry dialog box.)

1) In the first paragraph in the *Defining Desktop Publishing* section:

spreadsheets = subentry (main entry = *software*)
database = subentry (main entry = *software*)

2) In the second paragraph in the *Defining Desktop Publishing* section:

publishing = main entry
desktop = subentry (main entry = *publishing*)
printer = main entry
laser = subentry (main entry = *printer*)

3) In the third paragraph in the *Defining Desktop Publishing* section:

design = main entry

4) In the fourth paragraph in the *Defining Desktop Publishing* section:

traditional = subentry (main entry = *publishing*)

5) In the only paragraph in the *Initiating the Process* section:

publication = main entry
planning = subentry (main entry = *publication*)
creating = subentry (main entry = *publication*)
intended audience = subentry (main entry = *publication*)
content = subentry (main entry = *publication*)

6) In the third paragraph in the *Planning the Publication* section:

message = main entry

j. Click Close to close the Mark Index Entry dialog box.

4. Turn off the display of nonprinting characters.

5. Save **5-DTP**.

Inserting an Index

After marking all the text to be included in an index as main entries or subentries, the next step is to insert the index. The index should appear at the end of the document and generally begins on a separate page.

 Insert Index

To insert the index, position the insertion point at the end of the document and then insert a page break. With the insertion point positioned below the page break, type *INDEX*, and then press the Enter key. With the insertion point positioned at the left margin, click the References tab and then click the Insert Index button in the Index group. At the Index dialog box, shown in Figure 5.6, select formatting options and then click OK. Word inserts the index at the location of the insertion point with the formatting selected at the Index dialog box. Word also inserts section breaks above and below the index text.

Quick Steps

Insert Index
1. Click References tab.
2. Click Insert Index button.
3. Select format.
4. Click OK.

At the Index dialog box, specify how the index entries are to appear. The *Print Preview* section shows how the index will display in the document. The *Columns* measurement box has a default setting of *2*. With this setting applied, the index will display in two columns; this number can be increased or decreased.

Insert a check mark in the *Right align page numbers* check box and the *Tab leader* options become active. Use these options to apply leaders before page numbers. The default tab leader is a period. To choose a different leader, click the *Tab leader* option box arrow and then click a character at the drop-down list.

In the *Type* section, the *Indented* option is selected by default. With this setting applied, subentries will appear indented below main entries. Click *Run-in* and subentries will display on the same lines as main entries.

Click the *Formats* option box arrow to display a drop-down list of formatting options. At this list, click a formatting option and the *Print Preview* box displays how the index will appear in the document.

Figure 5.6 Index Dialog Box

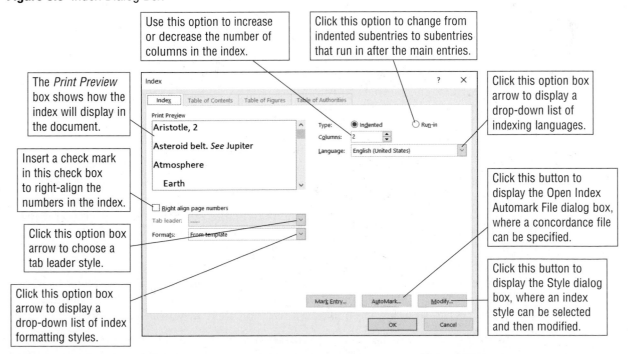

1. With **5-DTP** open, insert the index in the document by completing the following steps:
   a. Press Ctrl + End to position the insertion point at the end of the document.
   b. Insert a page break.
   c. With the insertion point positioned below the page break, type INDEX and then press the Enter key.
   d. Click the References tab.
   e. Click the Insert Index button in the Index group.
   f. At the Index dialog box, click the *Formats* option box arrow and then click *Modern* at the drop-down list.
   g. Click OK to close the dialog box.
   h. Click in the title *INDEX*, apply the Heading 1 style (located in the Styles group on the Home tab), and then press Ctrl + E to center the title.
2. Save **5-DTP** and then print the last page (the index page) of the document.
3. Close **5-DTP**.

1f

Check Your Work

Activity 3 **Mark Index Entries and Insert an Index**   **1 Part**

You will create bookmarks in a document on computers, mark entries for an index, and then insert an index in the document.

Using Other Options for Index Entries

The *Options* section of the Mark Index Entry dialog box provides additional options for marking text for an index. A bookmark can be marked as an index entry or text can be marked that refers readers to another index entry.

Indexing Topics that Appear on a Range of Pages Some topics in an index are found on a range of pages, not just one page. For instance, suppose the topic "information management" is discussed on pages 200–203 of your document. Instead of marking the term "information management" on each page where it appears, insert a bookmark for pages 200–203 and use the bookmarked text as the page range for the index entry. (Review Level 2, Chapter 4, for instructions on how to bookmark text.) To use the bookmarked text as the page range for the index entry, position the insertion point at the end of the bookmarked text, click the References tab, and then click the Mark Entry button in the Index group.

At the Mark Index Entry dialog box, type the index entry for the text and then click the *Page range* option in the *Options* section. Click the *Bookmark* option box arrow and then click the bookmark name at the drop-down list. Click the Mark button to mark the bookmark text and then close the dialog box.

Marking an Entry as a Cross-Reference Text that refers readers to another entry can be marked for inclusion in an index. For example, if the acronym *MIS* is used in a document to refer to the field of management information systems, the entries for *MIS* and *management information systems* can be cross-referenced in the index. To do this, select *MIS*, click the References tab, and then click the Mark Entry button in the Index group. At the Mark Index Entry dialog box, click *Cross-reference* in the *Options* section of the dialog box (to move the insertion point inside the text box), type *management information systems*, and then click the Mark button.

Activity 3 Marking Entries and Inserting an Index   Part 1 of 1

1. Open **Computers** and then save it with the name **5-Computers**.
2. Make the following changes to the document:
   a. Apply the Heading 1 style to the title *COMPUTERS*.
   b. Apply the Heading 2 style to the five headings in the document (*Speed, Accuracy, Versatility, Storage,* and *Communications*).
   c. Apply the Centered style set.
   d. Apply the Orange Red theme colors.
   e. Change the theme fonts to Candara.
3. Insert a bookmark for the *Speed* section of the document by completing the following steps:

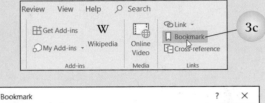

   a. Select text from the beginning of the heading *Speed* through the paragraph of text that follows the heading.
   b. Click the Insert tab.
   c. Click the Bookmark button in the Links group.

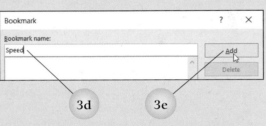

   d. At the Bookmark dialog box, type Speed in the *Bookmark name* text box.
   e. Click the Add button.
4. Complete steps similar to those in Step 3 to insert the following bookmarks:
   a. Select text from the beginning of the *Accuracy* heading through the paragraph of text that follows the heading and then create a bookmark named *Accuracy*.
   b. Select text from the beginning of the *Versatility* heading through the paragraph of text that follows the heading and then create a bookmark named *Versatility*.
   c. Select text from the beginning of the *Storage* heading through the paragraph of text that follows the heading and then create a bookmark named *Storage*.
   d. Select text from the beginning of the *Communications* heading through the two paragraphs of text that follow the heading and then create a bookmark named *Communications*.
5. Mark the *Speed* bookmark as an index entry that spans multiple pages by completing the following steps:

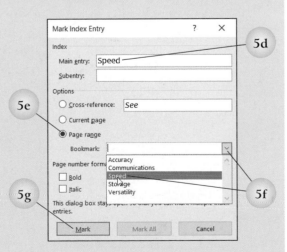

   a. Move the insertion point so it is positioned immediately following the only paragraph of text in the *Speed* section.
   b. Click the References tab.
   c. Click the Mark Entry button in the Index group.
   d. At the Mark Index Entry dialog box, type Speed in the *Main entry* text box.
   e. Click the *Page range* option.
   f. Click the *Bookmark* option box arrow and then click *Speed* at the drop-down list.
   g. Click the Mark button.

6. Complete steps similar to those in Step 5 to mark the following bookmarks as index entries: *Accuracy*, *Versatility*, *Storage*, and *Communications*.
7. With the Mark Index Entry dialog box open, mark the *first* occurrences of the following words (click the Mark All button) as main entries or subentries for the index:
   a. Mark *computers*, located in the first sentence of the first paragraph of text in the document, as a main entry.
   b. Mark *personal computers*, located in the second paragraph of text in the document, as a main entry.
   c. Mark *supercomputers*, located in the *Speed* section of the document, as a main entry.
   d. Mark *GIGO*, located in the *Accuracy* section of the document, as a main entry.
   e. Mark the following text located in the *Versatility* section:

   > *Human Genome Project:* main entry
   > *DNA:* main entry

   f. Mark the following text located in the *Communications* section:

   > *wireless devices:* main entry
   > *notebook computers:* subentry (main entry: *wireless devices*)
   > *cell phones:* subentry (main entry: *wireless devices*)
   > *local area network:* main entry
   > *wide area network:* main entry

   g. Click the Close button to close the Mark Index Entry dialog box.
8. Mark *microcomputers* as a cross-reference by completing the following steps:
   a. Press Ctrl + Home to move the insertion point to the beginning of the document.
   b. Select the word *microcomputers* in the first sentence of the second paragraph of text.
   c. If necessary, click the References tab.
   d. Click the Mark Entry button in the Index group.
   e. At the Mark Index Entry dialog box, click the *Cross-reference* option in the *Options* section and then type personal computers (after the word *See*).
   f. Click the Mark button.
   g. Click the Close button to close the Mark Index Entry dialog box.

9. Complete steps similar to those in Step 8 to mark the following text as cross-references:
   a. Select *LAN* in the second paragraph of text in the *Communications* section and cross-reference it to *local area network*.
   b. Select *WAN* in the second paragraph of text in the *Communications* section and cross-reference it to *wide area network*.
10. Close the Mark Index Entry dialog box and then turn off the display of nonprinting characters.
11. Insert the index in the document by completing the following steps:
    a. Position the insertion point at the end of the document.
    b. Insert a page break.
    c. With the insertion point positioned below the page break, press Ctrl + E, type INDEX, press the Enter key, and then press Ctrl + L.
    d. Click the References tab.
    e. Click the Insert Index button in the Index group.

Activity 4   Create an Index with a Concordance File for a Newsletter   3 Parts

You will create and then save a concordance file. You will then open a report containing information on designing newsletters and use the concordance file to create an index.

 Tutorial

Creating and Using a Concordance File

Quick Steps

Create Concordance File
1. Click Insert tab.
2. Click Table button and drag to create table.
3. In first column, type word or words for index.
4. In second column, type corresponding main entry and subentry.
5. Save document.

Creating and Using a Concordance File

Another method for creating an index is to create a concordance file and then use the information in it to create the index. Using a concordance file can be faster than marking every instance of a term or topic that appears frequently throughout a document.

A concordance file is a Word document that contains a two-column table with no text outside the table. In the first column of the table, enter the word or group of words to be indexed. In the second column, enter the corresponding main entry and subentry, if applicable, that should appear in the index. To create a subentry, type the main entry followed by a colon, a space, and then the subentry. Figure 5.7 shows an example of a concordance file.

In the concordance file shown in Figure 5.7, key terms and topics appearing in the document are listed in the first column (e.g., *World War I*, *Technology*, and *technology*). The second column lists the main entry (and subentry, if there is one), under which each term or topic will be indexed. For example, the terms *motion pictures*, *teletypewriters*, and *television* will all be indexed as subentries under the main entry *Technology*.

Use a concordance file to quickly mark text for an index in a document. To do this, open the document containing the text to be marked for the index, display the Index dialog box with the Index tab selected, and then click the AutoMark button. At the Open Index AutoMark File dialog box, double-click the concordance file name in the list box. Word turns on the display of nonprinting characters, searches the document for text that matches the text in the concordance file, and then marks it accordingly. After marking text for the index, insert the index at the end of the document, as described earlier.

Terms in the left column of the concordance file should be listed exactly as they appear in the document so that Word can find them for the index. For instance, to find all references to World War I, include the abbreviated form, WWI, in the concordance file. Since the search is case sensitive, list terms using a capital letter and a lowercase letter (technology and Technology). This way, if a term is capitalized at the beginning of a sentence, it will not be missed in the search. Also consider listing both singular and plural as well as multiple forms of a verb.

Figure 5.7 Sample Concordance File

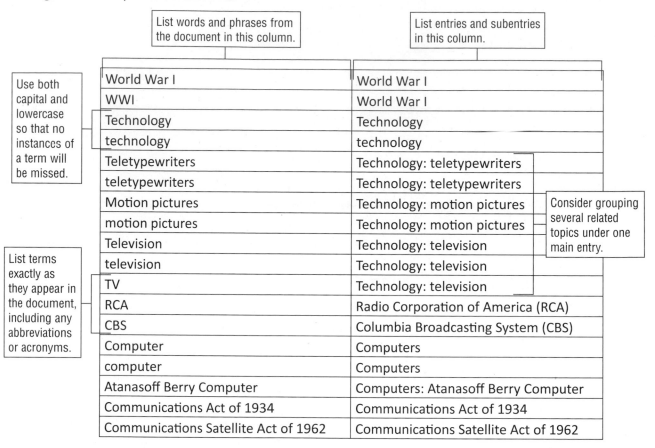

Activity 4a Creating a Concordance File

Part 1 of 3

1. At a blank document, create the text shown in Figure 5.8 as a concordance file by completing
   the following steps:
   a. Click the Insert tab.
   b. Click the Table button in the Tables group.
   c. Drag down and to the right until *2×1 Table* displays at the top of the grid and then click the left mouse button.

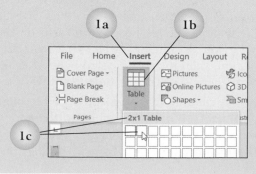

140 Word Level 3

Chapter 5 | Creating a Table of Authorities and Index

d. Type the text in the cells as shown in Figure 5.8, which continues on the next page. As you type the text shown in the figure, press the Tab key to move to the next cell. (Note that Word will automatically capitalize the first word in each cell of the table. To stop capitalizing automatically, hover over the capitalized word until the AutoCorrect options button displays. Click the button arrow and then click *Stop Auto-capitalizing First Letter of Table Cells*.)

2. Save the document and name it **5-CFile**.
3. Print and then close **5-CFile**.

 Check Your Work

Figure 5.8 Activity 4a

newsletters	Newsletters
Newsletters	Newsletters
software	Software
desktop publishing	Software: desktop publishing
word processing	Software: word processing
printers	Printers
laser	Printers: laser
Design	Design
communication	Communication
consistency	Design: consistency
ELEMENTS	Elements
Elements	Elements
elements	Elements
Nameplate	Elements: nameplate
nameplate	Elements: nameplate
Logo	Elements: logo
logo	Elements: logo
Subtitle	Elements: subtitle
subtitle	Elements: subtitle
Folio	Elements: folio
folio	Elements: folio
Headlines	Elements: headlines
headlines	Elements: headlines
Subheads	Elements: subheads
subheads	Elements: subheads
Byline	Elements: byline
byline	Elements: byline
Body Copy	Elements: body copy
body copy	Elements: body copy

continues

Figure 5.8 Activity 4a—*continued*

Graphics Images	Elements: graphics images
Graphics images	Elements: graphics images
audience	Newsletters: audience
Purpose	Newsletters: purpose
purpose	Newsletters: purpose
focal point	Newsletters: focal point

If AutoCorrect capitalization in tables was turned off during this activity, this feature may need to be turned back on. To do this, click the File tab and then click *Options*. At the Word Options dialog box, click *Proofing* in the left panel and then click the AutoCorrect Options button. At the AutoCorrect dialog box with the AutoCorrect tab selected, click the *Capitalize first letter of table cells* check box to insert a check mark. Click OK to close the dialog box and then click OK to close the Word Options dialog box.

Activity 4b Inserting an Index Using a Concordance File Part 2 of 3

1. Open **PlanNwsltr** and then save it with the name **5-PlanNwsltr**.
2. Mark text for the index using the concordance file you created in Activity 4a by completing the following steps:
   a. Click the References tab.
   b. Click the Insert Index button in the Index group.
   c. At the Index dialog box, click the AutoMark button.

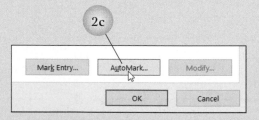

   d. At the Open Index AutoMark File dialog box, double-click **5-CFile** in the Content pane. (This turns on the display of nonprinting characters.)
3. Insert the index in the document by completing the following steps:
   a. Position the insertion point at the end of the document.
   b. Insert a page break.
   c. Type INDEX and then press the Enter key.
   d. Click the Insert Index button in the Index group.
   e. At the Index dialog box, click the *Formats* option box arrow and click *Formal* at the drop-down list, and then change the *Columns* measurement to *2*.
   f. Click OK to close the dialog box.
4. Apply the Heading 1 style to the title *INDEX*.
5. Turn off the display of nonprinting characters.
6. Save **5-PlanNwsltr** and then print only the index page.

> ● Check Your Work

Updating or Deleting an Index

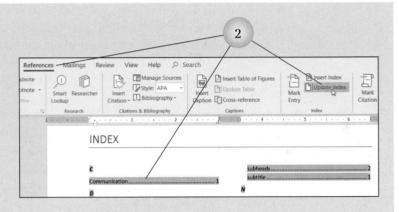

Update Index

Quick Steps

Update Index
1. Click in index.
2. Click Update Index button or press F9.

Delete Index
1. Select entire index.
2. Press Delete key.

If changes are made to a document after the index is inserted, update the index. To do this, click in the index and then click the Update Index button in the Index group or press the F9 function key. To delete an index, select the entire index using the mouse or keyboard and then press the Delete key.

Activity 4c Updating an Index   Part 3 of 3

1. With **5-PlanNwsltr** open, insert a page break at the beginning of the title *PLANNING A NEWSLETTER*.
2. Update the index by clicking in the index, clicking the References tab, and then clicking the Update Index button in the Index group.
3. Save **5-PlanNwsltr** and then print only the index page.
4. Close **5-PlanNwsltr**.

Check Your Work

Chapter Summary

- A table of authorities is a list of the citations in a legal brief or other legal document and the pages on which the citations appear.
- When marking text for a table of authorities, find the first occurrence of a citation, mark it as a full citation with the complete name, and then specify a short citation at the Mark Citation dialog box.
- Display the Mark Citation dialog box by clicking the Mark Citation button in the Table of Authorities group on the References tab or by using the keyboard shortcut Alt + Shift + I.
- Insert a table of authorities in a document with the Insert Table of Authorities button in the Table of Authorities group on the References tab.
- A table of authorities generally appears at the beginning of a document on a separate page.
- Delete a table of authorities by selecting the entire table and then pressing the Delete key.
- An index is a list of the topics in a document and the numbers of the pages where the topics appear.

- Mark the words and groups of words to be included in an index at the Mark Index Entry dialog box. Display this dialog box by clicking the Mark Entry button in the Index group on the References tab or by using the keyboard shortcut Alt + Shift + X.

- After all the words and groups of words have been marked as main entries and subentries, insert the index. Place it on a separate page at the end of the document.

- Insert an index in a document by clicking the Insert Index button on the References tab, selecting formatting at the Index dialog box, and then clicking OK.

- Text can be identified as a bookmark and then the bookmark can be marked as an index entry. This is especially useful when the text for an entry spans a range of pages.

- Mark text as a cross-reference to refer readers to another index entry.

- Key terms and topics that appear frequently in a document can be listed in a concordance file and then used in creating an index. A concordance file is a Word document that contains a two-column table. Using this table to create the index eliminates the need to mark every instance of a term or topic in a document.

- Update an index by clicking in the index, clicking the Update Index button in the Index group or pressing the F9 function key.

- Delete an index by selecting the entire index and then pressing the Delete key.

Commands Review

FEATURE	RIBBON TAB, GROUP	BUTTON	KEYBOARD SHORTCUT
Index dialog box	References, Index		
Mark Citation dialog box	References, Table of Authorities		Alt + Shift + I
Mark Index Entry dialog box	References, Index		Alt + Shift + X
Open Index AutoMark File dialog box	References, Index	, AutoMark button	
Table of Authorities dialog box	References, Table of Authorities		
update index	References, Index		F9
update table of authorities	References, Table of Authorities		F9

Word

Using Outline View

Performance Objectives

Upon successful completion of Chapter 6, you will be able to:

1. Display a document in Outline view
2. Collapse, expand, promote, demote, and assign levels in Outline view
3. Organize a document in Outline view
4. Assign levels at the Paragraph dialog box
5. Navigate in a document with assigned levels
6. Collapse and expand levels in Normal view
7. Move collapsed text
8. Collapse levels by default
9. Create a master document
10. Open and close a master document and its subdocuments
11. Expand, collapse, edit, insert, unlink, split, and merge subdocuments

Use Outline view to display specific titles, headings, and body text in a Word document. In this view, you can quickly see an overview of a document by collapsing parts of it so only specific titles and headings display. With the titles and headings collapsed, you can perform editing functions, including moving and deleting sections of a document.

For some documents, such as books and procedures manuals that contain many parts or sections, consider creating master documents and subdocuments. For example, if several people are working on one large document, each person can prepare a document and then those documents can be combined into a master document. In this chapter, you will learn how to use Outline view and how to create and edit master documents and subdocuments.

 Data Files

Before beginning chapter work, copy the WL3C6 folder to your storage medium and then make WL3C6 the active folder.

 The online course includes additional training and assessment resources.

Tutorial

Managing a
Document in
Outline View

Managing a Document in Outline View

When working in a large or complex document, consider using Outline view
to display heading levels, turn on or off the display of heading text formatting,
show only the first line of body text in the outline, and collapse or expand levels.
Outline view is useful for displaying the structure of the document and for
rearranging document content.

A title or heading formatted with the Heading 1 style displays as a level 1
heading in Outline view. A heading formatted with the Heading 2 style displays
as a level 2 heading, a heading formatted with the Heading 3 style displays as a
level 3 heading, and so on. If titles and headings in a document have not been
formatted with heading styles, heading level formatting can be applied in Outline
view with the *Outline Level* option box.

Displaying a Document in Outline View

 Outline

Q̃uick Steps

**Display Document in
Outline View**
1. Click View tab.
2. Click Outline button.

To switch to Outline view, click the View tab and then click the Outline button in
the Views group or use the keyboard shortcut Alt + Ctrl + O. Figure 6.1 shows
a document in Outline view that has heading styles applied to the titles and
headings. The figure also shows the Outlining tab, which contains options and
buttons for working in Outline view.

Figure 6.1 Document in Outline View

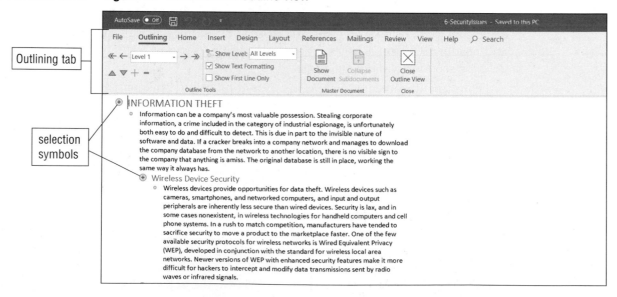

In Figure 6.1 (on page 146), the title *INFORMATION THEFT* is identified as a level 1 heading because the Heading 1 style was applied to it. The heading *Wireless Device Security* is identified as a level 2 heading because the Heading 2 style was applied to it. The paragraphs of text that follow the title and heading are identified as body text. Each heading shown in Figure 6.1 displays with a selection symbol (a gray circle containing a plus [+] symbol) immediately left of it. Click a selection symbol to select the heading and the body text below the heading.

Use buttons and options on the Outlining tab in Outline view to assign levels, promote and demote levels, show only specific levels, turn off the display of text formatting, and show only the first line of body text below a level. The buttons and options on the Outlining tab are described in Table 6.1.

Table 6.1 Outlining Tab Buttons and Options

Button/Option	Name	Action
⇐	Promote to Heading 1	Promotes text to the highest level of the outline
←	Promote	Promotes a heading (and its body text) by one level; promotes body text to the heading level of the preceding heading
Level 1 ▾	Outline Level	Assigns and displays the current level of text
→	Demote	Demotes a heading by one level; demotes body text to the heading level below the preceding heading
⇒	Demote to Body Text	Demotes a heading to body text
△	Move Up	Moves the selected item up within the outline
▽	Move Down	Moves the selected item down within the outline
+	Expand	Expands the first heading level below the currently selected heading
−	Collapse	Collapses body text into a heading and then collapses the lowest heading levels into higher heading levels
Show Level: All Levels ▾	Show Level	Displays all headings through the lowest level chosen
☑ Show Text Formatting	Show Text Formatting	Displays the outline with or without character formatting
☑ Show First Line Only	Show First Line Only	Switches between displaying all body text or only the first line of each paragraph

Collapsing and Expanding Levels

Quick Steps

Collapse and Expand Document
1. Display document in Outline view.
2. Click *Show Level* option box arrow.
3. Click level at drop-down list.

Hint Alt + Shift + _ is the keyboard shortcut to collapse an outline.

Hint Alt + Shift + + is the keyboard shortcut to expand an outline.

One of the major advantages of working in Outline view is being able to see a condensed outline of the document without all the text between the titles, headings, and subheadings. A level in an outline can be collapsed so that any text or subsequent lower levels temporarily do not display. Being able to collapse and expand headings in an outline provides flexibility in managing a document. With the levels collapsed, moving from one part of a document to another is faster. Collapsing levels is also helpful for maintaining consistency between titles and headings.

To collapse a document, click the *Show Level* option box arrow in the Outline Tools group on the Outlining tab and then click the desired level at the drop-down list. For example, if the document contains three levels, click *Level 3* at the drop-down list. Figure 6.2 shows the document used in Activity 1 collapsed so that only level 1 and level 2 headings display. When a title or heading that is followed by text is collapsed, a gray horizontal line displays beneath the title or heading, as shown in the figure. To redisplay all the text in the document, click the *Show Level* option box arrow and then click *All Levels* at the drop-down list.

In addition to the *Show Level* option box, the Collapse and Expand buttons on the Outlining tab can be used to hide and show specific headings and body text, respectively. Use the Collapse button on the Outlining tab to hide the body text below a heading and any lower level headings. Click the Expand button to display the body text below a heading and any lower level headings.

Figure 6.2 Collapsed Document

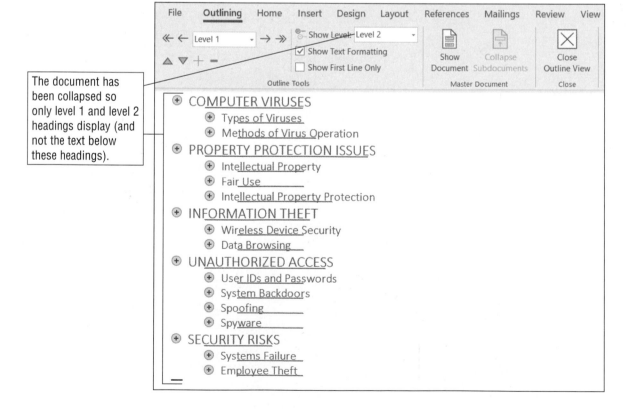

The document has been collapsed so only level 1 and level 2 headings display (and not the text below these headings).

1. Open **Security01** and then save it with the name **6-SecurityIssues**. (Heading 1 and Heading 2 styles have been applied to headings in the document.)

2. Display the document in Outline view by clicking the View tab and then clicking the Outline button in the Views group.

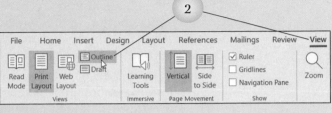

3. With the insertion point positioned at the beginning of the heading *INFORMATION THEFT*, notice that *Level 1* displays in the *Outline Level* option box.

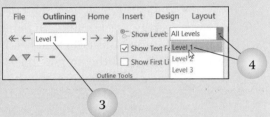

4. Display only level 1 headings by clicking the *Show Level* option box arrow and then clicking *Level 1* at the drop-down list.

5. Display level 1 and level 2 headings by clicking the *Show Level* option box arrow and then clicking *Level 2* at the drop-down list.

6. Turn off the display of heading style formatting by clicking the *Show Text Formatting* check box to remove the check mark.

7. Redisplay the formatting by clicking the *Show Text Formatting* check box to insert a check mark.

8. Show all the heading levels by clicking the *Show Level* option box arrow and then clicking *All Levels* at the drop-down list.

9. Click in the first paragraph of text below the heading *INFORMATION THEFT* and notice that *Body Text* displays in the *Outline Level* option box.

10. If necessary, display all the body text by clicking the *Show First Line Only* check box to remove the check mark.

11. Click in the heading *INFORMATION THEFT* and then collapse the body text below it and below the level 2 headings by clicking the Collapse button in the Outline Tools group.

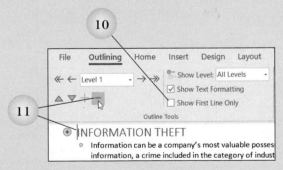

12. Click in the heading *Types of Viruses* and then collapse the body text by clicking the Collapse button.

13. Click the Expand button to expand the body text below the heading *Types of Viruses*.

14. Click in the heading *INFORMATION THEFT* and then click the Expand button.

15. Close Outline view by clicking the Close Outline View button on the Outlining tab.

16. Save **6-SecurityIssues**.

Promoting and Demoting Heading Levels

Quick Steps

Promote Level
1. Display document in Outline view.
2. Click in heading.
3. Click Promote to Heading 1 button or Promote button.

Demote Level
1. Display document in Outline view.
2. Click in heading.
3. Click Demote button.

💡 **Hint** Alt + Shift + Left Arrow is the keyboard shortcut to promote text to the next higher level.

💡 **Hint** Alt + Shift + Right Arrow it the keyboard shortcut to demote text to the next lower level.

Levels are assigned to titles and headings in Outline view based on the heading styles applied. Level 1 is assigned to titles and headings with the Heading 1 style applied, level 2 is assigned to headings with the Heading 2 style applied, and so on. The assigned level can be changed by promoting or demoting it. Click the Promote to Heading 1 button on the Outlining tab to promote text to level 1, and click the Promote button to promote a heading and its body text by one level. Click the Demote button to demote a heading by one level, and click the Demote Body Text button to demote a heading to body text.

Another method for promoting or demoting a heading in Outline view is to drag the selection symbol immediately left of the heading 0.5 inch to the left or right. The selection symbol for a level heading displays as a gray circle containing a plus symbol, and the selection symbol for body text displays as a smaller gray circle. For example, to demote text identified as level 1 to level 2, position the mouse pointer on the heading selection symbol immediately left of the level 1 text until the pointer turns into a four-headed arrow. Click and hold down the left mouse button, drag right with the mouse until a gray vertical line displays down the screen, and then release the mouse button. Complete similar steps to promote a heading. In addition, a heading can be promoted with the keyboard shortcut Alt + Shift + Left Arrow key and demoted with Alt + Shift + Right Arrow key.

Activity 1b Promoting and Demoting Heading Levels   Part 2 of 4

1. With **6-SecurityIssues** open, press Ctrl + Home to move the insertion point to the beginning of the document and then use the *Text from File* option at the Object button drop-down list on the Insert tab to insert the document **Security02**. (This document has heading styles applied to all the headings.)
2. Press Ctrl + Home to move the insertion point to the beginning of the document and then display the document in Outline view by clicking the View tab and then clicking the Outline button.
3. With the insertion point positioned at the beginning of the heading *SECURITY RISKS*, click the Promote to Heading 1 button to promote the heading to level 1.
4. Click in the heading *Systems Failure* and then click the Promote button to promote the heading to level 2.

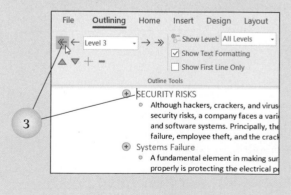

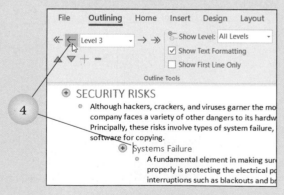

5. Click in the heading *Employee Theft* and then click the Demote button to demote the heading to level 2.
6. Promote the heading *PROPERTY PROTECTION ISSUES* using the mouse by completing the following steps:
   a. Position the mouse pointer on the selection symbol immediately left of the heading *PROPERTY PROTECTION ISSUES* until the mouse pointer turns into a four-headed arrow.
   b. Click and hold down the left mouse button, drag with the mouse to the left until a gray vertical line displays near the left side of the page (as shown in the image below), and then release the mouse button. (When you release the mouse button, check to make sure *Level 1* displays in the *Outline Level* option box.)

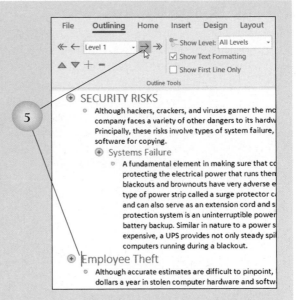

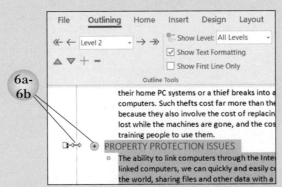

7. Click in the heading *Intellectual Property* and then demote it to level 2 by pressing Alt + Shift + Right Arrow.
8. Click in the heading *Fair Use* and then promote it to level 2 by pressing Alt + Shift + Left Arrow.
9. Click in the heading *Intellectual Property Protection* and then click the Demote button to demote the heading to level 2.
10. Click the Close Outline View button on the Outlining tab.
11. Save **6-SecurityIssues**.

Check Your Work

Assigning Levels

If heading styles have not been applied in a document, assigning heading levels in Outline view will apply them to the heading text. For example, assigning level 1 to a heading will apply the Heading 1 style. Assign a level by clicking the *Outline Level* option box arrow and then clicking a level at the drop-down list. Promoting or demoting also assigns levels.

1. With **6-SecurityIssues** open, press Ctrl + End to move the insertion point to the end of the document and then use the *Text from File* option at the Object button drop-down list to insert the document **Security03**. (This document does not have heading styles applied to the title or headings.)
2. Display the document in Outline view.
3. Click in the heading *UNAUTHORIZED ACCESS* and then click the Promote to Heading 1 button.
4. Click in the heading *User IDs and Passwords*, click the *Outline Level* option box arrow, and then click *Level 2* at the drop-down list.
5. Click in the heading *System Backdoors*, click the *Outline Level* option box arrow, and then click *Level 2* at the drop-down list.
6. Click in the heading *Spoofing* and then click the Promote button.
7. Click in the heading *Spyware*, click the *Outline Level* option box arrow, and then click *Level 2* at the drop-down list.
8. Click the Close Outline View button on the Outlining tab. (Notice that heading styles have been applied to the headings.)
9. Save **6-SecurityIssues**.

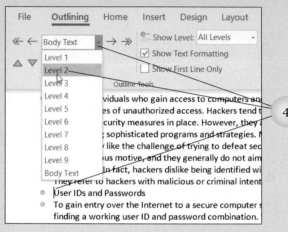

> Check Your Work

Organizing a Document in Outline View

Collapsing and expanding headings within an outline is only one of the useful features of Outline view. Outline view can also be used to organize a document. Move a heading level and any body text or lower heading levels move with the heading. Move a heading level with the Move Up button or Move Down button in the Outline Tools groups on the Outlining tab. For example, to move a level 2 heading below other level 2 headings, collapse the outline, click in the level 2 heading to be moved, and then click the Move Down button in the Outline Tools group until the level 2 heading is in the desired position.

A heading level can also be moved by dragging it with the mouse pointer. To do this, position the mouse pointer on the selection symbol immediately left of the heading until the pointer turns into a four-headed arrow, click and hold down the left mouse button, drag the heading to the new location, and then release the mouse button. As the heading is being moved, a gray horizontal line with an arrow attached displays. Use this horizontal line to help position the heading in the new location.

1. With **6-SecurityIssues** open, press Ctrl + Home to move the insertion point to the beginning of the document.
2. Display the document in Outline view.
3. Click the *Show Level* option box arrow and then click *Level 1* at the drop-down list.
4. Move the heading *COMPUTER VIRUSES* to the beginning of the document by clicking in the heading and then clicking the Move Up button three times.
5. Move the heading *SECURITY RISKS* to the end of the document by clicking in the heading and then clicking the Move Down button three times.
6. Click the *Show Level* option box arrow and then click *Level 2* at the drop-down list.
7. Move the *Spoofing* heading below *Spyware* by completing the following steps:
   a. Position the mouse pointer on the selection symbol immediately left of the heading *Spoofing* until the pointer turns into a four-headed arrow.
   b. Click and hold down the left mouse button, drag down with the mouse until the gray horizontal line with the arrow attached is positioned below *Spyware*, and then release the mouse button.

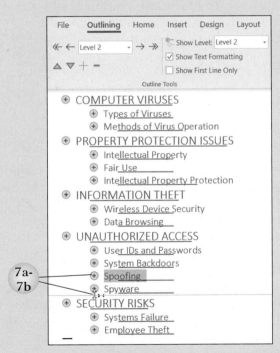

8. Save and then print the document. (This will print the collapsed outline, not the entire document.)
9. Click the *Show Level* option box arrow and then click *All Levels* at the drop-down list.
10. Click the Close Outline View button.
11. If necessary, remove any extra spacing above the *Spoofing* heading.
12. Save and then close **6-SecurityIssues**.

Assigning Levels at the Paragraph Dialog Box

Assigning a level to text in Outline view applies a heading style. In some situations, the headings in a document may contain specific formatting that should not be overwritten by heading styles. Assign a level to text that does not apply a heading style with the *Outline level* option box at the Paragraph dialog box. To use this option, position the insertion point in a heading and then click the Paragraph group dialog box launcher on the Home tab. At the Paragraph dialog box, click the *Outline level* option box arrow and then click a level option at the drop-down list. The drop-down list contains nine level options and a body text option.

Navigating in a Document with Assigned Levels

When levels are assigned to titles and headings with the *Outline level* option box at the Paragraph dialog box, the levels display in the Navigation pane with the Headings tab selected and can be used to navigate to specific locations in the document. Display the Navigation pane by clicking the View tab and then clicking the *Navigation Pane* check box in the Show group to insert a check mark. Click a title or heading in the Navigation pane to move the insertion point to that title or heading in the document.

Collapsing and Expanding Levels in Normal View

A document with levels assigned with the *Outline level* option box at the Paragraph dialog box can be viewed and edited in Outline view in the same manner as a document with heading styles applied. In addition to Outline view, levels can be collapsed or expanded in Normal view. To collapse levels in Normal view, position the mouse pointer on a heading level and a collapse triangle displays immediately left of the heading. The collapse triangle displays as a small solid dark triangle. Click the collapse triangle and any body text and lower level heading and body text below the level will collapse. To expand a collapsed level, position the mouse pointer on the heading and then click the expand triangle immediately left of the heading. The expand triangle displays as a small hollow right-pointing triangle.

Moving Collapsed Text

Collapse text and then move the heading and any body text or lower levels below the heading to a different location in the document. To move collapsed text, select the collapsed heading and then position the mouse pointer in the selected text. Click and hold down the left mouse button and then drag with the mouse. When dragging with the mouse, a thick black vertical line displays indicating where the text will be moved. Drag with the mouse until the vertical line displays in the desired position and then release the mouse button.

1. Open **Resumes** and then save it with the name **6-Resumes**.
2. Assign level 1 to the two titles in the document by completing the following steps:
   a. With the insertion point positioned at the beginning of the title *RESUME STYLES*, click the Paragraph group dialog box launcher.
   b. At the Paragraph dialog box, click the *Outline level* option box arrow and then click *Level 1* at the drop-down list.
   c. Click OK to close the dialog box.
   d. Scroll down the document, click in the title *RESUME WRITING*, and then press the F4 function key to repeat the last command.

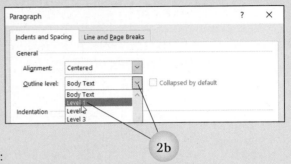

3. Assign level 2 to the five headings in the document by completing the following steps:
   a. Scroll up the document and then click in the heading *The Chronological Resume*.
   b. Click the Paragraph group dialog box launcher.
   c. At the Paragraph dialog box, click the *Outline level* option box arrow and then click *Level 2* at the drop-down list.
   d. Click OK to close the dialog box.
   e. Click in the heading *The Functional Resume* and then press the F4 function key.
   f. Click in the heading *The Hybrid Resume* and then press the F4 function key.
   g. Click in the heading *The Right Mix* and then press the F4 function key.
   h. Click in the heading *Information about the Job* and then press the F4 function key.
4. Press Ctrl + Home to move the insertion point to the beginning of the document.
5. Collapse the body text below the title by positioning the mouse pointer on the title *RESUME STYLES* and then clicking the collapse triangle immediately left of the title.
6. Collapse the body text below the second title by positioning the mouse pointer on the title *RESUME WRITING* and then clicking the collapse triangle immediately left of the title.
7. Move the title *RESUME WRITING* and all the body text and level 2 headings by completing the following steps:
   a. Select the title *RESUME WRITING*.
   b. Position the mouse pointer on the selected title and then click and hold down the left mouse button.
   c. Drag up with the mouse until a thick black vertical line displays left of the title *RESUME STYLES* and then release the mouse button.

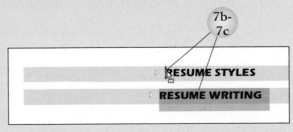

8. Expand the text below the title *RESUME STYLES* by positioning the mouse pointer on the title and then clicking the expand triangle immediately left of it.

9. Expand the text below the title *RESUME WRITING* by positioning the mouse pointer on the title and then clicking the expand triangle immediately left of it.

10. Navigate in the document by completing the following steps:

    a. Click the View tab and then click the *Navigation Pane* check box in the Show group to insert a check mark.

    b. If necessary, click the Headings tab in the Navigation pane.

    c. Click the heading *The Functional Resume* in the Navigation pane to move the insertion point to the beginning of the heading.

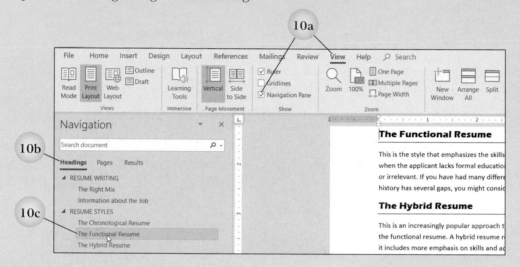

    d. Click the title *RESUME WRITING* in the Navigation pane to move the insertion point to the beginning of the title.

    e. Close the Navigation pane by clicking the *Navigation Pane* check box in the Show group on the View tab to remove the check mark.

11. Save **6-Resumes**.

Check Your Work

Collapsing Levels by Default in Normal View

Quick Steps

Collapse Level by Default

1. Position insertion point in title or heading.
2. Click Paragraph group dialog box launcher.
3. Click *Collapsed by default* check box to insert check mark.
4. Click OK.

If a collapsed document is closed and then opened, it opens with all the levels expanded. The Paragraph dialog box contains the *Collapsed by default* check box, which can be used to specify that a specific title or heading level should open in a collapsed manner. To use this option, position the insertion point in the title or heading, display the Paragraph dialog box, insert a check mark in the *Collapsed by default* check box, and then close the dialog box. Save and then close the document and each time it is opened, it opens with the specific title or heading level collapsed.

1. With **6-Resumes** open, make sure the insertion point is positioned at the beginning of the document.
2. Specify that all the body text and levels below the title *RESUME WRITING* should open collapsed by completing the following steps:
   a. Click the Home tab and then click the Paragraph group dialog box launcher.
   b. At the Paragraph dialog box, click the *Collapsed by default* check box to insert a check mark.
   c. Click OK to close the dialog box. (The body text and levels are collapsed below the title.)

3. Click in the title *RESUME STYLES* and then complete steps similar to those in 2a through 2c to specify that the title should open collapsed.
4. Save and then close **6-Resumes**.
5. Open **6-Resumes** and notice that the body text and levels below both titles are collapsed.
6. Print and then close **6-Resumes**. (Only the two headings will print.)

Activity 3 **Create a Master Document and Subdocuments with a Graphic Software Report**   **2 Parts**

You will create a master document from an existing document containing information on graphic and multimedia software and then create subdocuments with text in the master document. You will expand and collapse the document in Outline view and also edit subdocuments.

Creating a Master Document and Subdocuments

> **Hint** A master document is a container for text and graphics that points to subdocuments.

> **Hint** Word inserts a continuous section break before and after each subdocument.

Creating a Master Document

For a project that contains many parts or sections—such as a reference guide, procedures manual, or book—consider using a master document. A master document contains a number of separate documents referred to as *subdocuments*.

Creating a master document is useful in a situation in which several people are working on one project. Each person prepares a document for part of the project and then all the documents are combined in a master document. Working with a master document also allows for easier editing. Rather than work in one large document, changes are made in several subdocuments and then all the edits are reflected in the master document.

Creating a Master Document from an Existing Document

An existing document can be created as a master document. Text in the master document can be divided into subdocuments, which removes the subdocument text from the original document, creates new documents for the individual subdocuments, and inserts hyperlinks to the subdocuments in the master document. In this way, each subdocument can be assigned to an individual for editing. Any edits made to text in the subdocuments are automatically reflected in the master document.

To create a master document from an existing document, open the document; switch to Outline view; assign heading levels to titles and headings within the document, if necessary; and then click the Show Document button in the Master Document group. Select the headings and text to be divided into subdocuments and then click the Create button in the Master Document group. Text specified as a subdocument is enclosed within a box formed by thin gray lines and a subdocument icon displays in the upper left corner of the border.

Word creates a subdocument for each heading at the top level within the selected text. For example, if the selected text begins with level 1 text, Word creates a new subdocument at each level 1 heading in the selected text. Save the master document in the same manner as a normal document. Word automatically assigns a document name to each subdocument using the first characters in the subdocument heading.

Opening and Closing a Master Document and Its Subdocuments

Open a master document at the Open dialog box in the same manner as a normal document. Subdocument text in a master document displays collapsed in the master document, as shown in Figure 6.3. This figure displays the master document that you will create in Activity 3a. Notice that Word automatically converts subdocument names into hyperlinks. To open a subdocument, press and hold down the Ctrl key, click the subdocument hyperlink, and then release the Ctrl key.

Close a subdocument in the normal manner and if changes were made, a confirmation message will display. Closing a subdocument redisplays the master document and the subdocument hyperlink displays in a different color, identifying that the hyperlink has been used.

Figure 6.3 Master Document

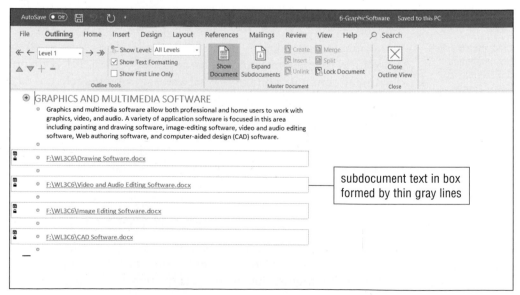

Expanding and Collapsing Subdocuments

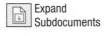
Expand Subdocuments

Collapse Subdocuments

Open a master document and its subdocuments automatically collapse. To expand the subdocuments, click the Expand Subdocuments button in the Master Document group on the Outlining tab. This expands the subdocuments and also changes the Expand Subdocuments button to the Collapse Subdocuments button.

Activity 3a Creating a Master Document and Collapsing Subdocuments   Part 1 of 2

1. Open **GraphicSoftware** and then save it with the name **6-GraphicSoftware**. (This document contains a title with the Heading 1 style applied and four headings with the Heading 2 style applied.)
2. Display the document in Outline view.
3. Create a subdocument for each level 2 heading and body text by completing the following steps:

   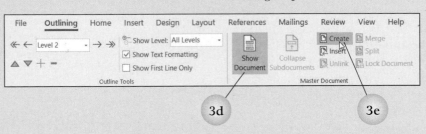

   a. Using the mouse, click the selection symbol immediately left of the heading *Drawing Software*. (This selects the heading and the body text below the heading.)
   b. If necessary, scroll down the document to the heading *CAD Software*.
   c. Press and hold down the Shift key, click the selection symbol immediately left of the heading *CAD Software*, and then release the Shift key.
   d. With all the level 2 headings and body text selected, click the Show Document button in the Master Document group on the Outlining tab.
   e. Click the Create button in the Master Document group.

4. Save the document by clicking the Save button on the Quick Access Toolbar.
5. Click the Collapse Subdocuments button. (This collapses the subdocuments and also changes the name of the button to *Expand Subdocuments*.)
6. Click the Close Outline View button.
7. Print the document. At the question asking if you want to open the subdocuments, click No. (The document will print collapsed, as displayed on the screen.)
8. Save and then close **6-GraphicSoftware**.

Check Your Work

Editing a Subdocument

The subdocuments created within a master document do not reside in the master document. Each subdocument is saved as an individual document and the master document contains a hyperlink to each one. Edit a subdocument by opening the subdocument, making the changes, and then saving and closing it. The changes made to the subdocument are reflected in the subdocument text in the master document. Another method for editing a subdocument is to open the master document, click the subdocument hyperlink, make the changes, and then save and close the subdocument.

Hint Edits made to a subdocument are reflected in the master document.

When subdocuments are created in a master document, the subdocument files are saved in the same location as the master document. The hyperlink to each subdocument in the master document reflects the location of the subdocument. For this reason, moving a subdocument to a different location will remove the link between the subdocument and the master document. When working with a master document, make sure the location of the master document and subdocuments remains consistent.

Activity 3b Editing Subdocuments

Part 2 of 2

1. Open **Drawing Software** from the WL3C6 folder on your storage medium. (This was one of the subdocuments created by Word in Activity 3a. Word used the names of the headings as the names of the subdocuments.)
2. Select and then delete the last sentence in the paragraph of text (the sentence that begins *Programs typically include a variety*).
3. Save and then close **Drawing Software**.
4. Open **6-GraphicSoftware**.
5. Open the subdocument **Drawing Software** by pressing and holding down the Ctrl key and then clicking the F:\WL3C6\Drawing Software.docx hyperlink. (The drive and/or path for the subdocument may vary.)
6. Notice that the last sentence in the paragraph of text has been deleted and then close **Drawing Software**.
7. Press and hold down the Ctrl key, click the F:\WL3C6\CAD Software.docx hyperlink, and then release the Ctrl key.
8. In the subdocument, position the insertion point immediately left of the first occurrence of *software* in the first sentence, type (CAD), and then press the spacebar.
9. Save and then close **CAD Software**.
10. Display the master document in Outline view.
11. Click the Expand Subdocuments button.
12. Scroll through the text and notice that the edits made to two of the subdocuments are reflected in the subdocuments.
13. Close Outline view.
14. Save, print, and then close **6-GraphicSoftware**.

GRAPHICS AND MULTIMEDIA SOFTWARE

Graphics and multimedia software allow both professional a and audio. A variety of application software is focused in this software, image-editing software, video and audio editing so computer-aide

file:///f:\wl3c6\drawing software.docx
Ctrl+Click to follow link

F:\WL3C6\Drawing Software.docx

F:\WL3C6\Video and Audio Editing Software.docx

5

8

CAD Software

Computer-aided design (CAD) software is a sophistic enable professionals to create architectural, enginee use the software to design buildings or bridges, and

Check Your Work

<table>
<tr><td>

Activity 4 **Create a Master Document and Subdocuments with a Newsletter Report**

</td><td>

2 Parts

</td></tr>
</table>

You will create a master document with an existing document containing information on creating newsletters and then create subdocuments with text in the master document. You will also insert a subdocument into the master document and then unlink, delete, and split the subdocument.

Quick Steps

Insert Subdocument
1. Open master document.
2. Change to Outline view.
3. Position insertion point above or below existing subdocument heading.
4. Click Insert button in Master Document group.
5. Navigate to folder containing document.
6. Double-click document.

 Insert

Inserting a Subdocument

In the previous activity, headings and body text in an existing document were divided into subdocuments. Another method for working with a master document is to insert documents in it as subdocuments. To insert a document as a subdocument, position the insertion point above or below the existing subdocument headings where the subdocument is to be inserted. (A subdocument cannot be inserted within body text.) Click the Insert button in the Master Document group on the Outlining tab. At the Insert Subdocument dialog box, navigate to the folder containing the document to be inserted and then double-click the document.

💡 **Hint** Use the insert button to assemble existing documents into a master document.

Activity 4a Creating a Master Document and Inserting Subdocuments

Part 1 of 2

1. Open **Newsletters** and then save it with the name **6-Newsletters**.
2. Display the document in Outline view.
3. Create a subdocument for each level 2 heading and body text by completing the following steps:
   a. Using the mouse, click the selection symbol immediately left of the heading *MODULE 1: DEFINING NEWSLETTER ELEMENTS.* (This selects the heading, the level 3 headings, and the body text below the headings.)
   b. Scroll down the document to the heading *MODULE 2: PLANNING A NEWSLETTER.*
   c. Press and hold down the Shift key and then click the selection symbol immediately left of the heading *MODULE 2: PLANNING A NEWSLETTER.*
   d. Click the Show Document button in the Master Document group on the Outlining tab.
   e. Click the Create button in the Master Document group.
4. Insert subdocuments in the master document by completing the following steps:
   a. Press Ctrl + End to move the insertion point to the end of the document.
   b. Click the Insert button in the Master Document group on the Outlining tab.

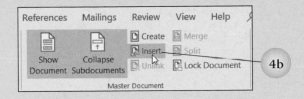

c. At the Insert Subdocument dialog box, navigate to your WL3C6 folder and then double-click *MODULE 3*.

d. Click the Insert button in the Master Document group.

e. At the Insert Subdocument dialog box, double-click *MODULE 4*.

5. Click the Save button on the Quick Access Toolbar.

6. Click the Collapse Subdocuments button in the Master Document group.

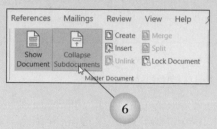

7. Close the Outline view.

8. Print the collapsed document. (At the question asking if you want to open the subdocuments, click No.)

9. Save and then close **6-Newsletters**.

Check Your Work

Unlinking a Subdocument

Quick Steps
Unlink Subdocument
1. Display master document in Outline view.
2. Expand subdocuments.
3. Click in subdocument to be unlinked.
4. Click Unlink button in Master Document group.

Split Subdocument
1. Display master document in Outline view.
2. Expand subdocuments.
3. Select specific text.
4. Click Split button in Master Document group.

Merge Subdocuments
1. Display master document in Outline view.
2. Expand subdocuments.
3. Select adjacent subdocuments.
4. Click Merge button in Master Document group.

Each subdocument is linked to the master document. A subdocument can be unlinked from the master document, which deletes the link and inserts the subdocument contents in the master document. To unlink a subdocument from the master document, expand the subdocuments, click in the subdocument to be unlinked, and then click the Unlink button in the Master Document group.

Splitting a Subdocument

A subdocument can be split into smaller subdocuments. To split a subdocument, expand the subdocuments, select the specific text to be split from the subdocument, and then click the Split button in the Master Document group on the Outlining tab. Word assigns a document name based on the first characters in the subdocument heading.

Merging Subdocuments

Several subdocuments in a master document can be merged into one subdocument. To merge subdocuments, expand the subdocuments and then click the subdocument icon of the first subdocument to be merged. Press and hold down the Shift key, click the subdocument icon of the last subdocument, and then release the Shift key. (The subdocuments must be adjacent.) With the subdocuments selected, click the Merge button in the Master Document group. Word saves the combined subdocuments with the name of the first subdocument.

 Unlink

 Split

Hint When subdocuments are merged, Word save the merged subdocument with the name of the first subdocument.

1. Open **6-Newsletters** and then display the document in Outline view.
2. Insert a subdocument by completing the following steps:
   a. Click the Show Document button.
   b. Click the Expand Subdocuments button.
   c. Position the insertion point on the blank line below the paragraph of text below the title *DESIGNING NEWSLETTERS*.
   d. Click the Insert button in the Master Document group on the Outlining tab.

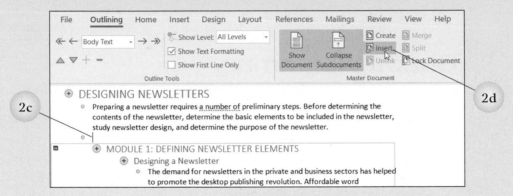

   e. At the Insert Subdocument dialog box, navigate to your WL3C6 folder and then double-click *NwsltrConsistency*.
3. Unlink the new subdocument so it becomes part of the master document by completing the following steps:
   a. Click in the paragraph of text below the heading *MAINTAINING CONSISTENCY*.
   b. Click the Unlink button in the Master Document group.
   c. Select and then delete the heading *MAINTAINING CONSISTENCY*. (The paragraphs should be separated only by a blank line.)
4. Delete the Module 2 subdocument by completing the following steps:
   a. Click the selection symbol immediately left of the heading *MODULE 2: PLANNING A NEWSLETTER*.
   b. Press the Delete key.
5. Split the Module 1 subdocument by completing the following steps:
   a. In the subdocument, edit the heading *Defining Basic Newsletter Elements* so that it displays as *MODULE 2: DEFINING BASIC ELEMENTS*.
   b. Click the heading *MODULE 2: DEFINING BASIC ELEMENTS* and then click the Promote button to change the heading from level 3 to level 2.

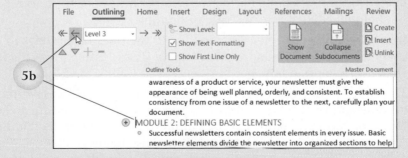

   c. Position the mouse pointer on the selection symbol immediately left of the heading *MODULE 2: DEFINING BASIC ELEMENTS* until the pointer turns into a four-headed arrow and then click the left mouse button.

d. With the text selected, click the Split button in the Master Document group.

e. Click the Save button on the Quick Access Toolbar.

f. Click the Collapse Subdocuments button in the Master Document group.

6. Click the Show Document button and delete the next page section break between the two paragraphs in the *DESIGNING NEWSLETTERS* section.

7. Close the Outline view.

8. Print the collapsed document. (At the message asking if you want to open the subdocuments, click No.)

9. Save and then close **6-Newsletters**.

 Check Your Work

Chapter Summary

- In a large or complex document, consider using Outline view to display the structure of the document and to rearrange document content. Display a document in Outline view by clicking the View tab and then clicking the Outline button in the Views group.

- A title or heading formatted with a heading style applied displays as that level in Outline view. For example, a title or heading formatted with the Heading 1 style displays as a level 1 heading.

- Use buttons and options on the Outlining tab in Outline view to display heading levels, turn on and off the display of heading text formatting, show only the first line of body text below a head level, collapse and expand levels, promote and demote heading levels, and assign levels.

- One of the major advantages of working in Outline view is being able to see a condensed outline of a document without all the text between titles, headings, and subheadings. Another advantage of working in Outline view is being able to maintain consistency between titles and headings.

- To collapse an entire document, use the *Show Level* option box to specify a level. For example, if a document contains two levels, click the *Level 2* option. To redisplay all the text in the document, click the *All Levels* option at the drop-down list.

- To collapse all the body text beneath a particular heading, click the Collapse button in the Outline Tools group on the Outlining tab. Click the Expand button to display all the body text.

- Promote or demote a title or heading in Outline view using the Promote to Level 1 button, Promote button, or Demote button or by dragging the selection symbol immediately left of a title or heading.

- If heading styles have not been applied to the titles or headings in a document, assigning levels in Outline view will apply styles. Assign a specific level at the *Outline Level* option box.

- The contents of a document can be rearranged in Outline view. To move a heading and the body text below it, select the heading and then click the Move Down or Move Up button in the Outline Tools group on the Outlining tab. A heading and the body text below it can also be moved by using the mouse pointer to drag the selection symbol immediately left of the heading to the desired position.

- Assign a level to text that does not apply a heading style using the *Outline level* option box at the Paragraph dialog box.

- When levels are assigned to titles and headings using the *Outline level* option at the Paragraph dialog box, the levels display in the Navigation pane with the Headings tab selected and can be used to navigate to specific locations in the document.

- A level can be collapsed in Normal view by clicking the collapse triangle immediately left of the level text. The collapse triangle displays as a small solid dark triangle and appears left of level text when the mouse pointer is positioned over the text.

- Expand a collapsed level in Normal view by clicking the expand triangle immediately left of the level text. The expand triangle displays as a small hollow right-pointing triangle.

- Collapsed text can be moved by selecting the collapsed heading and then dragging the heading with the mouse until a thick black vertical line displays in the new position.

- Specify that a level remain collapsed when a document is opened by inserting a check mark in the *Collapsed by default* check box at the Paragraph dialog box.

- A master document contains a number of separate documents called *subdocuments*. Create a master document or format an existing document as a master document in Outline view.

- Clicking the Show Document button and then clicking the Create button (both located in the Master Document group on the Outlining tab) causes Word to create a subdocument for each heading at the top level within the selected text.

- Save a master document in the same manner as a normal document. Word automatically assigns a document name to each subdocument using the first characters in the subdocument heading.

- Open and close a master document in the same manner as a normal document. To open a subdocument, open the master document, press and hold down the Ctrl key, click the subdocument hyperlink, and then release the Ctrl key.

- Use buttons in the Master Document group on the Outlining tab to create, insert, unlink, expand, collapse, merge, and split subdocuments.

Commands Review

FEATURE	RIBBON TAB, GROUP	BUTTON	KEYBOARD SHORTCUT
create master document	Outlining, Master Document		
collapse outline	Outlining, Outline Tools		Alt + Shift + _
collapse subdocuments	Outlining, Master Document		
demote to body text	Outlining, Outline Tools		
demote to next lower level	Outlining, Outline Tools		Alt + Shift + Right Arrow
expand outline	Outlining, Outline Tools		Alt + Shift + +
expand subdocuments	Outlining, Master Document		
insert subdocument	Outlining, Master Document		
move down outline level	Outlining, Outline Tools		Alt + Shift + Down Arrow
move up outline level	Outlining, Outline Tools		Alt + Shift + Up Arrow
Outline view	View, Views		Alt + Ctrl + O
Paragraph dialog box	Home, Paragraph		
promote to heading 1	Outlining, Outline Tools		
promote to next higher level	Outlining, Outline Tools		Alt + Shift + Left Arrow
show document	Outlining, Master Document		
split subdocument	Outlining, Master Document		
unlink subdocument	Outlining, Master Document		

Word

Microsoft®

Integrating and Sharing Documents and Data

Performance Objectives

Upon successful completion of Chapter 7, you will be able to:

1 Compare documents

2 Combine documents and show source documents

3 Embed and link objects between Excel and Word

4 Link objects at the Insert File dialog box

5 Use Paste Special options to specify formatting for pasted objects

6 Improve the accessibility of documents by using alternative text, header rows, and built-in styles

7 Share documents in the cloud, by email or fax, or as an online presentation

In a workgroup environment, multiple people may work on a document and make changes or revisions using tracked changes. The Compare feature can be used to compare two documents and display the differences between them as tracked changes. In addition, the Combine feature can be used to combine changed versions of a document with the original document.

Microsoft Office allows for an object from one application to be seamlessly integrated into another application. An object can be embedded in both the source and the destination application or an object can be linked. In this chapter, you will learn how to compare, combine, embed, and link documents as well as how to share documents. You will also learn how to improve the accessibility of documents.

 Data Files

Before beginning chapter work, copy the WL3C7 folder to your storage medium and then make WL3C7 the active folder.

The online course includes additional training and assessment resources.

You will compare the contents of a lease agreement and an edited version of the lease agreement. You will then customize compare options and compare the documents again.

 Tutorial

Comparing
Documents

 Compare

Quick Steps

Compare Documents
1. Click Review tab.
2. Click Compare button.
3. Click *Compare*.
4. Click Browse for Original button.
5. Double-click document.
6. Click Browse for Revised button.
7. Double-click document.
8. Click OK.

💡**Hint** Word does not change the documents being compared.

Comparing Documents

Word provides a Compare feature that will compare two documents and display the differences between them as tracked changes in the original document, the revised document, or in a new document. To use this feature, click the Review tab, click the Compare button in the Compare group, and then click *Compare* at the drop-down list. This displays the Compare Documents dialog box, shown in Figure 7.1. At this dialog box, click the Browse for Original button. At the Open dialog box, navigate to the folder that contains the original document and then double-click the document. Click the Browse for Revised button in the Compare Documents dialog box, navigate to the folder containing the revised document, and then double-click the document. Alternately, click the arrow in the *Original document* or *Revised document* option box to choose from recently viewed documents.

Viewing Compared Documents

Click OK at the Compare Documents dialog box and the compared document displays with the changes tracked. Other windows may also display, depending on the option selected at the Show Source Documents side menu. Display this side menu by clicking the Compare button and then pointing to *Show Source Documents*. Only the compared document may display or the compared document plus the Reviewing pane, original document, and/or revised document may display.

Figure 7.1 Compare Documents Dialog Box

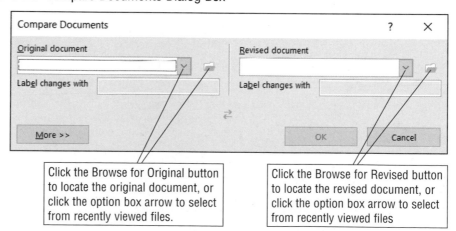

1. Close any open documents.
2. Click the Review tab.
3. Click the Compare button in the Compare group and then click *Compare* at the drop-down list.
4. At the Compare Documents dialog box, click the Browse for Original button.

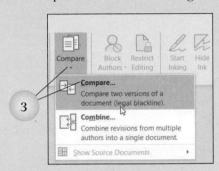 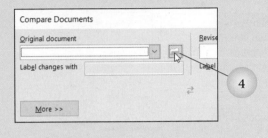

5. At the Open dialog box, navigate to your WL3C7 folder and then double-click *ComAgrmnt*.
6. At the Compare Documents dialog box, click the Browse for Revised button.

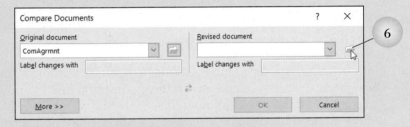

7. At the Open dialog box, double-click *EditedComAgrmnt*.
8. Click OK.
9. If the original and revised documents display along with the compared document, click the Compare button, point to *Show Source Documents* at the drop-down list, and then click *Hide Source Documents* at the side menu.
10. With the compared document active, print the document with the markup showing. (To make sure the markup prints with the document, click the first gallery in the *Settings* category at the Print backstage area and make sure a check mark appears before the *Print Markup* option.)
11. Close the Reviewing pane (displays with *Revisions* at the top of the task pane), if necessary.
12. Click the File tab and then click the *Close* option. At the message asking if you want to save changes, click the Don't Save button.

Customizing Compare Options

By default, Word compares the original document with the revised document and displays the differences as tracked changes. Change where track changes display and view other options by expanding the Compare Documents dialog box. Click the More button and additional options display, as shown in Figure 7.2.

Figure 7.2 Expanded Compare Documents Dialog Box

Use options in this section to control the level of comparison made between the original and revised documents.

Use options in this section to specify whether to show changes at the character or word level and in which document to show the changes.

Use options in this section to specify whether tracked changes should display in the original document, the revised document, or a new document.

Control the level of comparison that Word makes between the original and revised documents with options in the *Comparison settings* section of the dialog box. The *Show changes at* option in the *Show changes* section of the dialog box has two options—*Character level* and *Word level*. Choose the *Character level* option to show changes by character. Choose the *Word level* option and Word will show changes to whole words rather than individual characters within words. For example, if the letters *ed* are deleted from the end of a word, Word will display the entire word as a change rather than just the *ed*.

Use options in the *Show changes in* section of the dialog box to specify whether changes display in the original document, the revised document, or in a new document. Changes made to options in the expanded Compare Documents dialog box will be the defaults the next time the dialog box is opened.

Activity 1b Customizing Compare Options and Comparing Documents

Part 2 of 2

1. Close any open documents.
2. Click the Review tab.
3. Click the Compare button and then click *Compare* at the drop-down list.
4. At the Compare Documents dialog box, click the Browse for Original button.
5. At the Open dialog box, navigate to your WL3C7 folder and then double-click *ComAgrmnt*.
6. At the Compare Documents dialog box, click the Browse for Revised button.
7. At the Open dialog box, double-click *EditedComAgrmnt*.
8. At the Compare Documents dialog box, click the More button. (Skip this step if the dialog box displays expanded and a Less button displays above the *Comparison settings* section.)

9. Click the *Moves* check box and then click the *Formatting* check box to remove the check marks.
10. If necessary, click the *Word level* option in the *Show changes* section and click the *New document* option in the *Show changes in* section.
11. Click OK.
12. Print the document with markup showing.
13. Close the document without saving it.
14. Compare two documents and then return the compare options to the default settings by completing the following steps:

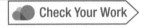

a. Close any open documents.
b. Click the Review tab.
c. Click the Compare button and then click *Compare* at the drop-down list.
d. At the Compare Documents dialog box, click the Browse for Original button.
e. At the Open dialog box, double-click **ComAgrmnt**.
f. At the Compare Documents dialog box, click the Browse for Revised button.
g. At the Open dialog box, double-click **EditedComAgrmnt**.
h. At the Compare Documents dialog box, click the *Moves* check box to insert a check mark and then click the *Formatting* check box to insert a check mark.
i. Click the Less button.
j. Click OK.
15. At the new document, accept all the changes.
16. Save the document and name it **7-ComAgrmnt**.
17. Print and then close the document.

> Check Your Work

Activity 2 Combine Lease Agreement Documents   2 Parts

You will open a lease agreement document and then combine edited versions of the agreement with the original document.

Combining
Documents

Quick Steps

Combine Documents
1. Click Review tab.
2. Click Compare button.
3. Click *Combine*.
4. Click Browse for Original button.
5. Double-click document.
6. Click Browse for Revised button.
7. Double-click document.
8. Click OK.

Combining Documents

If several people have made changes to a document, their changed versions can be combined with the original document. Each person's changed document can be combined with the original until all the changes have been incorporated into the original document. To do this, open the Combine Documents dialog box, shown in Figure 7.3, by clicking the Compare button on the Review tab and then clicking *Combine* at the drop-down list. The Combine Documents dialog box contains many of the same options as the Compare Documents dialog box.

At the Combine Documents dialog box, click the Browse for Original button, navigate to the specific folder, and then double-click the original document. Click the Browse for Revised button, navigate to the specific folder, and then double-click one of the documents containing revisions. Click the *Original document* option box arrow or the *Revised document* option box arrow and a drop-down list displays with the most recently selected documents.

Figure 7.3 Combine Documents Dialog Box

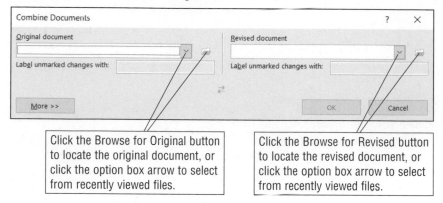

Click the Browse for Original button to locate the original document, or click the option box arrow to select from recently viewed files.

Click the Browse for Revised button to locate the revised document, or click the option box arrow to select from recently viewed files.

Combining and Merging Documents

Control how changes are combined with options at the expanded Combine Documents dialog box. This dialog box contains many of the same options as the expanded Compare Documents dialog box. Use options in the *Show changes at* section to specify if changes should display at the character or word level. Use options in the *Show changes in* section to specify if changes should show in the original document, the revised document, or a new document.

Activity 2a Combining Documents   Part 1 of 2

1. Close all the open documents.
2. Click the Review tab.
3. Click the Compare button and then click *Combine* at the drop-down list.
4. At the Combine Documents dialog box, click the More button to expand the dialog box.
5. At the expanded Combine Documents dialog box, click the *Original document* option in the *Show changes in* section.

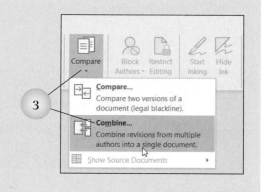

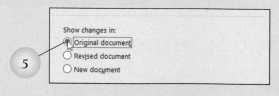

6. Click the Browse for Original button.
7. At the Open dialog box, navigate to your WL3C7 folder and then double-click *OriginalLease*.
8. At the Combine Documents dialog box, click the Browse for Revised button.
9. At the Open dialog box, double-click *LeaseReviewer1*.
10. Click OK.
11. Save the document and name it **7-CombinedLease**.

 **Check Your Work**

Showing Source Documents

Use options in the Show Source Documents side menu to specify which source documents to display. Display this side menu by clicking the Compare button and then pointing to *Show Source Documents*. Four options display at the side menu: *Hide Source Documents*, *Show Original*, *Show Revised*, and *Show Both*. With the *Hide Source Documents* option selected, the original and revised documents do not display on the screen; only the combined document displays. With the *Show Original* option selected, the original document displays in a side panel at the right side of the document. Choose the *Show Revised* option and the revised document displays in the panel at the right. Choose the *Show Both* option and the original document displays in a panel at the right side of the screen and the revised document displays in a panel below the original document panel. Synchronous scrolling is selected by default, so scrolling in the combined document causes simultaneous scrolling in the other document(s).

Activity 2b Combining and Showing Source Documents

Part 2 of 2

1. With **7-CombinedLease** open, click the Compare button, point to *Show Source Documents*, and then click *Hide Source Documents* at the side menu if necessary. (This displays the original document with the combined document changes shown as tracked changes.)
2. Click the Compare button, point to *Show Source Documents*, and then click *Show Original* at the side menu. (This displays the original document at the right, the original document with tracked changes in the middle, and the Reviewing pane at the left side of the screen.)
3. Click the Compare button, point to *Show Source Documents*, and then click *Show Revised*.
4. Click the Compare button, point to *Show Source Documents*, and then click *Show Both*. Scroll in the combined document and notice that the original document and revised documents scroll simultaneously.
5. Click the Compare button, point to *Show Source Documents*, and then click *Hide Source Documents*.
6. Close the Reviewing pane.
7. Click the Compare button and then click *Combine* at the drop-down list.
8. At the Combine Documents dialog box, click the Browse for Original button.
9. At the Open dialog box, double-click *7-CombinedLease*.
10. At the Combine Documents dialog box, click the Browse for Revised button.
11. At the Open dialog box, double-click *LeaseReviewer2*.
12. At the Combine Documents dialog box, click OK.
13. Save **7-CombinedLease**.
14. Print the document with markup showing.
15. Accept all the changes to the document.
16. Keep the heading *Damage to Premises* together with the next paragraph.
17. Save, print, and then close **7-CombinedLease**.

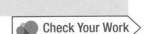 Check Your Work

Activity 3 **Embed and Link Objects between Excel and Word**   **3 Parts**

You will copy and embed Excel data into a Word document and then update the embedded data. You will also copy and link an Excel chart into a Word document and then update the data in the chart.

Embedding and Linking Objects

One of the reasons the Microsoft Office suite is used extensively in business is that it allows an object from one application in the suite to be seamlessly integrated into another application. For example, a chart depicting sales projections created in Excel can easily be added to a corporate report prepared in Word. An object can be text in a document, data in a table, a chart, a picture; or any combination of content to be shared between applications.

Integration is the process of adding objects from other sources to a file. Integrating an object is different from simply copying and pasting it. While it makes sense to copy and paste an object from one application to another when the content is not likely to change, if the content is dynamic, the copy and paste method becomes problematic and inefficient.

To illustrate this point, assume that one of the outcomes of presenting sales projections to the company's board of directors is revision of the projections; this means that the chart originally created in Excel has to be updated to reflect the new projections. If the first version of the chart was copied and pasted into Word, it will need to be deleted and then the revised Excel chart will need to be copied and pasted into the Word document again. Both Excel and Word will need to be opened and edited to reflect the changes in sales projections. In this case, copying and pasting the chart will not be efficient.

To eliminate the inefficiency of the copy and paste method, an object can be integrated between applications. The application that was used to create the object is called the *source* and the application to which the object is linked or embedded is called the *destination*.

Embedding and linking are two methods for integrating an object. *Embedding* an object means that the object is stored independently in both the source and the destination applications. When an embedded object is edited in the destination application, the source application opens to provide buttons and options for editing the object; however, the changes will not be reflected in the version of the object stored in the source application. If the object is changed in the source application, the changes will not be reflected in the version of the object stored in the destination application.

Linking inserts a code in the destination file that connects the destination to the name and location of the source object. The object is not stored within the destination file. When an object is linked, changes made to the content in the source application are automatically reflected in the destination application.

The decision to integrate an object by embedding or linking will depend on whether the content of the object is dynamic or static. If the content is dynamic, then linking the object is the most efficient method of integration.

Embedding an Object

An embedded object is stored in both the source and the destination applications. The content of the object can be edited in *either* the source or the destination; however, a change made in one will not be reflected in the other. The difference between copying and pasting and copying and embedding is that an embedded object can be edited in the destination application with the buttons and options of the source application.

Since an embedded object is edited within the source application, that application must reside on the computer when the file is opened for editing. When preparing a Word document that will be edited on another computer, determine whether the other computer has both Word and the source application before embedding any objects.

To embed an object, open both applications and both files. In the source application, click the object and then click the Copy button in the Clipboard group on the Home tab. Click the button on the taskbar that represents the destination application file and then position the insertion point where the object is to be embedded. Click the Paste button arrow in the Clipboard group and then click *Paste Special* at the drop-down list. At the Paste Special dialog box, click the source of the object in the *As* list box and then click OK.

Edit an embedded object by double-clicking it. This displays the object with the source application buttons and options. Make any changes and then click outside the object to close the source application buttons and options.

Quick Steps

Embed Object
1. Open source and destination applications and files.
2. Click object in source application.
3. Click Copy button.
4. Click taskbar button for destination application file.
5. Position insertion point in specific location.
6. Click Paste button arrow.
7. Click *Paste Special*.
8. Click source file format in *As* list box.
9. Click OK.

Activity 3a Embedding Excel Data in a Document

Part 1 of 3

1. Open **DIRevs** and then save it with the name **7-DIRevs**.
2. Open Excel and then open **DISales** from your WL3C7 folder.
3. Select the range A2:F9.
4. Click the Copy button in the Clipboard group on the Home tab.
5. Click the Word button on the taskbar.
6. Press Ctrl + End to move the insertion point to the end of the document.
7. Click the Paste button arrow and then click *Paste Special* at the drop-down list.
8. At the Paste Special dialog box, click *Microsoft Excel Worksheet Object* in the *As* list box and then click OK.
9. Save **7-DIRevs**.
10. Click the Excel button on the taskbar, close the workbook, and then close Excel.
11. With **7-DIRevs** open, double-click in any cell in the Excel data. (This displays the Excel buttons and options for editing the data.)
12. Click in cell E3 (contains the amount *$89,231*), type 95000, and then press the Enter key.
13. Click in cell F9 and then double-click the AutoSum button in the Editing group on the Home tab. (This inserts the total *$1,258,643* in the cell.)
14. Click outside the Excel data to remove the Excel buttons and options. (Make sure all columns and rows of the Excel worksheet are visible.)
15. Save, print, and then close **7-DIRevs**.

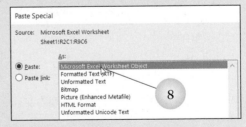

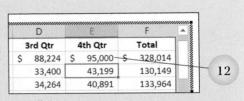

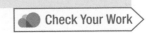

Linking an Object

If the content of the object to be integrated between applications is likely to change, link the object from the source application to the destination application. Linking the object establishes a direct connection between the source and destination applications. The object is stored only in the source application and the destination application contains a code that indicates the name and location of the source of the object. Whenever the document containing the link is opened, a message displays indicating that the document contains links and asking if the link should be updated.

To link an object, open both applications and application files. In the source application file, click the object and then click the Copy button in the Clipboard group on the Home tab. Click the button on the taskbar that represents the destination application file and then position the insertion point where the object is to be inserted. Click the Paste button arrow in the Clipboard group on the Home tab and then click *Paste Special* at the drop-down list. At the Paste Special dialog box, click the source application for the object in the *As* list box, click the *Paste link* option at the left side of the *As* list box, and then click OK.

Quick Steps

Link Object
1. Open source and destination applications and files.
2. Click object in source application.
3. Click Copy button.
4. Click taskbar button for destination application file.
5. Position insertion point.
6. Click Paste button arrow.
7. Click *Paste Special*.
8. Click source application for object in *As* list box.
9. Click *Paste link* option.
10. Click OK.

Activity 3b Linking an Excel Chart to a Document

Part 2 of 3

1. Open **NSSCosts** and then save it with the name **7-NSSCosts**.
2. Open Excel and then open **NSSDept%** in your WL3C7 folder.
3. Save the workbook and name it **7-NSSDept%**.
4. Copy and link the chart to the Word document by completing the following steps:
   a. Click the chart to select it.
   b. Click the Copy button.
   c. Click the Word button on the taskbar.
   d. Press Ctrl + End to move the insertion point to the end of the document.
   e. Click the Paste button arrow and then click *Paste Special* at the drop-down list.
   f. At the Paste Special dialog box, click the *Paste link* option.
   g. Click *Microsoft Excel Chart Object* in the *As* list box.

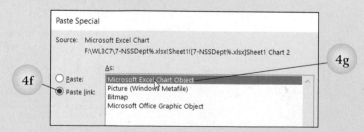

   h. Click OK.
5. Click the Excel button on the taskbar, close **7-NSSDept%**, and then close Excel.
6. With **7-NSSCosts** open, save, print, and then close the document.

Check Your Work

Editing a Linked Object

Edit a linked object in the source application in which it was created. Open the file containing the object, make the changes as required, and then save and close the file. If the source and destination applications are open at the same time, the changed content is reflected in both.

Activity 3c **Editing a Linked Excel Chart**   Part 3 of 3

1. Open Excel and then open **7-NSSDept%.xlsx**.
2. Make the following changes to the data:
   a. In cell B4, change *18%* to *12%*.
   b. In cell B6, change *10%* to *13%*.
   c. In cell B8, change *5%* to *8%*.
3. Click the Save button on the Quick Access Toolbar to save the edited workbook.
4. Close **7-NSSDept%** and then close Excel.
5. In Word, open **7-NSSCosts**.
6. At the message stating that the document contains links, click Yes. (Notice the changes made to the chart data.)
7. Save, print, and then close **7-NSSCosts**.

 Check Your Work

---

Activity 4   Linking and Pasting Data into a Document   2 Parts

You will open a company document and then use the Insert File dialog box to paste a file into the document as a linked object. You will also use the Paste Special dialog box to copy and paste the company name with formatting and copy and paste the company name and image as an object in a header.

Linking an Object at the Insert File Dialog Box

 Object

In addition to linking an object using the Paste Special dialog box, an object can be linked to a document at the Insert File dialog box. Display this dialog box by clicking the Insert tab, clicking the Object button arrow in the Text group, and then clicking the *Text from File* option. At the dialog box, specify the file to be linked to the open document, click the Insert button arrow, and then click *Insert as Link* at the drop-down list. The object in the identified file is inserted into the open document as a linked object. If changes are made to the content of the object in the original file, the content in the linked object will need to be updated. Update a link by clicking the object and then pressing the F9 function key or right-clicking the object and then clicking *Update Field* at the shortcut menu.

1. Open **ATSManagement**, save it with the name **7-ATSManagement**, and then close the document.
2. Open **ATSDocument** and then save it with the name **7-ATSDocument**.
3. Position the insertion point at the beginning of the heading *EMPLOYER COMMUNICATION*.
4. Link the table in *7-ATSManagement* as an object to the open document by completing the following steps:
   a. Click the Insert tab.
   b. Click the Object button arrow and then click *Text from File* at the drop-down list.
   c. At the Insert File dialog box, click *7-ATSManagement* in the Content pane.
   d. Click the Insert button arrow and then click *Insert as Link* at the drop-down list.

5. Save and then close **7-ATSDocument**.
6. Open **7-ATSManagement** and then make the following edits:
   a. Change the name *Genevieve Parkhurst* to *Noah Stein*.
   b. Change the extension *123* to *102*.

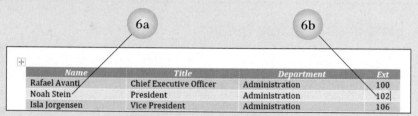

7. Save and then close **7-ATSManagement**.
8. Open **7-ATSDocument**.
9. Update the data in the table object by completing the following steps:
   a. Click in the table to select the table object.
   b. Press the F9 function key.
10. Save **7-ATSDocument**.

Check Your Work

Using Paste Special

Use options at the Paste Special dialog box shown, in Figure 7.4, to specify the formatting for pasted text and objects. Display the dialog box by clicking the Paste button arrow in the Clipboard group on the Home tab and then clicking *Paste Special* at the drop-down list. The options in the *As* list box vary depending on the cut or copied text or object and the source application. Text can be pasted with or without formatting and selected text can be pasted as an object. For example, in Activity 4b, text will be copied in one document and then pasted into another document without the formatting. Also in the activity, text and an image will be selected in one document and then pasted into another document as a Word object.

Figure 7.4 Paste Special Dialog Box

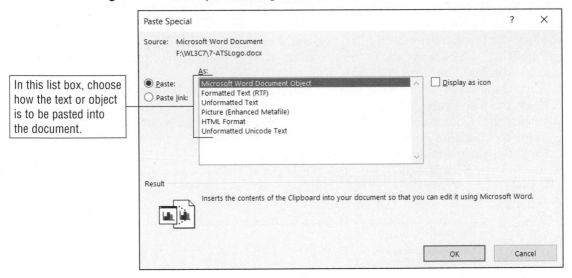

In this list box, choose how the text or object is to be pasted into the document.

Activity 4b Pasting Data Using the Paste Special Dialog Box

1. With **7-ATSDocument** open, press Ctrl + End to move the insertion point to the end of the document.
2. Open **ATSLogo** and then save it with the name **7-ATSLogo**.
3. Copy and paste the company name by completing the following steps:
   a. Select the company name *Advantage Transport Services*. (Select only the company name and not the image near the name.)
   b. Click the Copy button.
   c. Click the Word button on the taskbar and then click the *7-ATSDocument* thumbnail.
   d. With the insertion point positioned at the end of the document, click the Paste button arrow and then click *Paste Special* at the drop-down list.
   e. At the Paste Special dialog box, click the *Unformatted Text* option in the *As* list box.
   f. Click OK.

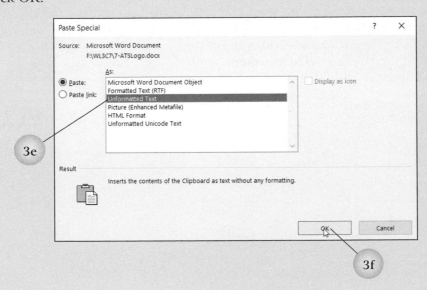

4. Copy the company name and image and then paste it as an object in the Header pane by completing the following steps:
   a. Click the Word button on the taskbar and then click the *7-ATSLogo* thumbnail.
   b. Press Ctrl + A to select the entire document (the company name plus the road image).
   c. Click the Copy button.
   d. Click the Word button on the taskbar and then click the *7-ATSDocument* thumbnail.
   e. Click the Insert tab.
   f. Click the Header button and then click *Edit Header* at the drop-down list.
   g. With the insertion point positioned in the Header pane, click the Home tab, click the Paste button arrow, and then click *Paste Special* at the drop-down list.
   h. At the Paste Special dialog box, click the *Microsoft Word Document Object* option in the *As* list box.
   i. Click OK.

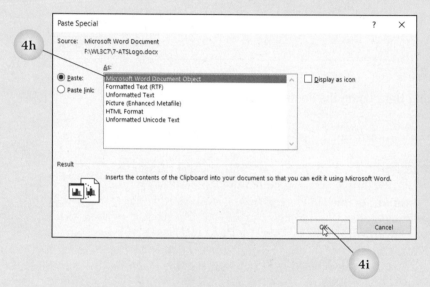

5. Increase the height of the pasted object by completing the following steps:
   a. Click the object to select it.
   b. Position the mouse pointer on the bottom middle sizing handle, click and hold down the mouse button, drag down approximately 0.25 inch, and then release the mouse button.
6. Close the Header pane by double-clicking in the document.
7. Save, print, and then close **7-ATSDocument**.
8. Close **7-ATSLogo**.

Check Your Work

You will open a document with information on Antarctic adventures and then run an accessibility check to identify issues that may make the document difficult to read and understand for someone with a disability, such as a visual impairment. You will then make changes to improve the accessibility of the document.

Tutorial

Tutorial Review:
Checking the
Accessibility and
Compatibility of a
Document

Quick Steps

Check Accessibility
1. Click File tab.
2. Click *Info* option.
3. Click Check for
   Issues button.
4. Click *Check
   Accessibility*.

Check for
Issues

Managing the Accessibility of a Document

The Americans with Disabilities Act (ADA) is a law that prohibits discrimination and guarantees that people with disabilities have the same opportunities as everyone else. To ensure that a Word document is accessible and ADA compliant, it should be formatted so that information in the document is accessible to assistive technology and screen readers.

As explained in Level 2, Chapter 1, Word's accessibility checker examines a document for content that someone with a disability, such as a visual impairment, might find difficult to access. Check the accessibility of a document by clicking the Check for Issues button at the Info backstage area and then clicking *Check Accessibility*.

In addition to checking images for alternative text, the accessibility checker examines a document for the most common accessibility problems and groups them into three categories: errors—content that is very difficult or impossible for people with disabilities to understand; warnings—content that makes a file difficult for people with disabilities to understand; tips—content that people with disabilities can understand but that can be better organized. Possible errors, warnings, and tips display in the Accessibility Checker task pane. In addition to these accessibility checker categories, consider other issues when making a document more accessible. The categories and other issues are identified in Table 7.1.

Creating Alternative Text for an Object

The first item in the *Errors* section, *Alt text*, refers to a text-based representation of an object. For example, if a document contains an image, alternative text can be added that describes the image. When creating alternative text for an object, describe the object accurately and succinctly and avoid phrases such as "Image of. . ." and "This is. . .".

The alternative text for an object will display when a screen reader is used to read the document or when the document is saved in a file format such as HTML (Hypertext Markup Language) or DAISY (Digital Accessible Information System). If a document is saved in a format that is easy to share or publish, such as PDF (Portable Document Format) or XML (Extensible Markup Language), then all the changes made to ensure accessibility are included.

A variety of methods are available for creating alternative text including using options in the Accessibility Checker task pane as well as the Alt Text button on the Picture Tools Format tab and the Drawing Tools Format tab. Create alternative text for a table at the Table Properties dialog box with the Alt Text tab selected.

Table 7.1 Accessibility Issues

Errors

Alt text: To pass the accessibility check, objects in a document—including pictures, images, tables, SmartArt, shapes, charts, embedded objects, and video and audio files—should have an alternative text description that can be read aloud by a screen reader. If an object is missing alt text, the Accessibility Checker will return an error message.

Table headers: The first row of a table should be clearly specified as the header row. A table header row provides context and helps readers navigate the data in a table.

Document structure: Long documents use styles to provide structure. Headings and/or a table of contents should be used to help organize the content. Creating a structure helps readers find information in the document.

Warnings

Meaningful hyperlink text: Hyperlink text should include a ScreenTip and should match the hyperlink target. Hyperlink text should provide a description of the destination, not just the URL.

Simple table structure: Tables must have a simple structure that does not include nested tables or merged or split cells. Tables should have a simple two-dimensional structure to be easily navigated and understood by readers.

Blank cells: Tables should not use blank cells for formatting or contain entirely blank rows or columns. Encountering blank cells may lead readers to think they have reached the end of the table.

Blank characters: Repeated blank characters (such as a series of blank spaces, tabs, or paragraphs) must be avoided. Blank characters may lead readers to think they have reached the end of the document. Paragraphs of text should not be separated with blank lines; paragraph styles should be applied.

Heading length: Headings should not contain too much information. Rather, keep them short (fewer than 10 words). Short, concise headings help readers navigate the document more easily.

Tips

Closed captions: Closed captions should be included for inserted audio and video files. Without closed captions, important information in audio or video files may not be accessible for people with disabilities.

Table layout: Tables must be structured for easy navigation and follow the appropriate reading order. For English, data in a table is read from left to right and top to bottom. Tabbing through the cells in a table will determine whether the information is presented in a logical order.

Watermarks: Avoid using watermarks on pages or images in a document. These may interfere with readability.

Heading order: All the headings should appear in the correct order. Use of correct heading levels allows readers to find information and navigate easily in the document.

Lists: Lists should be formatted with bullets using the Bullets button on the Home tab or formatted with numbers using the Numbering button on the Home tab.

Text color: If text colors are used in a document, provide contrast between the colors. Consider using the *Automatic* setting for text color. (Click the Font Color button arrow and then click *Automatic* at the drop-down gallery.)

Establishing a Header Row

The first row in a table should be established as a header row, so if the table flows onto a second page, the first row is repeated at the top. A header row helps identify the contents of the table. Specify the first row of a table as a header row by clicking in any cell in the first row and then clicking the Repeat Header Rows button in the Data group on the Table Tools Layout tab. Another method for specifying a header row is to insert a check mark in the *Repeat as header row at the top of each page* check box at the Table Properties dialog box with the Row tab selected. Display this dialog box by clicking the Table Tools Layout tab and then clicking the Properties button in the Table group.

 Properties

Using Built-in Styles

💡 *Hint* Keep headings relatively short and apply heading styles.

💡 *Hint* In a long document, consider including a heading every two pages at a minimum.

When preparing accessible documents, use the built-in heading styles to identify headings. Screen readers used by people with visual impairments recognize text with a heading style applied as a heading. Text with direct formatting applied, such as a larger font size or bold formatting, is not recognized as a heading by screen readers. Another advantage to applying built-in heading styles is that the person preparing the document can increase the font size of heading text by modifying the heading styles.

In addition to applying heading styles to make documents more accessible, apply body text styles. As with headings, the person preparing the document can modify the size of the body font and all the text in the document with that style applied will increase in size. Increasing the font size of text in a document makes the text easier to read for people with visual impairments.

Activity 5 Improving the Accessibility of a Document   Part 1 of 1

1. Open **BTZTAdventures** and then save it with the name **7-BTZTAdventures**.
2. Check the accessibility of the document by completing the following steps:
   a. Click the File tab and then, if necessary, click the *Info* option.
   b. At the Info backstage area, click the Check for Issues button and then click *Check Accessibility* at the drop-down list.
3. Add alternative text to the picture by completing the following steps:
   a. Click *Missing alternative text (1)* in the *Errors* section in the Accessibility Checker task pane. (This displays the item with missing alternative text in the document.)
   b. Click *Picture 3* in the task pane. (This selects the picture in the document.)
   c. Read the information near the bottom of the task pane that describes why the error should be fixed and how to fix it.

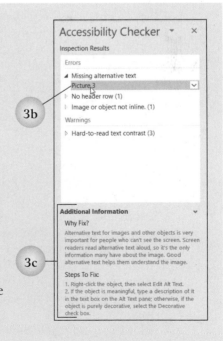

d. Click the down arrow at the right of *Picture 3* and then click *Add a description* at the drop-down list. (This opens the Alt Text task pane next to the Accessibility Checker task pane.)

e. Click in the text box in the Alt Text task pane and then type Adelie penguins on an iceberg in Antarctica.

f. Close the Alt Text task pane.

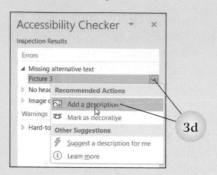
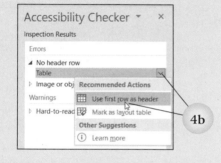

4. Add a header row to the table by completing the following steps:

a. Click *No header row (1)* in the *Errors* section in the Accessibility Checker task pane.

b. Click *Table* in the task pane, click the down arrow at the right of *Table*, and then click *Use first row as header* at the drop-down list.

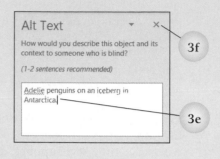

5. Format the picture to be in line with the text by completing the following steps:

a. Click *Image or object not inline. (1)* in the *Errors* section in the Accessibility Checker task pane.

b. Click *Picture 3* in the task pane, click the down arrow at the right of *Picture 3*, and then click *Place this inline* at the drop-down list.

6. Close the Accessibility Checker task pane.

7. Make the table in the document more accessible by completing the following steps:

a. Right-click the table and then click *Table Properties* at the shortcut menu.

b. At the Table Properties dialog box, click the Alt Text tab.

c. Click in the *Title* text box and then type Zenith Adventures.

d. Click in the *Description* text box and then type Four adventures offered by Zenith Adventures including number of days and prices.

e. Click OK to close the Table Properties dialog box.

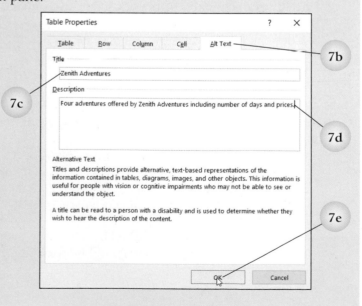

    f. Click in the first cell in the table and then click the Table Tools Layout tab.

    g. Click the Repeat Header Rows button in the Data group.

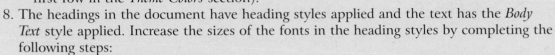

    h. Select the text in the first row and then change the font color to White, Background 1 (first column, first row in the *Theme Colors* section).

8. The headings in the document have heading styles applied and the text has the *Body Text* style applied. Increase the sizes of the fonts in the heading styles by completing the following steps:

    a. Press Ctrl + Home to move the insertion point to the beginning of the document. (The insertion point will be positioned immediately left of the title *BAYSIDE TRAVEL*.)

    b. Click the Home tab.

    c. Right-click the *Heading 1* style in the Styles group and then click *Modify* at the shortcut menu.

    d. At the Modify Style dialog box, click the *Font Size* option box arrow and then click *26* at the drop-down list.

    e. Click OK to close the Modify Style dialog box.

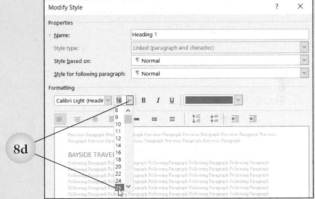

    f. With the insertion point still positioned at the beginning of the title *BAYSIDE TRAVEL*, click the *Heading 1* style. (This applies the new font size to the text.)

    g. Right-click the *Heading 2* style in the Styles group and then click *Modify* at the shortcut menu.

    h. At the Modify Style dialog box, click the *Font Size* option box arrow and then click *20* at the drop-down list.

    i. Click OK to close the Modify Style dialog box.

9. Increase the font size of the body text by completing the following steps:

    a. Click in the paragraph of text below the heading *Antarctic Zenith Adventures*.

    b. Click the More Styles button in the Styles group.

    c. Click *Apply Styles* at the drop-down gallery.

    d. At the Apply Styles window, make sure that *Body Text* displays in the *Style Name* text box. If not, select the text in the *Style Name* text box, type Body Text, and then press the Enter key.

    e. Click the Modify button in the Apply Styles window.

    f. At the Modify Style dialog box, make sure that *Body Text* displays in the *Name* text box.

    g. Click the *Font Size* option box arrow and then click *14* at the drop-down list.

    h. Click OK to close the Modify Style dialog box.

    i. Close the Apply Styles window.

10. Save, print, and then close **7-BTZTAdventures**.

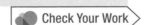
Check Your Work

Activity 6 Share a Report on Volcanoes

2 Parts

You will save a report on volcanoes to your OneDrive account and then send the document as an email attachment and present the document online.

Sharing a
Document

Sharing a Document

Word provides several options for sharing documents. Depending on the system and version of Microsoft Office, a number of options will be available for sharing, including sending a link to a document in the cloud, sending a presentation as an email attachment, or sharing the document as an online presentation.

Sharing in the Cloud

Word documents can be stored and shared online through a file hosting service, such as Microsoft OneDrive, or another shared location, such as a website or Microsoft SharePoint library. This is commonly referred to as *cloud storage* or *cloud sharing*.

Hint The person sharing the document is the only person who can change the settings for individuals in the group.

As discussed in Word Level 2, Chapter 8, to share a document, first save the document to a OneDrive account (or other shared location). Display file sharing options by clicking the Share button in the upper right corner of the Word window; by clicking the File tab and then clicking the *Share* option; or by clicking the File tab, clicking the *Info* option, and then clicking the Share button below the document name. At the Share window or task pane that displays, follow the instructions to send a link and invite others to view the document by typing in the email addresses of people to be invited. Specify if the document can be viewed and edited or only viewed and then share the document.

Sharing by Email or Fax

A copy of a Word document can be emailed to others as an attachment. Each recipient will receive a separate copy of the document, rather than having to access a shared file in the cloud. To share as an attachment, either open an email and then attach the file or click the Share button in the upper right corner of the Word window to view options for emailing the file using an Outlook email account.

A Word document can be converted to PDF or XPS format before being attached to an email. A PDF or XPS file has the advantage of being easily viewable and transferable on many platforms, and the content cannot be easily changed.

As an alternative to email, send a document as an internet fax. To use this option, the sender must be signed up with a fax service provider.

Note: To complete this activity, you need to have Outlook as your email provider. Check with your instructor to determine if you should complete this activity.

1. Open **Volcanoes** and then save it with the name **7-Volcanoes**.
2. Click the File tab and then click the *Share* option.
3. If the Share backstage area displays, click the *Email* option and then click the Send as Attachment button. If the Share window displays, click the Word Document button in the *Attach a copy instead* section of the window.
4. At the Outlook window, type your instructor's email address in the *To* text box.
5. Click the Send button.
6. Save **7-Volcanoes**.

Presenting a Document Online

Word includes the Present Online feature for sharing a document with others over the internet by sending a link to the people who will view the document in their own browsers. Using this feature requires having a network service to host the document. Microsoft provides the Office Presentation Service, which is available to anyone with a Windows Live ID (such as a OneDrive account) and Microsoft Office. (Depending on the system and version of Office, the Present Online feature may not be available at the Share backstage area.)

 Present Online

If the Present Online feature is available, present a document online by clicking the *Present Online* option at the Share backstage area and then clicking the Present Online button. At the Present Online window that displays, click the CONNECT button and enter your Windows Live ID user name and password, if necessary. When Word has connected to an account and prepared the document, the Present Online window will display with a unique link that Word created for the document. Click the Copy Link hyperlink in the Present Online window to copy the link and then paste it into an email that will be sent to the people who will view the document. If the person presenting the document online has an Outlook account, clicking the Send in Email hyperlink opens Outlook and the link can be pasted in the message window.

After everyone has opened the document link in a web browser, click the START PRESENTATION button in the Present Online window. People viewing the document do not need to have Word installed on their computers to view the document because the document displays through their web browsers.

 Edit

 Resume Online Presentation

When presenting a document online, the Present Online tab displays with options for sharing the document through OneNote, displaying the unique link to send to more people, editing the document, and ending the document presentation. When presenting a document online, make edits to it by clicking the Edit button in the Present Online group on the Present Online tab. A yellow message bar displays to indicate that the presentation is paused. Make edits to the document and then click the Resume button on the yellow message bar or click the Resume Online Presentation button in the Present Online group on the Present Online tab. Click the Resume button and the people viewing the document will see the edited version.

End Online Presentation

To end the presentation of a document, click the End Online Presentation button in the Present Online group on the Present Online tab. At the message indicating that all the people will be disconnected and asking if the online presentation should end, click the End Online Presentation button.

Activity 6b Presenting Online

Note: This is an optional activity. To complete the activity, the Online Presentation feature must be available and you must have a Windows Live ID account. Check with your instructor to determine if you should complete this activity. Depending on your system configuration and what services are available, the following steps will vary.

1. With **7-Volcanoes** open, click the File tab and then click the *Share* option.
2. At the Share backstage area, click the *Present Online* option and then click the Present Online button.

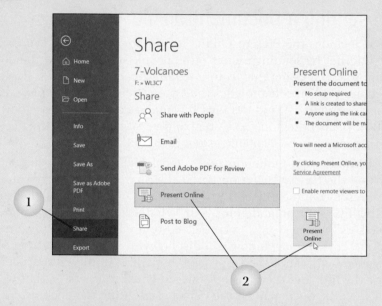

3. At the Present Online window that displays, click the CONNECT button. (If a CONNECT button does not appear, skip to Step 5.)
4. Type your user name and password in the Windows Security dialog box.
5. At the Present Online window with the unique link selected, click the Copy Link hyperlink.
6. Send the link to colleagues by opening an email account, pasting the link into a new message window, and then sending the email to the viewers. If you are using Microsoft Outlook, click the Send in Email hyperlink and Microsoft Outlook opens in a new message window with the link inserted in the message. In Outlook, send the link to the people you want to view the document.
7. When everyone has received the link, click the START PRESENTATION button at the Present Online window.

8. Edit one of the volcano names in the first table by completing the following steps:
   a. Click the Edit button in the Present Online group on the Present Online tab.

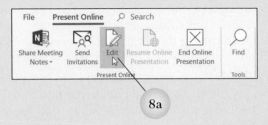

8a

b. Drag the button on the Zoom slider bar so the document displays at 100% view.
c. Scroll down the document to display the first table.
d. Select *Mt.* in the name *Mt. St. Helens* (in the first cell in the second row) and then type Mount.
e. Click the Resume button on the yellow message bar.

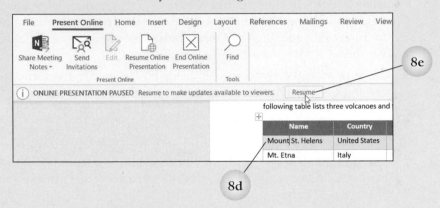

8e

8d

9. Click the End Online Presentation button on the Present Online tab.
10. At the message that displays stating that all the people will be disconnected if you continue, click the End Online Presentation button.
11. Increase the zoom of the document back to 100%.
12. Save, print, and then close **7-Volcanoes**.

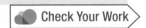 Check Your Work

Chapter Summary

- Use the Compare button in the Compare group on the Review tab to compare two documents and display the differences between them as tracked changes in the original document, the revised document, or a new document.

- Control how changes are combined with options at the expanded Compare Documents dialog box. Click the More button to display additional options.

- If several people have made changes to a document, their changed versions can be combined with the original document. Combine documents with options at the Combine Documents dialog box.

- Customize options for combining documents at the expanded Combine Documents dialog box. Click the More button to display additional options.

- Specify which source documents to display by clicking the Compare button in the Compare group on the Review tab, pointing to *Show Source Documents*, and then clicking an option at the side menu.

- An object created in one application in the Microsoft Office suite can be copied, linked, or embedded into another application in the suite. The application containing the original data or object is called the *source* application and the application in which it is inserted is called the *destination* application.

- An embedded data or an object is stored in both the source and the destination applications. Edit an embedded object by double-clicking the object. This displays the object with the source application buttons and options.

- A linked object is stored only in the source application. Link an object if the content in the destination application should reflect changes made to the object stored in the source application. Edit a linked object in the source application in which it was created.

- Data in one document can be linked to the open document at the Insert File dialog box by clicking the Insert button arrow in the dialog box and then clicking the *Insert as Link* option. Display the Insert File dialog box by clicking the Insert tab, clicking the Object button arrow, and then clicking the *Text from File* option.

- Use options at the Paste Special dialog box to specify the formatting for pasted text and objects. Display the Paste Special dialog box by clicking the Paste button arrow in the Clipboard group on the Home tab and then clicking *Paste Special* at the drop-down list.

- The accessibility checker reviews a document to identify content that people with disabilities might find difficult to read or understand. The accessibility checker examines a document and then displays issues in the Accessibility Checker task pane.

- The issues identified by the accessibility checker are grouped into three sections in the Accessibility Checker task pane. The *Error* section displays content that is very difficult or impossible for people with disabilities to understand, the *Warnings* section displays content that makes a file difficult for people with disabilities to understand, and the *Tips* section displays content that people with disabilities can understand but that can be better organized.

- Apply built-in heading styles and body text styles when preparing an accessible document.

- Use sharing options to send a link to a document in the cloud, send a document as an email attachment (such as a PDF or XPS file), or present a document online.

- Use the Present Online feature to share a document with others over the internet. Send a link to the people to view a document in a web browser.

Commands Review

FEATURE	RIBBON TAB, GROUP/OPTION	BUTTON, OPTION
accessibility checker	File, *Info*	, *Check Accessibility*
Combine Documents dialog box	Review, Compare	, *Combine*
Compare Documents dialog box	Review, Compare	, *Compare*
Insert File dialog box	Insert, Text	, *Text from File*
Paste Special dialog box	Home, Clipboard	, *Paste Special*
Share backstage area or window	File, *Share*	
show source documents	Review, Compare	, *Show Source Documents*

Microsoft®
Word

Customizing Word

Performance Objectives

Upon successful completion of Chapter 8, you will be able to:

1. Customize the Quick Access Toolbar
2. Customize the ribbon
3. Import and export Quick Access Toolbar customizations
4. Import and export ribbon customizations
5. Customize Word Options
6. Display and customize account information

Microsoft Word can be personalized by customizing features such as the Quick Access Toolbar and ribbon. Buttons can be added and removed from the Quick Access Toolbar and new tabs and groups can be added to the ribbon. Word can also be customized with options at the Word Options dialog box. In this chapter, you will learn how to customize the Quick Access Toolbar and ribbon, how to customize Word at the Word Options dialog box, and how to customize account information.

 Data Files

Before beginning chapter work, copy the WL3C8 folder to your storage medium and then make WL3C8 the active folder.

The online course includes additional training and assessment resources.

Tutorial

Customizing the
Quick Access
Toolbar

  Customize
Quick Access
Toolbar

Quick Steps

**Customize Quick
Access Toolbar**

1. Click Customize
   Quick Access Toolbar
   button.
2. Insert check mark
   before each button
   to be added.
3. Remove check mark
   before each button
   to be removed.

Customizing the Quick Access Toolbar

The Quick Access Toolbar contains buttons for some of the most commonly performed tasks. By default, the toolbar contains the Save, Undo, and Redo buttons. Some basic buttons can be easily added to or removed from the Quick Access Toolbar with options at the Customize Quick Access Toolbar drop-down list. Display this list by clicking the Customize Quick Access Toolbar button at the right side of the toolbar. Insert a check mark before each button to be added to the toolbar and remove the check mark from each button to be removed from the toolbar.

The Customize Quick Access Toolbar button drop-down list includes an option for moving the location of the Quick Access Toolbar. By default, the Quick Access Toolbar is above the ribbon. To move the toolbar below the ribbon, click the *Show Below the Ribbon* option at the drop-down list.

Buttons or commands from a tab can be added to the Quick Access Toolbar. To do this, click the tab, right-click the button or command, and then click *Add to Quick Access Toolbar* at the shortcut menu.

Activity 1a **Customizing the Quick Access Toolbar**   Part 1 of 4

1. Open **InterfaceApps** and then save it with the name **8-InterfaceApps**.
2. Add the New button to the Quick Access Toolbar by clicking the Customize Quick Access Toolbar button at the right of the toolbar and then clicking *New* at the drop-down list.
3. Add the Open button to the Quick Access Toolbar by clicking the Customize Quick Access Toolbar button and then clicking *Open* at the drop-down list.
4. Click the New button on the Quick Access Toolbar. (This displays a new blank document.)
5. Close the document.
6. Click the Open button on the Quick Access Toolbar to display the Open backstage area.
7. Press the Esc key to return to the document.
8. Move the Quick Access Toolbar by clicking the Customize Quick Access Toolbar button and then clicking *Show Below the Ribbon* at the drop-down list.
9. Move the Quick Access Toolbar back to the default position by clicking the Customize Quick Access Toolbar button and then clicking *Show Above the Ribbon* at the drop-down list.

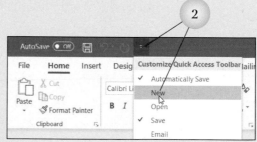

10. Insert the Margins and Themes buttons on the Quick Access Toolbar by completing the following steps:
    a. Click the Layout tab.
    b. Right-click the Margins button in the Page Setup group and then click *Add to Quick Access Toolbar* at the shortcut menu.
    c. Click the Design tab.
    d. Right-click the Themes button in the Themes group and then click *Add to Quick Access Toolbar* at the shortcut menu.

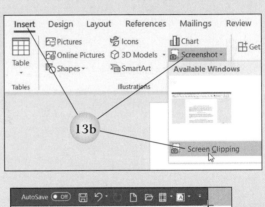

11. Change the top margin by completing the following steps:
    a. Click the Margins button on the Quick Access Toolbar and then click *Custom Margins* at the drop-down list.
    b. At the Page Setup dialog box, change the top margin to 1.5 inches and then click OK.

12. Change the theme by clicking the Themes button on the Quick Access Toolbar and then clicking *View* at the drop-down gallery. (You will need to scroll down the gallery to find the *View* theme.)

13. Create a screenshot of the Quick Access Toolbar by completing the following steps:
    a. Click the New button on the Quick Access Toolbar. (This displays a new blank document.)
    b. Click the Insert tab, click the Screenshot button in the Illustrations group, and then click *Screen Clipping* at the drop-down list.
    c. In a few moments, **8-InterfaceApps** displays in a dimmed manner. Click and hold down the left mouse button, drag down and to the right from the upper left corner of the screen to capture the Quick Access Toolbar, and then release the mouse button.
    d. With the screenshot image inserted in the document, print the document and then close the document without saving it.

14. Save **8-InterfaceApps**.

> Check Your Work

The Customize Quick Access Toolbar button drop-down list contains some of the most commonly used buttons. However, many other buttons can be inserted on the toolbar. To display the buttons available, click the Customize Quick Access Toolbar button and then click *More Commands* at the drop-down list. This displays the Word Options dialog box with *Quick Access Toolbar* selected in the left panel, as shown in Figure 8.1. Another method for displaying this dialog box is to click the File tab, click *Options*, and then click *Quick Access Toolbar* in the left panel of the Word Options dialog box.

To reset the Quick Access Toolbar to the default (Save, Undo, and Redo buttons), click the Reset button in the lower right corner of the dialog box and then click *Reset only Quick Access Toolbar* at the drop-down list. At the message that

Figure 8.1 Word Options Dialog Box with *Quick Access Toolbar* Selected

Click a command in the list box at the left and then click the Add button to display the command in the list box at the right.

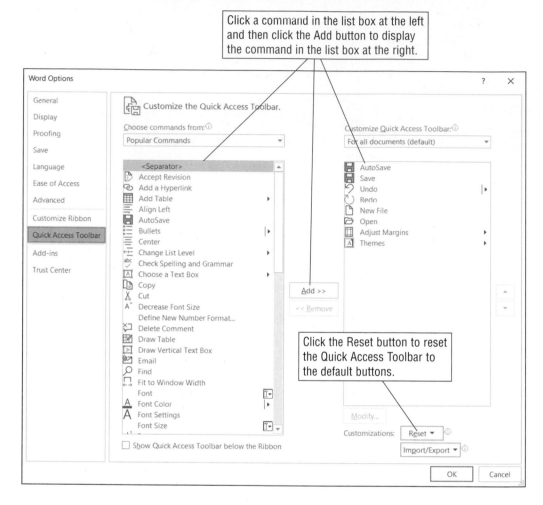

Click the Reset button to reset the Quick Access Toolbar to the default buttons.

displays asking if the Quick Access Toolbar shared between all documents should be restored to its default contents, click Yes.

The Quick Access Toolbar can be customized for all documents or for a specific document. To customize the toolbar for the currently open document, display the Word Options dialog box with *Quick Access Toolbar* selected, click the *Customize Quick Access Toolbar* option box arrow, and then click the *For (document name)* option, where the name of the currently open document displays.

The *Choose commands from* option has a default setting of *Popular Commands*. At this setting, the list box below the option displays only a portion of all the commands available to insert as buttons on the Quick Access Toolbar. To display all the commands available, click the *Choose commands from* option box arrow and then click *All Commands*. The drop-down list also contains options for specifying commands that are not currently available on the ribbon, as well as commands on the File tab and various other tabs.

To add a button to the Quick Access Toolbar, click the command in the list box at the left side of the dialog box and then click the Add button between the two list boxes. Continue inserting buttons and then click OK to close the dialog box.

1. With **8-InterfaceApps** open, reset the Quick Access Toolbar by completing the following steps:
   a. Click the Customize Quick Access Toolbar button at the right of the Quick Access Toolbar and then click *More Commands* at the drop-down list.
   b. At the Word Options dialog box, click the Reset button at the bottom of the dialog box and then click *Reset only Quick Access Toolbar* at the drop-down list.

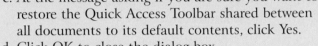

   c. At the message asking if you are sure you want to restore the Quick Access Toolbar shared between all documents to its default contents, click Yes.
   d. Click OK to close the dialog box.
2. Add buttons to the Quick Access Toolbar for the currently open document by completing the following steps:
   a. Click the Customize Quick Access Toolbar button and then click *More Commands*.
   b. At the Word Options dialog box, click the *Customize Quick Access Toolbar* option box arrow and then click *For 8-InterfaceApps* at the drop-down list.
   c. Click the *Choose commands from* option box arrow and then click *All Commands*.
   d. Scroll down the list box and then click the *Close File* command. (Commands are listed in alphabetical order.)
   e. Click the Add button between the two list boxes.

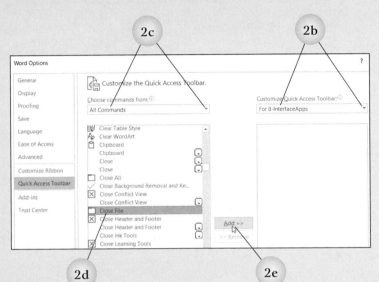

   f. Scroll up the list box and then click *Add a Footer*.
   g. Click the Add button.
   h. Click OK to close the dialog box.
   i. Check the Quick Access Toolbar and notice that the two buttons display along with the default buttons.
3. Insert a footer by completing the following steps:
   a. Click the Add a Footer button on the Quick Access Toolbar.
   b. Click *Integral* at the drop-down list.
   c. Select the name in the footer and then type your first and last names.
   d. Double-click in the document.
4. Save and then print **8-InterfaceApps**.
5. Close the document by clicking the Close button on the Quick Access Toolbar.

Check Your Work

Tutorial

Customizing the
Ribbon

Customizing the Ribbon

Just as the Quick Access Toolbar can be customized, the ribbon can be customized by creating a new tab and inserting groups with buttons on the tab. To customize the ribbon, click the File tab and then click *Options*. At the Word Options dialog box, click *Customize Ribbon* in the left panel and the dialog box displays as shown in Figure 8.2.

With options at the *Choose commands from* drop-down list, choose to display only popular commands, which is the default, or choose to display all commands, commands not on the ribbon, and all tabs or commands on the File tab, main tabs, tool tabs, and custom tabs and groups. The commands in the list box vary depending on the option selected at the *Choose commands from* option drop-down list. Click the *Customize the Ribbon* option box arrow and a drop-down list displays with options for customizing all tabs, only main tabs, or only tool tabs. By default, *Main Tabs* is selected.

Figure 8.2 Word Options Dialog Box with *Customize Ribbon* Selected

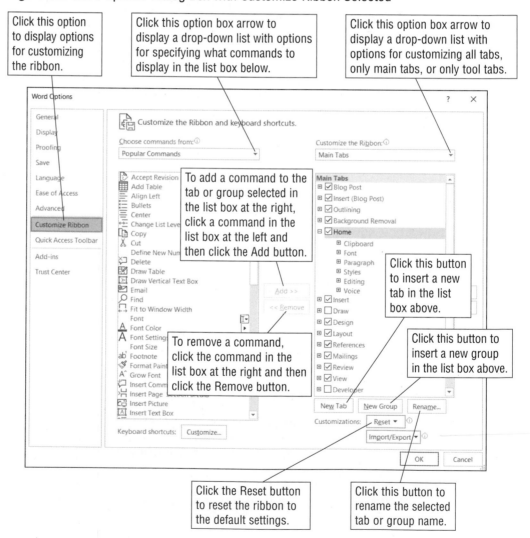

Creating a New Tab

Add a command to an existing tab or create a new tab and then add commands in groups on the tab. To create a new tab, click the tab name in the list box at the right side of the Word Options dialog box that will precede the new tab and then click the New Tab button below the list box. This inserts a new tab in the list box along with a new group below the new tab. Move the new tab up or down in the list box by clicking the new tab and then clicking the Move Up or Move Down button. Both buttons display to the right of the list box.

Renaming a Tab or Group

Rename a tab by clicking the tab in the list box and then clicking the Rename button below the list box at the right. At the Rename dialog box, type a new name for the tab and then click OK. The Rename dialog box can also be displayed by right-clicking the tab name and then clicking *Rename* at the shortcut menu.

Complete similar steps to rename a group. Click the group name and then click the Rename button (or right-click the group name and then click *Rename* at the shortcut menu) and a Rename dialog box displays containing a variety of symbols. Use the symbols to identify new buttons in the group, rather than the group name.

Adding Commands to a Tab Group

Add commands to a tab group by clicking the group name on the tab, clicking the command in the list box at the left, and then clicking the Add button between the two list boxes. Remove commands in a similar manner. Click the command to be removed from the tab group and then click the Remove button between the two list boxes.

Removing a Tab or Group

Remove a tab by clicking the tab name in the list box at the right and then clicking the Remove button between the two list boxes. Remove a group in a similar manner.

Resetting the Ribbon

If the ribbon has been customized by adding tabs and groups, all customizations can be removed by clicking the Reset button below the list box at the right side of the dialog box. Click the Reset button and a drop-down list displays with two options: *Reset only selected Ribbon tab* and *Reset all customizations*. Click the *Reset all customizations* option and a message displays asking if all ribbon and Quick Access Toolbar customizations for this program should be deleted. At this message, click Yes.

1. Open **8-InterfaceApps** and then add a new tab and a new group by completing the following steps:

   a. Click the File tab and then click *Options*.

   b. At the Word Options dialog box, click *Customize Ribbon* in the left panel.

   c. Click *View* in the list box at the right side of the dialog box. (Do not click the check box before *View*.)

   d. Click the New Tab button below the list box. (This inserts a new tab below *View*.)

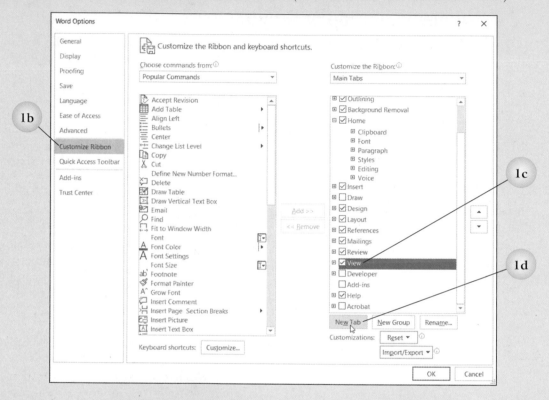

2. Rename the tab and group by completing the following steps:

   a. Click *New Tab (Custom)*. (Do not click the check box.)

   b. Click the Rename button below the list box.

   c. At the Rename dialog box, type your initials in the *Display name* text box and then click OK.

   d. Click *New Group (Custom)* below the tab with your initials.

   e. Click the Rename button.

   f. At the Rename dialog box, type IP Movement in the *Display name* text box and then click OK. (Use *IP* to stand for *insertion point*.)

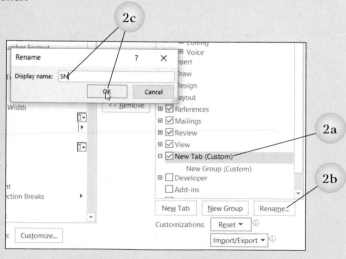

3. Add buttons to the IP Movement (Custom) group by completing the following steps:
   a. Click *IP Movement (Custom)* in the list box at the right side.
   b. Click the *Choose commands from* option box arrow and then click *Commands Not in the Ribbon* at the drop-down list.
   c. Scroll down the list box at the left side of the dialog box (which displays alphabetically), click the *End of Document* command, and then click the Add button. (This inserts the command below the *IP Movement (Custom)* group name.)
   d. With the *End of Line* command selected in the list box at the left side of the dialog box, click the Add button.
   e. Scroll down the list box at the left side of the dialog box, click the *Page Down* command, and then click the Add button.
   f. Click the *Page Up* command in the list box and then click the Add button.
   g. Scroll down the list box, click the *Start of Document* command, and then click the Add button.
   h. With the *Start of Line* command selected in the list box, click the Add button.
4. Click OK to close the Word Options dialog box.
5. Move the insertion point in the document by completing the following steps:
   a. Click the tab containing your initials.
   b. Click the End of Document button in the IP Movement group.
   c. Click the Start of Document button in the IP Movement group.
   d. Click the End of Line button.
   e. Click the Start of Line button.

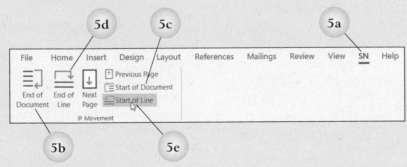

6. Create a screenshot of the ribbon with the tab containing your initials the active tab by completing the following steps:
   a. Make sure your tab is active and then press Ctrl + N to display a new blank document.
   b. Click the Insert tab, click the Screenshot button in the Illustrations group, and then click *Screen Clipping* at the drop-down list.
   c. In a few moments, the **8-InterfaceApps** document displays in a dimmed manner. Click and hold down the left mouse button, drag down from the upper left corner of the screen and to the right to capture the Quick Access Toolbar and the buttons on the tab containing your initials, and then release the mouse button.
   d. With the screenshot image inserted in the document, print the document and then close the document without saving it.
7. Save **8-InterfaceApps**.

Check Your Work

Importing and Exporting Customizations

Export Customizations
1. Click File tab.
2. Click *Options*.
3. Click *Customize Ribbon*.
4. Click Import/Export button.
5. Click *Export all customizations*.
6. At File Save dialog box, navigate to folder.
7. Click in *File name* text box.
8. Type name.
9. Press Enter.

Import Customizations
1. Click File tab.
2. Click *Options*.
3. Click *Customize Ribbon* or *Quick Access Toolbar*.
4. Click Import/Export button.
5. Click *Import customization file*.
6. At File Open dialog box, navigate to folder.
7. Double-click file.
8. Click Yes.

If the ribbon and/or Quick Access Toolbar have been customized, these customizations can be exported for use on other computers or devices by saving them to an export file. To export customizations to the ribbon and Quick Access Toolbar, display the Word Options dialog box with *Customize Ribbon* or *Quick Access Toolbar* selected in the left panel, click the Import/Export button below the list box at the right side of the dialog box, and then click *Export all customizations* at the drop-down list. At the File Save dialog box that displays, navigate to the desired folder, type a name for the file in the *File name* text box, and then press the Enter key or click the Save button. By default, Word saves the file type as *Exported Office UI file (*.exportedUI)*.

To import a ribbon and Quick Access Toolbar customization file, display the Word Options dialog box with *Customize Ribbon* or *Quick Access Toolbar* selected in the left panel, click the Import/Export button, and then click *Import customization file* at the drop-down list. At the File Open dialog box, navigate to the folder containing the customization file and then double-click the file. (The file name will display with the *.exportedUI* file extension.) At the message that displays asking if all existing ribbon and Quick Access Toolbar customizations for this program should be replaced, click Yes.

Activity 1d   Exporting Customizations and Resetting the Ribbon and Quick Access Toolbar

Part 4 of 4

1. With **8-InterfaceApps** open, export your ribbon and Quick Access Toolbar customizations to a file by completing the following steps:
   a. Click the File tab and then click *Options*.
   b. Click *Customize Ribbon* in the left panel at the Word Options dialog box.
   c. Click the Import/Export button that displays below the list box at the right side of the dialog box and then click *Export all customizations* at the drop-down list.

   d. At the File Save dialog box, navigate to your WL3C8 folder.
   e. Click in the *File name* text box. (This selects the file name.)
   f. Type CustomRibbon&QAT and then press the Enter key.

2. Reset the Quick Access Toolbar and ribbon by completing the following steps:
a. Click the Reset button below the list box at the right side of the dialog box and then click *Reset all customizations* at the drop-down list.

b. At the message asking if you want to delete all ribbon and Quick Access Toolbar customizations, click Yes.
c. Click OK to close the Word Options dialog box. (The buttons you added to the Quick Access Toolbar will display while this document is open.)
3. Save and then close **8-InterfaceApps**.

Activity 2 Customize Word and Account Options and Display the Windows Feedback Window

5 Parts

You will open a travel document, change options at the Word Options dialog box, make changes to the document, and then restore the default options at the Word Options dialog box. You will also customize and display account options.

Tutorial

Customizing Word Options

Quick Steps

Customize Word Options
1. Click File tab.
2. Click *Options.*
3. Click option in left panel.
4. Make customization choices.
5. Click OK.

Customizing Word Options

Customize Word at the Word Options dialog box. Display the dialog box by clicking the File tab and then clicking *Options.* The Word Options dialog box displays with a number of options in the left panel.

The Word Options dialog box, like many other dialog boxes in Word, contains a Help button in the upper right corner. Click this button, which displays as a question mark (?), and the Microsoft Office support website opens with information about the options in the dialog box.

Customizing General Options

By default, the Word Options dialog box displays with *General* selected in the left panel, as shown in Figure 8.3. Use options in the Word Options dialog box with *General* selected to turn the Mini toolbar and live preview features on and off, specify the ScreenTip style, change user information, choose a different Office background and theme, and specify start-up options.

Open Word and the Word opening screen displays by default. This screen contains a Recent list and templates for creating a document. To have Word open directly to a blank document, remove the check mark from the option *Show the Start screen when this application starts.*

Figure 8.3 Word Options Dialog Box with General Selected

Click the options in this panel to display customization features and commands.

Click this button to display the Microsoft Office support website with information about available options.

With *General* selected in the left panel, options display for customizing the user interface and personalizing Microsoft Office, start-up, and real-time collaboration.

Word Options

General
Display
Proofing
Save
Language
Ease of Access
Advanced
Customize Ribbon
Quick Access Toolbar
Add-ins
Trust Center

General options for working with Word.

User Interface options

When using multiple displays: ⓘ
- ● Optimize for best appearance
- ○ Optimize for compatibility (application restart required)

☑ Show Mini Toolbar on selection ⓘ
☑ Enable Live Preview ⓘ
☑ Update document content while dragging ⓘ
ScreenTip style: [Show feature descriptions in ScreenTips ▾]

Personalize your copy of Microsoft Office

User name: [Student Name]
Initials: [SN]
☐ Always use these values regardless of sign in to Office.
Office Background: [No Background ▾]
Office Theme: [Colorful ▾]

Office intelligent services

Intelligent services bring the power of the cloud to the Office apps to help save you time and produce better results. To provide these services, Microsoft needs to be able to collect your search terms and document content.
☑ Enable services

About intelligent services   Privacy statement

LinkedIn Features

Use LinkedIn features in Office to stay connected with your professional network and keep up to date in your industry.
☑ Enable LinkedIn features in my Office applications ⓘ

[OK] [Cancel]

Activity 2a   Customizing General Options

Part 1 of 5

1. At a blank document, customize Word options by completing the following steps:
   a. Click the File tab and then click *Options*.
   b. At the Word Options dialog box with *General* selected in the left panel, click the *Show Mini Toolbar on selection* check box to remove the check mark.
   c. Click the *Enable Live Preview* check box to remove the check mark.
   d. Make a note of the name in the *User name* text box and then select the name and type Sylvia Porter.
   e. Make a note of the initials in the *Initials* text box and then select the initials and type SP.
   f. Click the *Always use these values regardless of sign in to Office* check box to insert a check mark.
   g. Click the *Office Background* option box arrow and then click *Calligraphy* at the drop-down list.
   h. Click the *Office Theme* option box arrow and then click *White* at the drop-down list.

i. Click the *Show the Start screen when this application starts* check box to remove the check mark.

j. Click OK to close the dialog box.

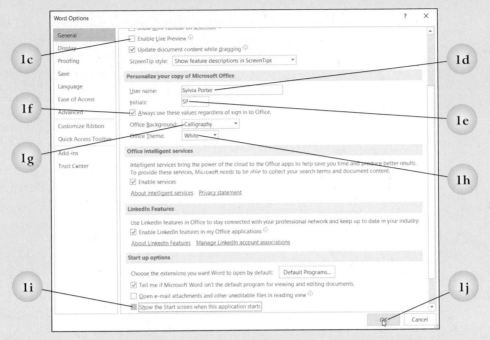

2. Close Word and then reopen Word. Notice that a blank document displays, rather than the Word opening screen.

3. Open **BTAfricaStudy** and then save it with the name **8-BTAfricaStudy**.

4. Select any text in the document and notice that the Mini toolbar does not display because this feature is turned off.

5. With the text still selected, click the *Font* option box arrow and then hover the mouse pointer over the font options in the drop-down gallery. Because the live preview feature is turned off, the text in the document does not display the font over which the mouse pointer is hovering.

6. Insert a user name field by completing the following steps:

a. Press Ctrl + End to move the insertion point to the end of the document.

b. Click the Insert tab.

c. Click the Quick Parts button in the Text group and then click *Field* at the drop-down list.

d. At the Field dialog box, scroll to the bottom of the *Field names* list box and then double-click *UserName*.

7. Save **8-BTAfricaStudy**.

Check Your Work

Customizing Display Options

Click the *Display* option in the left panel and the Word Options dialog box
displays options for how document content appears on the screen and when it is
printed, as shown in Figure 8.4.

Chapter 6 in Level 1 contained information on turning on and off the display
of white space that separates pages in Print Layout view by double-clicking the
white space or the line separating two pages. The display of white space between
pages can also be turned on or off with the *Show white space between pages in Print
Layout view* option at the Word Options dialog box. The display of highlighting
and ScreenTips can also be turned on or off at the dialog box.

Customizing Proofing Options

Click the *Proofing* option in the left panel and the Word Options dialog box
displays options for customizing AutoCorrect and the spelling and grammar
checker. Some of these options were used in previous chapters.

Figure 8.4 Word Options Dialog Box with *Display* Selected

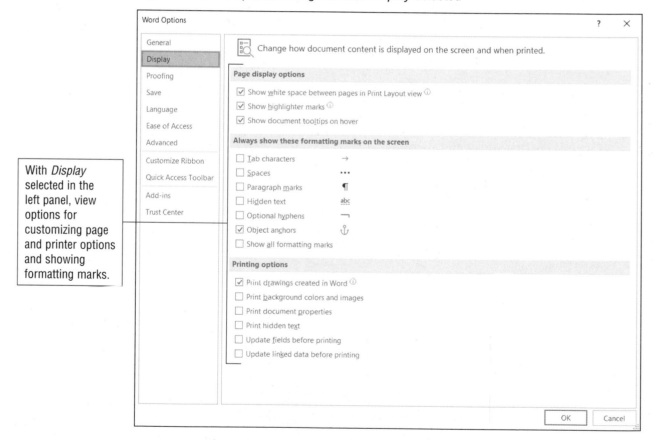

With *Display*
selected in the
left panel, view
options for
customizing page
and printer options
and showing
formatting marks.

Customizing Save Options

Click the *Save* option in the left panel and the Word Options dialog box displays options for customizing how and where documents are saved, as shown in Figure 8.5. The format in which files are saved can be changed from the default *Word Document* to another format, such as a previous version of Word or a Word template, web page, or plain text. The default locations for saving documents and AutoRecover files can also be changed. These save options are also available with the *Save as type* option at the Save As dialog box. The difference is that changing the file save format with the *Save files in this format* option at the Word Options dialog box with *Save* selected changes the default for all future documents.

Figure 8.5 Word Options Dialog Box with *Save* Selected

With *Save* selected in the left panel, options display for saving documents, editing offline, and preserving fidelity when sharing the document.

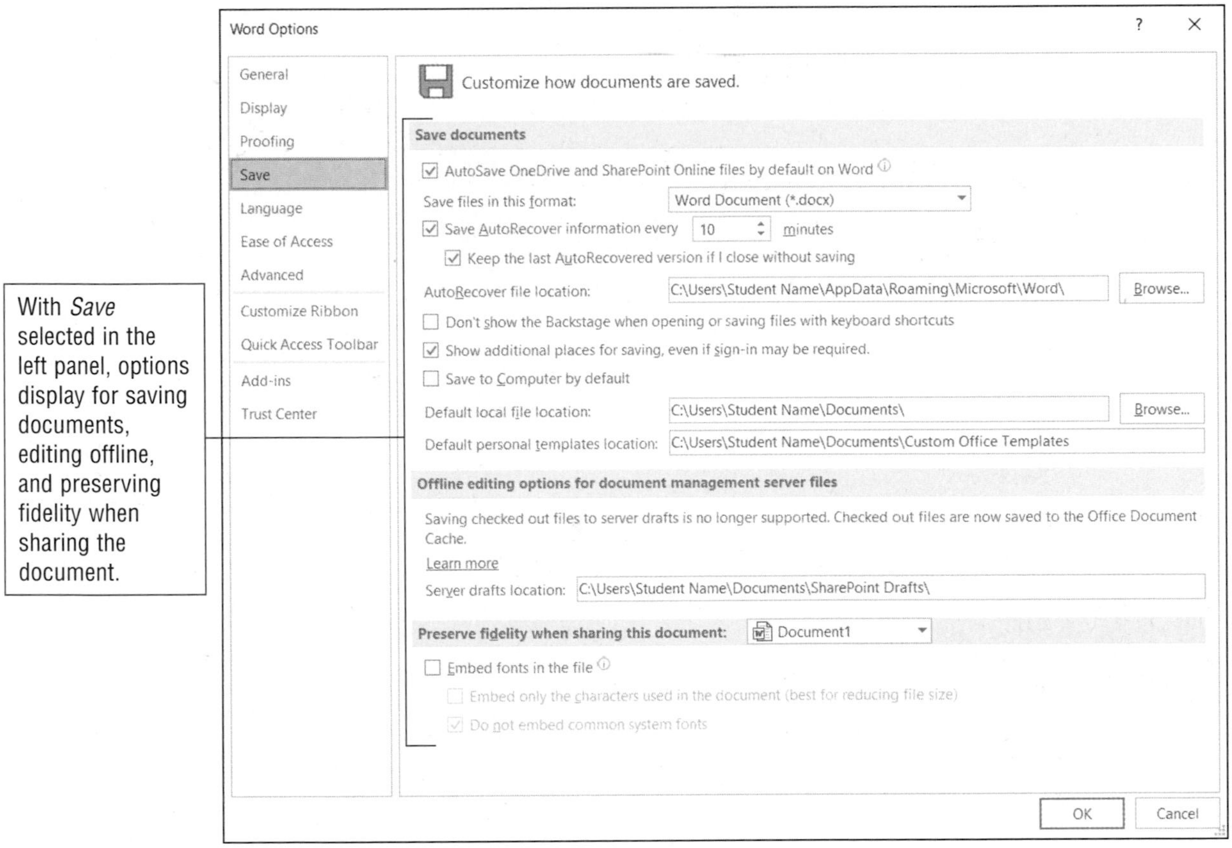

Activity 2b Customizing Save Options

Part 2 of 5

1. With **8-BTAfricaStudy** open, click the File tab and then click *Options*.
2. At the Word Options dialog box, click the *Display* option in the left panel and then look at the options available.
3. Click the *Proofing* option in the left panel and then look at the options available.

4. Click the *Save* option in the left panel.
5. Change the default local file location by completing the following steps:
   a. Make note of the current default local file location.
   b. Click the Browse button right of the *Default local file location* option box.

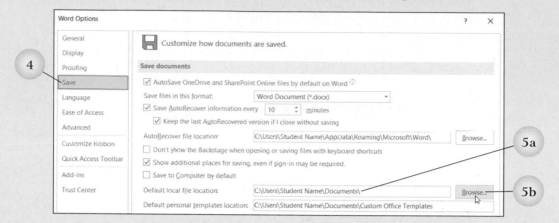

c. At the Modify Location dialog box, click *Desktop* to navigate to the desktop.

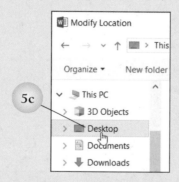

   d. Click OK.
6. Click OK to close the Word Options dialog box.
7. Save, print, and then close **8-BTAfricaStudy**.
8. Close Word and then reopen Word.
9. At a blank document, press the F12 function key to display the Save As dialog box. (Notice that the default save location is the desktop.)
10. Click the Cancel button to close the Save As dialog box.

Check Your Work

Customizing Language Options

The Word Options dialog box with the *Language* option selected, as shown in Figure 8.6, contains options for specifying editing and proofing languages and the display language for Word. The *Choose Editing Languages* section of the dialog box indicates the current editing and proofing languages as well as the keyboard layout. Other languages can be added to the dialog box by clicking the option box arrow below the list of editing languages. At the drop-down list that displays, click a specific language and that language will display in the list box. If a language has not been installed, click the <u>Not installed</u> hyperlink and a website will open from which a language accessory pack can be downloaded.

The *Choose Display Language* section of the dialog box shows the current display language, as established by Microsoft Windows. The display language is the language Office uses for displaying elements such as menu items, commands, and tabs. This default language can be changed by clicking another language in the list box and then clicking the Set as Default button.

Figure 8.6 Word Options Dialog Box with *Language* Selected

Use options in this section to specify the editing and proofing language as well as the keyboard layout language.

Use options in this section to specify the display language for elements such as menu items, commands, and tabs.

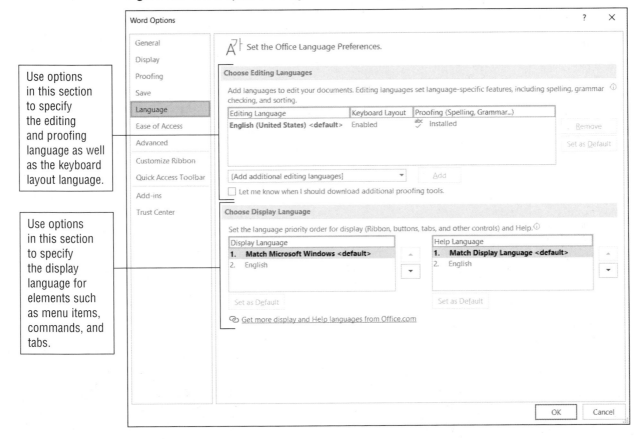

Customizing Advanced Options

Figure 8.7 shows the Word Options dialog box with the *Advanced* option selected. With the *Advanced* option selected, the Word Options dialog box displays a number of sections that identify ways to customize Word. Included are sections for changing editing options; specifying how text is cut, copied, and pasted in a document; specifying what document content to show; and customizing the display and printing of a document, among others.

Figure 8.7 Word Options Dialog Box with *Advanced* Selected

With *Advanced* selected in the left panel, options display for customizing editing and pasting options; specifying image size and quality; showing document content; and customizing display, print, save, layout, and general options.

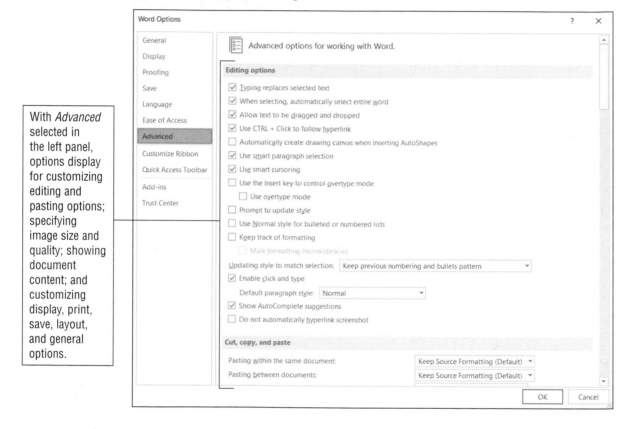

Activity 2c Customizing Advanced Options

Part 3 of 5

1. Open **8-BTAfricaStudy**.
2. Click the File tab and then click *Options*.
3. At the Word Options dialog box, click the *Advanced* option in the left panel.
4. Make the following changes to the options in the dialog box:

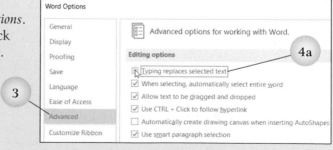

a. Click the *Typing replaces selected text* check box in the *Editing options* section to remove the check mark.
b. Scroll down the dialog box to the *Cut, copy, and paste* section and then click the *Use the Insert key for paste* check box to insert a check mark.
c. Scroll down the dialog box to the *Show document content* section and then click the *Show text boundaries* check box to insert a check mark.

d. Scroll down the dialog box to the *Display* section, select the current number in the *Show this number of Recent Documents* measurement box, and then type 5.
5. Click OK to close the dialog box.
6. At the document, notice the boundary lines around paragraphs of text. These lines display because a check mark was inserted in the *Show text boundaries* check box.
7. Double-click the word *African* in the heading *African Study Adventure*, type Bayside Travel, and then press the spacebar. (The typed text did not replace the selected word, *African*. This is because the check mark was removed from the *Typing replaces selected text* check box.)

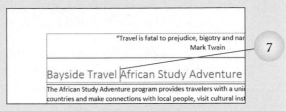

8. Copy and paste text by completing the following steps:
   a. Select text from the beginning of the heading *Disneyland Adventure* and the four bulleted items that follow it and then press Ctrl + C.
   b. Position the insertion point at the beginning of the heading *Cancun Adventure* and then press the Insert key on the keyboard. (The Insert key pastes the copied text because a check mark was inserted in the *Use the Insert key for paste* check box.)
9. Save, print, and then close **8-BTAfricaStudy**.

Customizing Add-ins and Trust Center Options

Click the *Add-ins* option and the Word Options dialog box displays add-ins, which are supplemental options that add custom commands and specialized features to Office applications. With the *Trust Center* option selected in the left panel of the Word Options dialog box, the <u>Microsoft Trustworthy Computing</u> hyperlink displays. Click this hyperlink to display the Trust Center web page at the microsoft.com website. At the Word Options dialog box with the Trust Center option selected, click the Trust Center Settings button and the Trust Center dialog box displays with options for specifying macro settings.

Activity 2d **Displaying Add-ins and Trust Center Options and Returning Options to the Default Settings**

Part 4 of 5

1. Open a blank document, click the File tab and then click *Options*.
2. At the Word Options dialog box, click the *Add-ins* option and then look at the options available in the dialog box.
3. Click the *Trust Center* option and then click the <u>Microsoft Trustworthy Computing</u> hyperlink.
4. Look at the information on Microsoft's Trust Center web page and then close the web browser.
5. At the Word Options dialog box, click the *General* option.
6. Click the *Show Mini Toolbar on selection* check box to insert a check mark.
7. Click the *Enable Live Preview* check box to insert a check mark.
8. Click the *Show the Start screen when this application starts* check box to insert a check mark.

9. Select the current name in the *User name* text box and then type the original name.

10. Select the current initials in the *Initials* text box and then type the original initials.

11. Click the *Office Background* option box arrow and then click *No Background* at the drop-down list.

12. Click the *Office Theme* option box arrow and then click *Colorful* at the drop-down list.

13. Click the *Always use these values regardless of sign in to Office* check box to remove the check mark.

14. Change the default file location back to the original setting by completing the following steps:
    a. Click the *Save* option in the left panel of the Word Options dialog box.
    b. Click the Browse button right of the *Default local file location* option box.
    c. At the Modify Location dialog box, navigate to the original location.
    d. Click OK.

15. Click the *Advanced* option in the left panel of the Word Options dialog box and then make the following changes:
    a. Click the *Typing replaces selected text* check box to insert a check mark.
    b. Scroll down the dialog box to the *Cut, copy, and paste* section and then click the *Use the Insert key for paste* check box to remove the check mark.
    c. Scroll down the dialog box to the *Show document content* section and then click the *Show text boundaries* check box to remove the check mark.
    d. Scroll down the dialog box to the *Display* section, select the current number in the *Show this number of Recent Documents* measurement box, and then type 50.

16. Click OK to close the Word Options dialog box.

Customizing Account Information

Click the File tab and then click the *Account* option and account information displays in the Account backstage area, similar to what is shown in Figure 8.8. The *User Information* section contains hyperlinks for changing the user photo and information, signing out of all Office applications, and switching accounts. The *Office Background* and *Office Theme* options in the Account backstage area are the same as the options at the Word Options dialog box with *General* selected. The *Connected Services* section displays any services, such as a OneDrive account, that are currently connected.

The *Product Information* section of the Account backstage area displays information about Office, such as the Office product and available applications. Click the Manage Account button to display an option for creating or managing one account for all Microsoft products. If a Microsoft account has not been established, clicking the Manage Account button will display the Office Online sign-in page. At this page, sign into an existing Microsoft account or click the Sign up Now hyperlink to create an account.

The *Product Information* section contains buttons for displaying information about Office and Office updates. Use buttons in this section to turn on or off automatic renewal (for Office 365), manage Office updates, display information about the Word application, and see what's new with updates.

Figure 8.8 Account Backstage Area

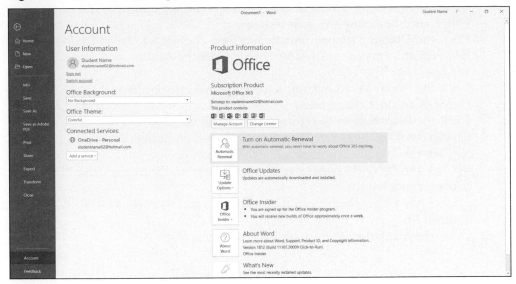

Activity 2e Displaying and Customizing Account Information

Note: Before completing this activity, check with your instructor to determine whether you have access to account information on the computer.

1. Make sure a blank document displays.
2. Click the File tab and then click the *Account* option.
3. At the Account backstage area, click the *Office Background* option box arrow and then click *Spring* at the drop-down list.
4. Click the *Office Theme* option box arrow and then click *Black* at the drop-down list.
5. Click the Update Options button in the *Product Information* section and then click *View Updates* at the drop-down list.

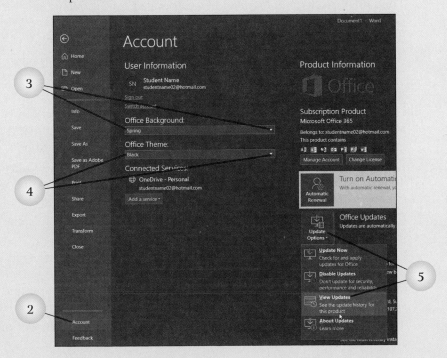

6. View the information that displays in a web browser on new and improved features in Office and then close the web browser.
7. Click the Update Options button and then click *About Updates* at the drop-down list.
8. Read the information in the Automatic Updates window and then click OK to close the window.
9. Click the About Word button, look at the information that displays about Word, and then click OK to close the window.
10. Click the Back button to return to the blank document.
11. Change back to the Office default background and colors by completing the following steps:
    a. Click the File tab and then click the *Account* option.
    b. Click the *Office Background* option box arrow and then click the *No Background* option at the drop-down list.
    c. Click the *Office Theme* option box arrow and then click the *Colorful* option at the drop-down list.
12. Close the blank document without saving changes.

Chapter Summary

- Customize the Quick Access Toolbar with options at the Customize Quick Access Toolbar button drop-down list and options at the Word Options dialog box with *Quick Access Toolbar* selected.

- Insert a button or command on the Quick Access Toolbar by right-clicking the button or command and then clicking *Add to Quick Access Toolbar* at the shortcut menu.

- Use options at the Word Options dialog box with *Quick Access Toolbar* selected to display all the options and buttons available for adding to the Quick Access Toolbar and to reset the Quick Access Toolbar to the default. The Quick Access Toolbar can be customized for all documents or for a specific document.

- The Quick Access Toolbar can be customized for all documents or a specific document with the *Customize Quick Access Toolbar* option at the Word Options dialog box with *Quick Access Toolbar* selected in the left panel.

- Add a button to the Quick Access Toolbar by clicking a command in the list box at the left side of the Word Options dialog box with *Quick Access Toolbar* selected in the left panel.

- Use options at the Word Options dialog box with *Customize Ribbon* selected to add a new tab and group, rename a tab or group, add a command to a new group, remove a command from a tab group, and reset the ribbon.

- Export a file containing customizations to the ribbon and/or Quick Access Toolbar with the Import/Export button at the Word Options dialog box with *Customize Ribbon* or *Quick Access Toolbar* selected.

- Customize Word options at the Word Options dialog box. Display the dialog box by clicking the File tab and then clicking *Options*.

- Use options at the Word Options dialog box with *General* selected to turn the Mini toolbar and live preview features on or off, specify the ScreenTip style, change user information, choose a different Office background and theme, and specify start-up options.

- The Word Options dialog box with *Display* selected contains options for specifying how document content appears on the screen and when it is printed.

- Use options at the Word Options dialog box with *Proofing* selected to customize AutoCorrect and the spelling and grammar checker.
- The Word Options dialog box with *Save* selected contains options for customizing how and where documents are saved.
- The Word Options dialog box with the *Language* option selected contains options for specifying editing and proofing languages and the display language for Word.
- Click *Advanced* in the left panel of the Word Options dialog box to display a number of sections for identifying ways to customize Word, such as changing editing options; specifying how text is cut, copied, and pasted; specifying what document content to show; and customizing the display and printing of a document.
- The Word Options dialog box with *Add-ins* selected displays options for adding custom commands and specialized features to Office applications.
- The Word Options dialog box with *Trust Center* selected in the left panel displays a link to the Office.com website as well as a button to displaying the Trust Center dialog box with options for specifying macro settings.
- The Account backstage area contains options for changing user information and the Office background and theme. It also contains product information, Office updates, and information about Word. Display this backstage area by clicking the File tab and then clicking the *Account* option.

Commands Review

FEATURE	RIBBON TAB	OPTION	BUTTON
Account backstage area	File	*Account*	
Customize Quick Access Toolbar			⏷
Word Options dialog box	File	*Options*	

Index

Customize Keyboard dialog box, 9, 66–67

Customize Quick Access Toolbar button, 194, 195

customizing

    account information, 212–214

    compared document options, 169–171

    importing and exporting, 202–203

    Quick Access toolbar, 194–197

    ribbon, 198–201

    Word options, 203–212

        add-ins options, 211–212

        advanced options, 210–211

        display options, 206

        general options, 203–205

        language options, 209

        proofing options, 206

        save options, 207–208

        Trust Center options, 211–212

custom style sets

    changing default setting, 19

    deleting, 20

    saving, 18–20

D

data

    editing grouped data, 93–94

    pasting with Paste Special dialog box, 179–180

data source file

    elements of, 39

    finding records in, 55–56

    merging main document

        with Access database table source file, 48

        with Excel worksheet data source file, 46–47

        with Word table data source file, 45–46

    selecting records in, 52–54

    sorting records in, 49–51

date picker content control

    customizing, 103–104

    inserting, 96–98

Date Picker Content Control button, 97

default style set, changing, 19

Define New List Style dialog box, 21–22

Demote button, 147, 150

Demote to Body Text button, 147, 150

demoting heading levels, 150–151

Design Mode, displaying form in, 89

Design Mode button, 89

destination, 174

Developer tab, 86

    displaying, 88

display options, customizing, 206

documents

    accessibility management, 181–185

    combining, 171–173

    comparing documents, 168–171

    copying macros between documents and templates, 74–75

    copying styles between templates and, 34–35

    creating master document, 157–164

    embedding objects, 174–178

    linking objects in, 176

    managing in Outline view, 146–157

    master document, 157–164

    merging, 172

navigating, with assigned levels, 154

opening and filling form document, 91–92

saving as template, 14

saving macro-enabled, 73–75

sharing, 186–189

subdocuments, 157–164

Drop-Down Form Field button, 107, 112

Drop-Down Form Field Options dialog box, 112

drop-down list content control

    inserting, 99

    specifying, 100–102

Drop-Down List Content Control button, 99

drop-down list form field, creating with Legacy Tools, 112–115

E

Edit button, 187

editing

    linked object, 177

    macros, 79–81

    subdocuments, 160

Edit Recipient List button, 49

email, for sharing document, 186–187

embedding

    defined, 174

    Excel data in document, 175

    objects, 174–175

End Online Presentation button, 188

Excel

    embedding data in document, 175

    linking chart to document, 176

    merging main document with Excel worksheet data source file, 46–47

Expand button, 147

expanding

levels

in Normal view, 154

in Outline view, 148–149

subdocuments, 159

Expand Subdocuments button, 159

exporting, customizations, 202–203

F

fax, for sharing document, 186–187

Field dialog box, 76

fields

adding Fill-in field, 40–42

check box form field, 109–110

check box form field options, 115–117

drop-down list form field, 112

inserting If…Then…Else… field, 43–45

Merge Record # field, 42

recording macro with Fill-in field, 76–78

text form field, 107–109

text form fields, 118–120

Fill-in field

inserting in main document, 40–42

recording macro with, 76–78

running macro with, 78–79

Filter and Sort Dialog Box, 50, 52, 54, 55

forms

defining groups in, 89

designing, 86–87

displaying in Design mode, 89

content controls in, 88, 86–104

check box, 99

combo box, 99

date picker, 96–98

drop-down list, 99

picture, 96–98

setting properties of, 99–104

editing grouped data in, 93–94

filling in, with form fields, 110–111

form template, 87–88

editing protected form template, 104–106

mailing list form template, 90–91

protecting template, 96, 110

placeholder text in, 95–96

printing data in, 111–112

using Developer tab to create, 88

using Legacy Tools to create, 107–111

form fields, 110–111

check box form field, 109–110

drop-down list form field, 112–115

customizing form field options, 112–120

text form fields, 107–108, 118–120

using tables to create, 95

formatting

with styles, 3–35

applying, 4–6

creating style, 6–16

displaying all styles, 16–17

displaying styles in style set, 4

managing styles, 31–35

modifying predesigned style, 12–13

multilevel list style, 21–24

revealing style formatting, 17–18

saving custom style set, 18–20

Style Inspector task pane, 29–31

table style, 25–29

Form Field Help Text dialog box, 112

Form Field Shading button, 107, 108

G

general options, customizing, 203–205

group

defining, 89–91

editing grouped data, 93–94

Group button, 89

H

header row, establishing, 183

Heading 1 style, 4, 5

Heading 2 style, 4, 5

heading levels, in Outline view

assigning levels, 151–152

expanding and collapsing, 148–149

moving, 152–153

overview of, 146, 147

promoting and demoting, 150–151

headings, in Outline view, assigned levels at Paragraph dialog box

assigning, 154–157

collapsing and expanding levels in Normal view, 154

collapsing levels by default, 156

moving collapsed text, 154

navigating in document with, 154

with fields

    inputting text during merge, 40–42

    inserting If...Then...Else... field, 43–45

    inserting Merge Record # field, 42

merging main document

    with Access database table source file, 48

    with Excel worksheet data source file, 46–47

    with Word table data source file, 45–46

sorting, selecting and finding records in data source file, 49–56

Mail Merge Recipients dialog box, 49–50

main document file

    adding Fill-in field, 40–42

    elements of, 39

    merging with data source file

        with Access database table source file, 48

        with Excel worksheet data source file, 46–47

        with Word table data source file, 45–46

Manage Styles dialog box, 31–33

Mark Citation button, 126

Mark Citation dialog box, 126–127

Mark Entry button, 132

Mark Index Entry dialog box, 132–134

master document, 157–164

    creating, from existing document, 157–158

    opening and closing, 158

    subdocuments

        editing, 160

        expanding and collapsing, 159

        inserting, 161–162

        merging, 162

        splitting, 162–164

        unlinking, 162–164

    uses/benefits of, 157

Match Fields button, 46

Merge button, 162

merge documents, 171–173

Merge Record # field, 42

merging. *See also* mail merge

    subdocuments, 162

Modify Style dialog box, 12–13

More Styles button, 6

Move Down button, 147, 152

Move Up button, 147, 152

Multilevel List button, 21

multilevel list style

    creating, 21–24

    modifying, 28

N

navigating, document with assigned levels, 154

New Tab button, 199

Normal.dotm, 81–82

Normal style, 4, 5

Normal view, collapsing and expanding levels in, 154

No Spacing style, 4, 5

O

Object button, 177

objects

    creating alternative text for, 181

    defined, 174

    editing linked object, 177

    embedding, 174–175

    linking, 176

    linking, at Insert File dialog box, 177–178

    opening

document based on template, 14

    master documents and subdocuments, 158

Organizer dialog box, 34–35, 74, 75

Outline button, 146

    buttons and options in Outlining tab, 146–147

Outline Level option, 147

Outline view

    assigned levels at Paragraph dialog box

        assigning, 154–157

        collapsing and expanding levels in Normal view, 154

        collapsing levels by default, 156

        moving collapsed text, 154

        navigating in document with, 154

    assigning levels, 151–152

    benefits/uses of, 145, 146

    collapsing levels, 148–149

    demoting heading levels, 150–151

    display document in, 146–147, 149

    expanding levels, 148–149

    moving headings, 152–153

    organizing document in, 152–153

    promoting heading levels, 150–151

Outlining tab, buttons and options in, 146–147

P

Paragraph dialog box, assigned levels

    assigning, 154–157

styles, 3–35

applying, 4–6

copying between documents and templates, 34–35

creating

assigning keyboard shortcut to style, 9–12

based on existing formatting, 6–7

based on existing style, 6

new style, 7–8, 10–12

custom style sets

changing default setting, 19

deleting, 20

saving, 18–20

displaying all styles, 16–17

displaying styles in style set, 4

managing, 31–33

modifying

applied style, 15–16

predesigned style, 12–13

multilevel list style

creating, 21–24

modifying, 28

renaming, 34

revealing style formatting, 17–18

saving in template, 14–15

Style Inspector task pane, 29–31

table style

creating, 25–28

modifying, 28–29

updating template with updated style, 22

Styles task pane, 4–5

subdocuments

defined, 157

editing, 160

expanding and collapsing, 159

inserting, 161–162

merging, 162

opening and closing, 158

splitting, 162–164

unlinking, 162–164

Subtitle Emphasis style, 4, 5

Subtitle style, 4, 5

survey form template, editing and filling in, 105–106

T

tab

creating new, 199

removing, 199

renaming, 199

table of authorities

creating, 126–131

deleting, 128

example of, 126

inserting, 127–131

marking citations, 126–127

overview of, 126

updating, 128

Table of Authorities dialog box, 127–128

tables

creating alternative text for, 181

establishing header row, 183

Tables feature, creating form using, 95

table style

creating, 25–28

modifying, 28–29

templates

copying macros between documents and templates, 74–75

copying styles between documents and, 34–35

creating application form, 108

form template

creating, 87–88

editing protected, 104–106

mailing list form template, 90–91

protecting, 96

open document based on, 14

protecting, with Legacy Tools, 110

saving macro-enabled, 61

saving styles in, 14–15

survey template

editing and filling in, 105–106

inserting controls in, 101–102

updating, with updated styles, 22

text

creating alternative text for image or table, 181

inputting during mail merge, 40–42

text form field

customizing with Legacy Tools, 118–120

inserting in form, with Legacy Tools, 107–108

Text Form Field button, 107

Text Form Field Options dialog box, 118

Text level formatting option box, 29

Title style, 4, 5

Trust Center dialog box, 73

Trust Center options, customizing, 211–212

U

Unlink button, 162

unlinking, subdocuments, 162–164

Update Index button, 143

Update Options button, 213

Interior Photo Credits

Page GS-1, (banner image) © lowball-jack/GettyImages; *page GS-1, (in Figure G.1)* all images courtesy of Paradigm Education Solutions; *page GS-2,* © irbis picture/Shutterstock.com; *page GS-3,* © th3fisa/Shutterstock.com; *page GS-4,* © goldyg/Shutterstock.com; *page GS-5,* © Pressmaster/Shutterstock.com.